I0712010

THE
FOUNDATIONS
TO
BEYOND

What must Human Beings know about being human?

<u>**Special Thanks to:**</u>

Alyssa M. for editing and proofreading
Kezia M. for book cover words arrangement

<u>**And a big Thank You to you, the reader, for reading this book**</u>

If you know of friends and family members who would benefit from this content, a free portion of this book is available at the author's official Facebook page:

<u>https://www.facebook.com/authorLK</u>

Thanks for reading!

<u>**If we are serious about solving the world's problems, where would be an effective place to start?**</u>

In 2015, the United Nations adopted a set of Sustainable Development Goals as a call to action to achieve peace and prosperity for all. These goals include good health, well-being, quality education, and gender equality. However, what is needed to achieve all these?

Human effort is needed. The interplay of human ingenuity and compassion for one another is crucial for the sustainable development of our societies. Most importantly, we need human development. We need people to know more. By fostering knowledge and understanding, individuals can distinguish between positive actions and those that are harmful. Then through knowledgeable deliberation and free choice, they can create environments that unlock positive potential.

As you read through this book, you will come to realize that many societal problems have their roots in human development. Scientific findings have shown that individuals can be set on debilitating life paths even before birth. Human development is an invisible force that affects every person throughout their lifespan.

Scientists have recognized the importance of human development and put in more than a century of research to understand how humans grow, thrive, or form negative outcomes. I do not dare claim such tremendous efforts as my own. But what I have done is organize some of their insights so that anybody can easily understand human development.

Specifically, more than a thousand science papers were read so that you do not have to. In closing, we may now have the closest thing to answering the age-old questions:

Why do people behave the way they do?
How can we do better?

PART II

Adverse Life-trajectories

PROLOGUE

As I hopped around classes in different university faculties, I stumbled upon a course with an interesting title: 'Lifespan human development.' Intrigued, I signed up for the course without knowing what to expect. It was foreign territory, given that I did not have any psychology knowledge.

Class began, and I remained incognito as I was probably the only non-psychology student there. I still vividly remember that first lesson. The professor began by playing a video of teenagers passing a basketball around, and we were asked to count the number of times the ball was passed. Obeying the instruction, I counted silently, as did many others.

By the end of the video, we attempted to give the correct answer. However, the video followed up with a surprising question, 'Did you notice the moonwalking bear?' The clip was replayed, and we saw that a person in a bear costume was actually moonwalking between the teenagers passing the ball. It shocked me. We were so engrossed in counting the ball passes that our perceptions were preoccupied, and we didn't notice the bear. The professor then continued her lesson on how a human being's capabilities worked, how such capabilities were developed, and how such capabilities can be affected by the actions of others.

When I finished the lesson, I thought to myself, 'why do people not know this? Why do we rely on myths to answer why people behave the way they do?' The answers were in front of us all along.

Over time, as I attended the lessons, it became clear that our actions as friends, family, parents, teachers or even strangers have impacts that extend to the human development of others. It also dawned on me how little people know about the consequences of their actions on others. Think a simple snub is harmless? Think excluding someone or socially isolating them is harmless? By the end of this book, you will be able to answer these questions. But before that, you may be wondering, 'are people molded by behaviors, or are they determined by their personalities?'

Nature or Nurture?

There is some evidence that differences in maternal care were linked to differences in offspring gene activation [1].

A review of 'epigenetics,' how one's environment affects how their genes work, noted that abused children displayed changes to a gene linked to stress responses [2]. But the influence of the environment on genes may not stop there. For example, there is preliminary evidence that one's learning experience is associated with DNA methylation, meaning adding a methyl group to nucleotides within the brain's hippocampus, and if gene methylation is inhibited, there can be memory impairments to that learning experience [3].

Similarly, early-life stress, postnatal malnutrition, and maternal separation can have persisting effects, creating various gene methylations associated with cognitive impairments in memory performance, intelligence, and attention [4].

As we can see, both nurture and nature can influence a person's development. However, that does not mean a person can only be influenced by others or have no choice but to be determined by their inborn genes. One may also develop intrapersonal intelligence. But this does not mean that one's environment cannot debilitate one's development or create disadvantages.

The Snowball Called Development

At this juncture, you may ask, 'why development?' The answer may be best illustrated by the development of a person's 'Theory of mind.'

A person with a developed 'Theory of mind' is able to recognize and reason about the thoughts, beliefs, and emotions of others [5]. For example, persons without a developed theory of mind may fail in a false-belief task. Not only may these persons fail to recognize that another person does not possess the knowledge they do, but they also may not recognize that a person's beliefs may not accurately reflect a reality that has undergone change [6].

The theory of mind development was predicted by a child's verbal intelligence and early interactions with a mother with mind-mindedness [7]. Mind-mindedness refers to accurately reading an infant's mental state during the infant's behavior and commenting on it to the said infant [7]. For example, if a mother accurately commented to a child, 'do you want this toy?' in response to a child's behavior and the comment was consistent with the child's mental state of such a desire, the mother would have demonstrated mind-mindedness.

The same experiment found that mere exposure to 'psychological-state language' was insufficient if the comments were not accurate [7]. Thus, in order to develop a child's theory of mind, we are looking at empathetic parenting that discusses the child's feelings. The same parental mind-mindedness is also associated with a healthy, secure parent-child attachment [7].

Neuroscience has shown that even though the neural structures of the theory of mind are not directly related to the neural structures of empathy, they are interconnected through other regions [8]. Theory of mind is said to be related to the cognitive portions of empathy (i.e., inferring another's mental state), and every empathic response would activate both the emotional and cognitive components even if the regions work autonomously [8].

In other words, if a parent's mind-mindedness is linked to a child's development of a theory of mind, a child with impaired empathy may

4

cultivate the same in their own children. But the implications may not stop there.

In one study, children with emotional or behavioral problems tended to have parents with lower perspective-taking (empathy) [9]. This relationship was mediated by a child's lower-developed social competence [9]. Conversely, parental empathy was associated with higher child social competence [9]. This suggests that empathy could have repercussions beyond 'theory of mind' development.

It was also proposed that the development of mental state understanding is important for meta-cognition, the ability to regulate and think about one's own thinking [10].

This is important because young children may hold various thinking fallacies. For example, when young children were asked what was in a candy box, they answered candy. However, when shown that the box actually contained pencils and asked what they thought was inside before the reveal, some children would answer 'pencils' [10]. This highlights the tendency for young children to retroactively revise their beliefs based on new information, assuming it to be a prior belief.

You may have met adults who changed their views but insisted that their new view was what they had all along. This could be due to a lack of metacognition to evaluate their false belief. Or perhaps they had an emotional need that prevented them from acknowledging their mistake. The former suggests a lack of metacognition, which could have stemmed from a lack of a developed theory of mind, which may lead to various thinking fallacies which may or may not be overcome later. Once again, the repercussions may not stop there.

Children, who scored higher in their false-belief tasks, like being able to recognize the differences in their feelings and those of others, were observed to be more socially competent [10].

Going further, social intelligence and emotional intelligence, which respectively means being able to empathize with others and regulate one's own emotions, were said to be related to cultural intelligence but may not necessarily apply in new cultural settings [11]. For example, a socially intelligent compliment in one culture could be considered harassment in another [11]. Cultural intelligence requires processes that acquire new rules and information [11].

Meta-cognitive strategies are central to cultural intelligence since a person has to look beyond their own cultural lens to comprehend another culture [11]. This cultural intelligence is likely needed for people to be socially competent within a new culture. Put together, these imply that various intelligences could rely on one another. In addition, certain aspects of these intelligences, like empathy, could go on to impact one's moral reasoning and development.

As we can see, a single developmental aspect like the theory of mind can be implicated in the developmental snowball, including empathy, social competence, metacognition, and moral development. All of these have an impact on a person's behavior and, in turn, the health of the societal institutions they exist in. As such, what underlies a moral and positive institution is a multitude of developmental efforts and access to such development is likely critical for societal peace and well-being.

<u>Unequal Access to Development</u>

Even when there is access to education, students from disadvantageous family environments may underperform academically. Even worse, teachers attribute a student's difficulties to an unchangeable lack of intelligence. Such attributions are incorrect and reflect a lack of scientific knowledge. But more importantly, such attributions may have repercussions on a student.

Along with a teacher's misattributions, poor academic results may be all the evidence a student needs to construct a poor academic self-concept.

6

This self-concept can be long-lasting. For example, a friend in his late 20s once said, 'I am not good at studying.' In other words, his poor academic self-concept has persisted into his adulthood.

Such self-condemnation begs the question, 'was it wholly the fault of the student if he or she did not perform academically?' Scientific findings hint that it is not.

In one study, academic self-concept was found to have reciprocal effects on academic results [12]. This was in line with another study that found academic self-competence and self-determination to be positively associated with academic motivation and, in turn, academic performance [13].

To clarify, self-determination here includes the students' feelings that 'school does not feel like a prison' and that they attend school out of personal choice rather than being forced to. This hints that harsh and authoritarian teaching could actually achieve the opposite effect of helping students improve. As such, unequal access to development can manifest in terms of unequal access to effective learning environments. Furthermore, students labeled as 'problematic' or 'slow' may face unequal access to constructive teacher behavior.

Ultimately, teachers themselves need positive development to gain the necessary knowledge and demeanor to be effective teachers. Only then can we truly improve the unequal access to development, at least in this aspect.

So what could equal access to development mean?

<u>Equal access means Availability, Accessibility, and Alternatives</u>

The first step is, of course, to create a developmental initiative so that it becomes *'available.'* But even if an initiative is available, individuals may be excluded due to discrimination, or they may be unaware due to poor information flow. Therefore, an opportunity only becomes available when it is inclusive and made aware of. For example, continued education opportunities can be made available for at-risk adolescents who drop out of school.

However, even if a developmental opportunity exists, it may not be *'accessible.'* The costs of taking up an opportunity can be prohibitive. For example, student loans can be overly expensive, causing students to overwork while juggling their education, or experience poor mental health [14]. However, accessibility does not pertain solely to affordability. Individuals may have important responsibilities of supporting their family financially or providing care for their dependents.

As such, the accessibility of development depends on the support we can provide to help people manage their costs and responsibilities.

Lastly, we need to recognize that developmental initiatives are not one-size-fits-all. They do not provide equal benefits to each person. Thus, *alternatives* are required so that people have choices that provide them with sufficient benefits.

As such, when we think of human development, we think about meeting the diverse developmental needs of different persons. This, of course, includes at-risk persons. It means providing available and accessible choices so that no one could only be isolated, marginalized, exploited, or debilitated by their environments.

However, this does not mean demanding conformance to a single developmental path. There are two main reasons for this.

Firstly, positive development is unlikely to succeed if people are denied the opportunities to think and act. In other words, people do not mature in their thinking or cognitive abilities. As such, avoiding building an unreflective idolization of ideologies and beliefs makes sense because such idolization denies development.

The second reason is not so straightforward. It is a reasoning that is prevalent throughout this book. In this book, you will notice that the possible solutions are much shorter than the explained problems. This is the case even when a study finds a program to be effective. Why is this so?

Scientific studies often have a limitation in their generalizability due to their sample population being limited to specific cultures and demographics. Therefore, a scientific finding may not be directly applicable to other cultures or demographics. Similarly, solutions that have worked for one culture or demographic may not work for another, and could even be considered culturally inappropriate. It is essential to acknowledge these limitations and approach scientific research and problem-solving with a cultural lens that considers the diverse needs and perspectives of different communities. By doing so, we can better understand the unique needs of various cultures and demographics and develop solutions that are inclusive and effective for everyone.

The difference here is that even though scientific findings may provide us with an adequate exploration of a problem's risk factors, a solution that is based on a different or unknown constellation of issues could set up a solution for failure. Thus, any solution listed should be used as an idea only, and any solution has to be tailored to the situations and risks faced by the participants to be effective.

Similarly, a fixed developmental path can be ineffective or detrimental because it disregards individual differences and risk factors.

I once observed an aid program making the same mistake during their 'outreach.' The program aimed to target those living in poverty but invited participants through television broadcasts, phone calls, SMS, and newspapers, asking them to visit a website for more information.

But having worked with those in severe poverty, I noticed that many did not own a television or phone, let alone have internet access. Some were even illiterate! So how could the program expect to reach those persons through such means?

Even with an invitation, people may not seek help as they may feel ashamed of doing so. As such, there are many operational and emotional aspects to consider, and crafting a solution is not as simple as we may think.

A good solution must also consider the costs borne by the different stakeholders. For example, it is counterproductive to the societal well-being sought after if the social workers alleviating the situation experience poor mental health due to toxic workplace cultures.

At this juncture, we now possess a clearer picture of how to utilize the information presented in this book. Let us begin proper. Let us begin to demystify, 'what must human beings know about being human?'

<u>PART I</u>

The Cognitive Building Blocks
Of the Human Experience

<u>What must Human Beings know about being human?</u>

<u>#1</u>

Do children in low-income families face a disadvantage in cognitive development?

According to one study, only a third of poor families provided a comparable level of intellectual stimulation and emotional support as families that were not poor [15].

In another study, children from the most impoverished families and disadvantaged home environments showed a decline in intelligence scores as they grew older [16]. This was substantiated by another study that found a link between disadvantaged socio-economic status and lower intellectual growth [17]. In contrast, a disadvantaged home environment exerted a constant disadvantage on intellectual skills, predicting early intellectual performance [17]. These findings suggest that children from poor families have limited access to learning resources and intellectual stimulation.

Research suggests that a child's cognitive intelligence is influenced by the quality of their environment [18]. While genes play a role in the stability of cognitive intelligence [18], intelligence may not be entirely predetermined. Improving the quality of a child's environmental is likely to have a positive impact on their cognitive development.

- Brain development is vulnerable to the deprivation of stimulation [19]. This deprivation can lead to differences in brain synapse quantity, density, and selection of synapse connections, where this selection can mean the regression of certain synapse connections over time [19]. However, mere exposure to a high-information environment is insufficient. One has to interact with that environment [19].

14

- The experiences in the environment lead to neural activity that selectively preserves synapse connections [19]. This suggests that individuals who have exposure to intellectual information and are engaged by that experience may display differences in brain development compared to those who are disengaged or live in an information-deprived environment.

Possible Initiatives

✓ Provide resources that assist parents in mitigating their challenges in providing intellectual stimulation. This includes providing economic support to ensure the accessibility of developmental opportunities to young persons.

<u>What must Human Beings know about being human?</u>

<u>#2</u>

Can parental behavior cause retardation?

In more recent times, retardation has fallen from the tradition prevalence of 2-3% to about 1%, but there were differences between country states, where observed retardation rates went as high as 3% [20].

Cultural familial retardation is believed to affect 75% of all persons facing retardation [21]. It is the retardation that arises due to some form of psychosocial disadvantage [21]. This means that many of its causes are actually preventable.

Cultural familial retardation arises in environments that are impoverished – economically, psychologically, and socially [22]. Factors such as low infant birthweight [23], fetal exposure to alcohol [24], poor prenatal care, maternal malnourishment, and trauma can all contribute to a cumulative effect on a child's intelligence [22].

In addition, the intelligence impairments from fetal alcohol exposure tended to be enduring, even though a small portion of persons, about one in eight, showed significant improvements in IQ scores over time [25]. As such, these prenatal sources of retardation may cause lasting brain damage that could have been easily prevented.

- Postnatal conditions like the lack of childhood stimulation i.e., severe isolation and neglect, can cause serious retardation [22]. Parents may also have limited communication skills to stimulate their child's language acquisition and cognitive development [22].

Children with retardation were found to have higher levels of learned helplessness [21]. Children with learned helplessness believe that they have no control over an outcome [21]. This, in turn, leads to deficits in effort initiation and perseverance [21]. This was particularly the case in failure conditions. Children with retardation displayed a significant decline in effective strategies after they received negative feedback [21]. This highlights that helplessness can hinder one's efforts.

- Conversely, those who attributed unfavorable outcomes to their efforts, i.e., viewing failures as reversible, showed low levels of helplessness [21].

So far, we have seen that psychological risks can accompany retardation, but what about the outcomes in other life aspects?

- In one study, persons with moderate to severe mental retardation experienced poor employment outcomes. Specifically, less than 12% were employed [26].

- Another study also found that the development of social functioning decreased when mental retardation severity increased [27].

- A separate study reported that persons with severe mental retardation were more likely to have lower incomes, face problems in learning achievement, and were less likely to be married or have more than six friends or relatives with whom they were in regular contact [28].

- However, the study did not find significant differences in terms of social life satisfaction between those with intellectual impairment and those without [28]. Interestingly, the study also noted that social outcomes and employment outcomes varied widely across studies [28].

- These findings suggest that people who experience retardation can still thrive. The adaptive skills that can be developed include communication skills, daily living skills, and social intelligence, all of which can be impacted by deficits in intellectual functioning [29].

- In one study into participants at heightened risk of neurodevelopmental problems, the development of adaptive behavior was predicted by the amount of nurturance that participants received [30].

<u>Possible Initiatives</u>

✓ Institutions build parental knowledge on high-quality prenatal care to prevent child retardation. These institutions may intervene in pre-natal and post-natal drug abuse, alcohol use, and other behavioral risks that parents pose to their children. We should aim to achieve 100% prevention of parental behaviors that lead to child mental retardation.

✓ Establish early detection programs that provide high-quality support for individuals with mental retardation, including young children programs that offer adaptive development to compensate for deficits in home environments. We should aim to achieve access to adaptive skills development for 100% of persons who experience mental retardation.

<u>What must Human Beings know about being human?</u>

<u>#3</u>

Can one's learning environment be detrimental to learning?

Negative learning environments can be characterized by negative teacher interactions. Threatening and dismissive teaching, low teacher responsiveness to student needs, and low teacher likeability by students were all negatively linked to students' perceived learning [31].

- Specifically, negative teacher interactions and poor course organization were linked to the students' negative feelings toward the teachers' instructional methods and, in turn, lower perceived learning [31].

- Low teacher responsiveness to student needs was linked to lower student interest and, in turn, lower perceived learning [31].

- The likeability of a teacher was linked to the students' learning performance, defined as their self-evaluated knowledge and their desire to learn more [31]. Student learning performance was linked to students' interest, which was linked to perceived learning [31].

It was said that students might associate their poor performance in a subject with their personal failure, leading them to engage in other activities that are seen as rewarding and doable [32]. Students view their learning abilities negatively and become less motivated. These negative self-perceptions, which can be influenced by negative teacher interactions, can hinder effective study strategies and reinforce poor learning outcomes.

- Affirming this, it was found in one study that students' self-perceptions of low intellectual capabilities and learning competence were associated with the negative beliefs that high costs would be incurred if they sought help from their teachers and classmates for their academic difficulties [33]. They believed they would receive negative attitudes from those they sought help from and be considered stupid [33]. This, in turn, translates into avoidance of help-seeking [33]. As a result, individuals who need help the most do not get the help they need.

- This aligns with the 'vulnerability' hypothesis, which suggests that individuals with low self-esteem would have a greater need to avoid situations that threaten their worth. This can be a vicious cycle.

- It was said that students who experience inadequacy and helplessness and anticipate a loss of status and esteem might experience anxiety that impairs academic performance [34].

- The study also found that correlations with test anxiety included poor self-esteem, fears of negative evaluation, and perception of teachers as negative or unfriendly [34]. Test anxiety was, in turn, related to poorer performance across different tests [34].

- It was said that students might experience fear and anticipate that learning will result in shame and humiliation [35]. Once again, this inhibits helpful behaviors towards learning.

Students who do not believe that they possess what it takes to succeed academically and who do not believe that they have control over their academic success were less likely to be engaged in learning [36]. These beliefs of capacity and control over academic achievement were found to be associated with student engagement, which was, in turn, associated with academic performance [36]. Academic performance may then exert reciprocal effects on the students' self-beliefs of their capacity.

- As we can see, beliefs like 'I am not smart' and 'I can't get good grades no matter what I do' can adversely affect one's academic achievement.

- Furthermore, self-beliefs of capacity interact with what students believe is an effective strategy for academic achievement (e.g., effort, ability, and powerful others like teachers) [36]. This implies that students' confidence in a teacher's teaching methods and involvement with their learning can contribute to engagement.

- Additionally, a student's perceived control was associated with positive teacher involvement and whether helpful feedback was given [36].

- Conversely, poor teacher-student interactions could lead to negative beliefs about learning. Wrong answers can be punished. Mistakes can lead to humiliation. Furthermore, teachers tended to attribute students' poor performance to factors that are internal to the student, like effort and ability, rather than teacher or school issues such as the teacher's instructional methods [37]. The reverse is true. Teachers tended to attribute good student performance to good instructional methods [37].

- Simultaneously, teachers frequently categorize their students as either 'good' or 'poor,' creating distinctions based on their ability and potential for success [37]. This can lead to teachers attributing the achievements of 'good' students, who are labeled as 'high ability,' to their innate abilities, while dismissing the accomplishments of 'low ability' students as mere luck or effort [37]. Such labeling practices increase the likelihood of students developing negative self-beliefs, putting them at greater risk of experiencing academic setbacks.

- It was said that many schools were failing to engage their students. They failed to provide social environments that were conducive to healthy psychosocial development and learning [38]. Furthermore, it was reported that within some studies, as high as 40% to 60% of high school students were chronically disengaged from their studies [38].

This disengagement may seem unimportant, but student motivation is important in learning. Even the type of motivation matters. Within certain education systems, students can be focused on outperforming others to aggrandize their ability at their peers' expense [39]. This is known as a *performance goal* orientation.

This can be compared to a '*mastery goal*' orientation where students focus on building their understanding and appreciation of the subject matter [39]. Learning goals affect cognitive self-regulation, including learning engagement and progress monitoring [39]. Specifically, students with mastery goals were reportedly engaged in more self-regulated learning [39].

- One study investigated in a slightly different direction. The study found that children with helplessness and children with mastery goals displayed different behaviors during failure conditions. When persons with mastery goals failed, they tended to exhibit solution-focused behaviors like self-instruction and monitoring [40]. They expressed positivity and enjoyment of the challenge and believed they could eventually reach a workable solution [40]. In the face of failure feedback, they improved their performance and even strategy sophistication [40].

- Conversely, children with helplessness ruminated about the cause of their failure and spent little time searching for ways to overcome the failure [40]. In the face of failure, children with helplessness subsequently displayed decreased performance and decreased use of effective strategies [40]. A portion of them even abandoned helpful strategies altogether [40]. All of these suggest that the effects of failure can accumulate. Children with helplessness also attributed their failures to a lack or loss of ability, whereas those with mastery goals did not [40]. So how does this relate to performance goals?

- In one study, persons, who were in performance goal conditions, meaning to gain favorable judgments of their competence and avoid negative ones, and told that they had 'low ability,' displayed similar strategy deterioration and negative emotions to those found in learned helplessness [41]. Furthermore, 'low ability' persons in performance goal conditions made more attributions, mostly attributing failure to uncontrollable causes like their ability [41].

One study found that performance goals can be further separated into performance-approach goals and performance-avoidance goals [42]. Participants who were highly afraid of failure were more likely to adopt a performance-avoidance or performance-approach goal [42].

While adopting a performance-approach goal was associated with high grades, adopting a performance-avoidance goal was associated with poor grades [42]. In addition, the adoption of a performance-approach and performance-avoidance goal led to low intrinsic motivation [42]. In contrast, individuals who prioritized mastery goals and had low focus on performance goals reported the highest levels of intrinsic motivation [42].

- In this study, intrinsic motivation was measured by the students' enjoyment and meaning in class [42]. Thus, the link between performance goals and low intrinsic motivation hints at low engagement.

It was said that students who hold mastery goals, for example, having the desire to learn something for themselves, can see learning as a means to better understand the world [43]. A mastery goal orientation was found to be positively linked to the use of deep processing strategies, which were said to lead to understanding and retention [43].

24

Conversely, learning for the sake of demonstrating superior ability in relation to others was found to be positively linked to the use of surface-level processing strategies like memorizing [43]. Surface-level strategies can be used to pass school tests but do not require students to understand the material [43].

Moving on, beliefs that impede learning may not be formed solely due to negative classroom environments. It was found that parental attitudes play a key role in shaping children's academic self-perceptions [44]. Parents' dissatisfaction with their children's academic performance and the low importance placed on academic success were related to the children's poorer perception of academic competence [44].

Children perceived themselves to be more academically competent when their parents valued the children's academic success and were more satisfied with the children's school performance [44]. These findings highlight the importance of parents providing supportive and constructive involvement in their child's education.

Now that we have seen how teachers and parents can construct a child's beliefs that are detrimental to learning, what do we need to consider to create a constructive learning environment?

The earlier a school cultivates the students' self-belief that they have the capacity to do well, the earlier they may become engaged and feel accomplishment in learning [45]. This is because there is a longitudinal influence. The previous year's engagement and perceived self-competence influenced the next year's engagement and self-competence, and furthermore, predicted the next year's academic achievement [45]. In turn, higher academic achievement was followed by an increased likelihood of engagement the next year [45].

- High-quality instruction and supportive teaching develop student engagement and self-confidence in their capacity [45]. The resulting engagement can mean high levels of participation, interest, perseverance, positive learning values, and effort [45]. Engaged students may then learn more and retain more.

- Children as young as two years old may begin to differentiate between 'success' and 'failure'. They feel positive self-evaluative emotions during a task's success and negative self-evaluative emotions during failure [46]. Additionally, children tended to seek adult approval when they succeeded, but avoided adult attention when they failed [46]. This implies that children may regard adult approval and disapproval as important. Managing these emotions and providing appropriate adult approval may influence a child's learning goals, self-concept, and task perseverance.

At the same time, the feedback that children receive is important. Its importance can even be seen during infancy. For example, infants who used baby walkers that blocked visual sensory of leg movements were slower to learn to walk [47]. This was in comparison to infants who did not use baby walkers and instead received visual feedback on their leg movements [47].

- The frequent use of baby walkers was also found to predict lower infant mental development, though the infants eventually caught up as they aged and became increasingly mobile outside of their walkers [47]. The effect on mental development was proposed to be due to lower exploratory access, and the effect may not be short-lived.

- The frequent use of a walker continued to predict lower mental development for as long as ten months after the initial usage [47]. This highlights the possible impacts of deprivating sensory information and feedback, which could similarly impact other forms of learning and development.

On top of helpful feedback, it matters if schools and parents espouse learning goals.

- In one study, high school students, who perceived more mastery structures in their classroom, experienced more positive changes in their subject self-efficacy [48]. Conversely, students, who perceived more performance-focused structures, experienced more negative changes in their subject self-efficacy [48]. Classroom mastery structures were also moderately correlated to student mastery goals [48].

- In a mastery-focused classroom, teachers may focus on intellectual development and learning importance [48]. They may also recognize the students' attempts at trying. Teachers in performance-focused classrooms may instead focus on the student's grades, relative ability, and correct answers [48].

- Students with more mastery goals experienced more positive changes to their subject self-efficacy and GPA as they transitioned school years [48]. The students' performance goals were not related to such changes across academic years [48].

- Furthermore, students with parents who espoused at least one mastery goal demonstrated significantly higher math GPAs than those whose parents did not [48]. There was no such difference whether the parents held a performance goal or not.

- In addition, another study found that the belief that one's intelligence is malleable was positively associated with positive beliefs toward effort-making such as, 'If I work hard, I can get better at it' [49]. The belief of intelligence malleability was also associated with learning goals such as, 'I do school work because I like to learn new things,' low helplessness attributions such as, 'I am not smart enough,' and higher positive strategies such as, 'I will work harder from now on' [49].

- To be more specific, incremental intelligence belief was linked to learning goals and, in turn, positive strategies [49]. Another path was found where incremental intelligence belief was linked to positive effort beliefs like, 'The harder you work at something, the better you will be at it,' and in turn, lower helplessness attributions, where the latter two were linked to positive strategies [49].

- All of these have possible effects on actual academic achievement. Having incremental intelligence belief at the beginning of junior high school predicted higher mathematics grades at the end of the second year [49].

- All in all, it was found that teaching students to recognize the malleability of their intelligence was an effective intervention that encouraged positive motivation in a large proportion of the participants, leading even to the reversal of downward trajectories in grades over time [49]. In contrast, students in the control group, who endorsed unchangeable intelligence, continued on a downward trajectory [49].

- In the same experiment, both the intervention and control groups were provided with anti-stereotypic thinking and study skills that could help them study better [49]. However, given that only the intervention group reversed their downward trajectory, it was likely that providing anti-stereotypic thinking and studying skills were insufficient. But that is not to say stereotypes may not adversely affect performance.

In one experiment, individuals in a stereotype-threat situation were made aware of a relevant 'lower ability' stereotype, and they experienced impaired performance [50]. Interestingly, an individual does not need to be chronically targeted by the stereotype or have an internalized belief of intellectual disadvantage [50]. It was sufficient if the relative superiority of another group was made relevant and salient [50]. However, that is not to say being the target of chronic stereotyping would not evoke a stereotype-threat. It is certainly possible for one to become disengaged or disidentified with the threatened domain [50].

- It was further found that stereotype threat had a greater effect when individuals valued the subject or domain that is under threat [50]. This highlights that inculcating the importance of academics can backfire.

We have seen that believing in the malleability of intelligence could lead to an improvement in academic performance. However, could expertise knowledge compensate for lower intelligence to lead to high performance?

In one experiment into the age-old argument of effort versus aptitude, it was found that expertise, namely domain knowledge, reduced but did not fully eliminate the relationship between aptitude (IQ) and recall performance [51]. Higher IQ and expertise affected recall tasks that benefited from strategy, but only expertise affected recall tasks that did not [51]. However, low-aptitude experts had almost equal performance to high-aptitude experts in most tasks, and both groups outperformed High IQ novices [51]. This highlights that effort is indeed a resource that can make up for existing differences in intelligence.

- When children have detailed knowledge of a subject domain, they can more efficiently process information in that domain, more effectively apply strategies, and incorporate new information more easily [52]. This basically means that as one builds knowledge in a subject, one can learn things in that subject more effectively. Experts can learn more than novices when studying new information in the domain [52]. Expert knowledge can even allow a child to perform like an adult expert and outperform adult novices [52]. Similarly, adults at lower levels of aptitude (IQ of 80) performed complex classification and reasoning in their expert domains [52].

- Furthermore, rich domain-specific knowledge exerts influence on the development of memory, capacities, strategies, and the monitoring of learning [52]. The act of processing materials for knowledge leads to the automatic usage and sophistication of learning strategies, eventually diminishing the need for intentional strategies [52].

- With increasing expertise, not only does knowledge quantity increase, but knowledge becomes more accessible as concepts become linked to one another. This knowledge structure may affect our processing performance as our knowledge becomes more cohesive [52].

- All of these support that a mastery orientation that develops a child's domain expertise would empower a child to learn new materials more easily while developing their domain-based intelligence, even if one's general aptitude is lower.

So far, most of what we have covered pertained to studying as a means of learning. But could people also learn when they are not studying?

At the extreme, parents may become overly restrictive, disallowing their children from participating in healthy amounts of play. Play is so important that the United Nations recognize it as a right of a child [53]. The benefits of play include a child's cognitive development, specifically problem-solving and divergent thinking [54]. Divergent thinking is also known as creativity.

Furthermore, social play was found to be related to the development of social skills, including social cooperation, perspective-taking, and communication [54]. Play may also be implicated in emotional development, possibly reducing anxiety [54].

- For example, when there is sociodramatic play, such as pretend play with a friend or a group, a child may display the capacity to take on a complementary role and share meaning [55]. This sharing of meaning is said to reflect the sophistication of a young child's 'theory of mind' [55].

- In another study, chronically neglected and play-deprived children displayed social immaturity and patterns of disturbing behaviors [56]. Children just sat rocking, staring into vacant space. One threw playing bricks, unaware of the dangers it posed to other children [56]. Social play helped these children recover and become more social, finding safety in social interaction and developing in their own ways [56].

- The mentioned social-emotional developments may have important repercussions on a child's well-being. For example, emotion regulation was found to predict the number of mutual friendships [57]. Behavior regulation, which included 'others-oriented' behaviors like conflict management and recognition of emotional cues, predicted popularity [57]. In turn, these social relations may provide further opportunities to develop social competencies. Importantly, these relationships may enhance one's self-worth, provide context for distress alleviation, and build positive adjustment [57].

- As we can see, if we narrowly define learning as studying, we would neglect the development of critical capabilities.

<u>Possible Initiatives</u>

✓ Schools may train teachers to achieve supportive teacher interactions and responsiveness to student needs. Teachers buffer against negative learning beliefs, which include helplessness and the lack of control and ability. Teachers must become trained to avoid misattributing poor academic performances to a child's internal factors like aptitude. Instead, they should help their students cultivate knowledge of malleable intelligence, anti-stereotypic thinking, and studying techniques.

✓ In addition, schools may adopt a mastery-based structure rather than a performance goal structure. This may combine with good course organization to make the class understandable, meaningful, and interesting. In this manner, teachers can engage and motivate their students.

✓ Programs may create opportunities for parents and teachers to explore the value of the children's learning and become involved positively. They may also become aware of the benefits of mastery goals and encourage children to strive for them. For that, they may teach students that it is acceptable to try and fail and give constructive feedback to aid in the sophistication of strategy.

✓ The famous Terman study into gifted children gives further insights into the needed nurturance. The study found that exceptional school achievement required far more than intelligence. It required a high-quality school climate, a high proportion of capable and inspiring teachers, and a conscious effort to discover strengths and motivate students [58].

✓ In the Terman study, high achievers displayed all-around mental and social adjustment [58]. They also displayed four volition traits: prudence, self-confidence, perseverance, and desire to excel [58]. In other words, they were focused on their goals [58] and felt confident about their ability rather than inferior. They were well-adjusted rather than maladjusted. This means that students' psychological and social well-being are important for school achievement. Furthermore, school achievement was linked to 'stability' rather than 'instability' and the absence of disturbing conflict rather than presence [58].

✓ While schools may not resolve the students' familial conflict, they may provide access to options that students may use to better handle their adverse environments. This may include emotional and behavioral regulation skills. However, the students' mental and social adjustment should be pursued as the primary concern, though it may be incidentally conducive to school achievement.

<u>What must Human Beings know about being human?</u>

<u>#4</u>

Can one's social environment be detrimental to learning?

The developmental pathway of a child's academic failure may begin from home. Coercive parenting practices may promote maladaptive youth behavior that contradicts effective interpersonal interactions with peers [59].

In one study, peer acceptance was positively correlated with academic achievement [59]. Conversely, aggression-disruptiveness was negatively related to peer acceptance and academic achievement [59].

- Path analysis highlights that low family socioeconomic status was related to a child's early aggressive-disruptive behavior, which was, in turn, linked to association with friends who were aggressive-disruptive during preadolescence, which, in turn, was linked to lower school commitment during adolescence [59]. All of these factors were linked to poorer academic achievement [59].

- Conversely, early academic achievement was a predictor of lower child aggressive-disruptiveness, higher prosocial behaviors, peer acceptance, and later academic achievement [59]. This affirms that there are benefits if students find early academic achievement to be engaging.

- In another study, early aggressive behavior was found to be related to higher risks of peer rejection, friendlessness, and victimization that persisted over time [60]. Later on, children with chronic relational adversity were more likely to have higher loneliness, internalizing problems, i.e., anxiety, depression, and withdrawal, and externalizing problems, i.e., aggression and delinquent behaviors [60].

- These problems were mediated by the formation of negative social self-concepts, including poor self-acceptance and self-liking [60]. Similarly, another mediating factor was the formation of negative beliefs about peers [60]. Rejected and victimized children viewed others as anti-social, hurtful, and domineering rather than pro-social, kind, and helpful [60]. The internalizing and externalizing problems that result highlight the poor psychological and social adjustment of children, which cannot be helpful toward their academic achievement.

- In another study, child rejected status was found to have a direct negative relationship with grades [61]. Rejected children were reported to receive lower levels of peer support, had fewer efforts in learning, and were seen as less pro-social and more irresponsible [61].

- In this study, being pro-social referred to how often a student was considerate to others or helped others to learn. Whereas one's perceived support from peers referred to whether their peers cared about their feelings or how much they learned [61].

- Perceived peer support, learning efforts, pro-social goals and behaviors, responsible goals, and academic grades were significantly interrelated [61]. This supports the notion that academic performance may be affected by the social support one receives.

- Similarly, the lack of closeness with parents was found to be related to early delinquent behaviors, peer rejections, and association with delinquent peers [62]. The said lack of closeness can include the lack of interactions, encouragement, and compliment from parents [62]. In addition, the lack of closeness to parents was related to low child self-esteem [62]. In particular, rejection by peers and low self-esteem mediated the link between closeness to parents and joining up with delinquent peers [62]. In other words, children may join up with others who were rejected due to their unmet socio-emotional needs. In this manner, one's unmet socio-emotional needs may contribute to poor school commitment.

So far, we have seen that those who do not perform well in school may be at higher risk of developing social behaviors that lead to peer rejection. This may, in turn, be detrimental to academic performance. But what about those who perform well in school? Could a social environment punish those who perform well?

The answer is yes. A behavior observed was the derogatory labeling of students who scored well. This was first observed in high-performing African American students within their school populations [63]. However, this phenomenon was not limited to that group [63]. Any group can be at risk.

In this 80's study, African American students, who studied hard, got good grades, spoke standard English, volunteered, and read poetry, were considered 'acting white' and were hated by their African American peers [63]. Furthermore, these students were labeled 'punks' and 'brainiacs' and faced exclusion, ostracism, and even physical assault [63]. As a result, students reduced their academic efforts and concealed their ability to conform to their peers' performance to participate in their group [63]. In this manner, social pressures from poor-performing groups discouraged academic performance.

- But why would these groups do so? It was proposed that the poor-performing groups had formed a collective oppositional identity, viewing academic behaviors as 'joining the enemy' [63]. Such identities can be constructed due to the structural disadvantages faced in society. For example, it was said that African Americans faced a job ceiling in the past even when they had good education achievements [63]. This led them to question the value of their learning and education.

- It was also recounted that a teacher doubted an African American student who presented a good piece of work. The teacher accused him of plagiarism, which he denied, and he was given a grade that indicated the teacher's disbelief. The student never tried again. His grades dived, and his interest in school diminished [63]. As we can see, peer pressure, unequal opportunities, and ability doubting can kill students' motivation.

- It is conceivable that ability doubting could also occur between peers, where peers put down another based on their self-beliefs of what they themselves are incapable of. Ability-doubting narratives could include, 'Do not act smart,' 'Do not try to achieve what you are incapable of,' and 'You are not as good as you think.' One may even argue that an ingrained performance-goal culture influences these social behaviors.

In addition, toxic cultures may punish non-conformity.

In a study that interviewed 'nerds,' one participant described her middle school peers as stereotyping, narrow-minded, and judgmental [64]. Furthermore, individuals who were different in any way often faced difficulties fitting in [64]. This was a common theme highlighted in the study.

The study also described how middle school peers emphasized trendiness and traditional gender roles, such as competition and masculinity for boys and attractiveness and relationships for girls [64]. Those who displayed these traits would be popular and given high peer status, whereas those who did not meet the standards would be excluded, ridiculed, or shunned [64]. As a result, unpopular teens recalled feeling like 'social outcasts.' In this manner, peer cultures can perform derogatory labeling and dismiss one's academic efforts by questioning one's coolness, masculinity, femininity, or even worth.

In another study, gifted students reported experiencing more sadness and lower satisfaction with the quality of their social support, which refers to the availability of people they could rely on and those who let them know that they were valued and loved [65].

- In addition, the grades of gifted students were moderately and negatively correlated to high psychoticism [65]. Conversely, their grades moderately and positively correlated to conscientiousness, hope, joviality, and their attitudes toward school [65]. Again, this highlights the importance of mental and social well-being in academic achievement.

In the worst case, social exclusion may be performed against people who do not conform to group norms. It may even reach the point of collective bullying, which may include rumor spreading and ignoring the bullied [66]. In a study with student participants from two junior high schools, as high as 80% of the participants reported being involved in bullying either as a bully, witness, or victim [66]. Some thought that it was alright to bully a victim as other students were doing the same [66].

In another study, high or increasing victimization was found to be associated with an increased likelihood of bullying involvement [67]. This means that youths bullied by peers were at increased risk of victimizing others [67]. The bullying behaviors measured here included hitting, spitting, name-calling, threatening, ignoring or excluding a person, and recruiting someone to bully another [67].

The same study found that bullies, including those who transitioned from victims to bullies or bullies to victims, displayed higher delinquency rates [67]. Additionally, those on an increasing bullying trajectory displayed higher overall rates of delinquency and self-harm [67]. This highlights that both bullies and victims may be more vulnerable to anti-social trajectories.

You may be wondering, 'Are bullies developed?' After all, we have seen that victims may transition to bullies, possibly due the traumatic experiences of being bullied. But a better question could be, 'Does underdevelopment support bullying perpetration?'

To begin answering that question, let us look at the tendencies of young children. While it was found that young children tended to be egocentric, meaning they are unable to see a situation from another's point of view, there have been experiments that challenged this notion [68]. One such experiment was Yarrow & Zahn-Waxler's 1977 study into the capacity of compassion and pro-social behavior in young children [68].

Though it was not universal, it was found that young children can display responsiveness to others' need states [69], notably when there is clear situational context and emotional display. Of course, non-prosocial responses were also displayed in many instances [69].

The complication is that there were children who succeeded in perspective-taking tests but failed to respond pro-socially, but there were also children who responded pro-socially but failed in perspective-taking tasks [69].

Yarrow & Zahn-Waxler proposed that this phenomenon was due to the differences in child experience. Specifically, non-aggressive children displayed increased sensitivity to the feeling states of others when they also had increased experiences of aggression by others [69].

Consistent with Yarrow & Zahn-Waxler, there were other experiments that showed that children had no difficulty decentering from their own perspective when they had the right knowledge and context interpretation [68].

But even so, the lack of consistent correspondence between perspective-taking and pro-social behavior indicates that compassion may not solely depend on perspective-taking.

With that said, failure in perspective-taking can be brought into adulthood, especially when there is incongruence in emotional states between persons [70], like when one is sad and one is happy.

Egocentrism may come in a different form. People may struggle to set aside their privileged knowledge to better discern another person's knowledge state [71]. They fail to recognize the privileged and subjective nature of what they know, assuming that others believe what they believe.

Such egocentrism may be linked to a false-consensus bias where people overestimate how common their belief really is [71]. However, even when people know that another party does not share their knowledge, they may be unable to prevent their knowledge from twisting their understanding of the other's perspective [71]. This may lead people to distort new information to fit in with their pre-existing theory [71].

So what does egocentrism have to do with bullying?

In one study, bullies displayed higher levels of moral disengagement compared to victims and outsiders [72]. However, the underlying mechanism of this disengagement can be argued to be of egocentric reasoning. To elaborate, it was found that a bully's personal motive was sufficient to justify their detrimental behavior towards others. Bullies reported feeling pride and indifference, and they valued the personal benefits from such behaviors [72].

- Only 30% of the bullies showed some awareness of their detrimental impact on the victims [72]. Instead, they were more concerned with personal consequences [72]. Such consequences may include punishment, which may be absent. Taken together, these findings suggest that bullies may have difficulty seeing the perspectives and feelings of others that differ from their own [72].

- As a result, egocentrism may lead to bullies having difficulty recognizing the negative impact of their aggressive behavior. They may feel little negative emotions in response to another's distress and lack any sense that bullying for personal benefit is morally wrong [72]. Additionally, bullies may feel a lack of personal responsibility [72], denying the consequences for their victims and justifying their behavior as a 'harmless joke.'

- As we can see, it is possible that bullies have not outgrown a child's state of egocentrism.

One study also found that bullies tended to be popular persons who were socially preferred by their peers [73]. This was in comparison to the victims [73]. Still, some studies found that bullies had average or slightly below-average popularity instead [74]. Regardless, it is possible that bullies enjoy social admiration for their bullying and they bully others to enhance their social dominance and status [73].

- Victims, on the other hand, tended to be unpopular persons who were without a friend in their class or even disliked by their peers [74]. Victims tended to be non-aggressive persons whose passiveness signals their 'worthlessness' to bullies and informs their bullies that they would not retaliate if attacked or insulted [74].

- Bullies were also found to have higher self-esteem but lower pro-social behavior [73]. This implies that bullies may view their victims to be inferior or of lower status. Such views reinforce their rationalizations for bullying.

- In another study, a classroom's bullying by popular and non-popular adolescents was found to be positively correlated [75]. Furthermore, bullying by popular persons accounted for the acceptance of bullying behaviors by their peers [75]. In other words, bullying by popular adolescents promoted bullying by non-popular persons. One explanation was that non-popular people imitated popular peers to increase their chances of being part of a popular group and enhance their status [75].

- It was also found that a behavior becomes more likely or less likely to be peer accepted depending on the popular peers' behavior [75]. Thus in this manner, bullying also became a less frowned upon behavior.

- Obviously, bullying in a classroom indicates a dysfunctional culture. Classes with high levels of bullying by popular adolescents were higher in peer rejection [75]. These classes were also lower in peer acceptance [75]. This hints at a culture that is mired in stereotyping that harms class relations.

<u>Possible Initiatives</u>

✓ School programs can raise students' awareness of social behaviors such as labeling and doubting others' abilities, which can be detrimental to academic achievement.

✓ Programs provide anti-stereotypic training against the peer stereotyping, peer-conformity pressures, and popularity herd mentality that leads to bullying. In place of these, social skills and pro-social reasoning can be cultivated for positive peer relationships.

✓ Anti-bullying programs may explicitly create awareness of victim recounts and consequences. This is done to build perspective-taking. The brain's temporoparietal junction, associated with a person's theory of mind, can be activated simply by reading stories that describe another person's thoughts and beliefs [76]. In this manner, we may foster perspective-taking to achieve student behaviors that are conducive to mutual socio-emotional well-being.

42

✓ Similarly, a parental program may cultivate parents' sensitivity toward child feelings with the aim of fostering positive parent-child relationship. Such relationships are important for the development of a child's conscience [77]. After all, perspective-taking may be insufficient to stop the enactment of detrimental peer-to-peer behavior for personal motives.

- Conscience is said to be preceded by a child's eagerness and willingness toward parental discipline and guidance [77]. A parent's sensitive caregiving and gentle disciplining through inductive explanations foster a child's willingness and cooperation toward parental guidance [77].

- As opposed to positive parenting, power-assertive parenting hurts a child's internalization of moral behavior due to the child's anger and resentment towards the parent [77]. Unsurprisingly, power-assertive parenting was linked to a child's less mature moral conduct [77]. Conversely, a positive parent-child relationship of mutual trust, cooperation, and positive feelings fosters the moral emotion of guilt [77]. Such relationships were associated with a child's internalized conduct [77].

- Both moral emotion and internalized moral conduct make up self-regulation, where children perform rule-compatible behaviors in the absence of surveillance [77]. Healthy guilt may then support altruism, responsibility-taking, and pro-social relationship with parents, teachers, and peers [77].

- Furthermore, it was said that warm parents, who are sensitive to their child's feelings and teach their child about emotions, promote the child's competence in understanding and regulating emotions [78]. This, in turn, promotes the child's social competence [78]. Conversely, parents who express high levels of anger during frustrating situations are less likely to provide a good example of effective emotional regulation strategies [78]. This highlights the importance of cultivating parental emotional regulation.

✓ Lastly, programs may not only aid parents in cultivating emotional regulation but also skills of emotional coaching. One study found that parents' emotional coaching buffered the children's loneliness and relationship pessimism that arose from poor peer relationships and low respect from peers [79]. But regardless of emotional coaching, a lack of reciprocal friendship continued to be associated with higher loneliness [79]. Still, emotional coaching could improve a child's emotional well-being, reducing their need to associate with at-risk peers or adopt attitudes that are incompatible with academic commitment.

<u>What must Human Beings know about being human?</u>

<u>#5</u>

Is intelligence changeable?

To start with, an excessive emphasis on intelligence can lead to issues when individuals are labeled and judged based on their intellectual abilities. This can be problematic because IQ tests may be misused and people may fail to acknowledge the diversity of intelligences that exist.

While it was found that general intelligence had a moderate to high correlation with academic performance [80], a narrow and blind emphasis on IQ is a problematic practice that fails to recognize the complexity of human cognitive performance.

To illustrate, some organizations impose employment tests that entail speed-based assessments of numeric ability, verbal ability, inductive reasoning, and deductive reasoning. However, the problem with such intelligence tests is that a number of these mental abilities were found to taper off and decline from the age of 39 to 46 [81]. Furthermore, a significant proportion of persons showed a significant decline in one or two abilities from as early as age 32 [81].

In addition, perception speed declined rapidly from as early as age 25 [81]. This means that speed-based and abstract intelligence tests that do not account for age complexities, like those that measure mental abilities through unfamiliar geometric patterns, can discriminate against adult persons as their intelligence comes from other sources. It was found that after accounting for declining perception speed, age differences in *fluid intelligence* were significantly reduced [81]. In contrast, *crystallized abilities* tended to increase as one grew older [81].

Fluid intelligence here referred to the speed of learning and reasoning in novel situations [82]. It was said to be the raw information processing power for new information [82]. However, we will soon see that processing information in real life actually depends on more than fluid intelligence. Again, fluid intelligence tended to fluctuate within the lifespan in tandem with physical maturation and decline [82]. This is in line with the decline in mental abilities we saw earlier.

Conversely, crystallized intelligence tended to accompany the increase in fluid intelligence but not its decline [82]. Crystallized intelligence reflects mental abilities like verbal comprehension and communication and represents the brain's network of information and skills gained through learning and reasoning [82].

Intelligence tests typically involve tasks that require participants to process information and solve problems, which are thought to be indicative of their cognitive abilities [82]. However, at the core of such information processing and problem-solving lies the limitations of both short-term and long-term working memory [83]. In essence, working memory refers to the amount of information that can be recalled, sustained, and processed during the problem-solving process, and it is also thought to play a role in decision-making and concept formation [83].

However, short-term working memory was traditionally considered the only memory resource available [83]. Short-term working memory can solve a problem, but the memory relating to the problem becomes poor once the task is completed [83]. In other words, the memory is temporary. Similarly, when we do speed-based abstract intelligence tests, we are likely using short-term working memory.

Conversely, a much larger working memory was observed in complex cognitive tasks. At times, more than twenty active units were observed compared to four active short-term memory units [83]. This means that our working memory capacity, i.e., problem-solving capacity, is far greater than the traditionally assumed short-term memory capacity. In other words, if we use intelligence tests that measure mental capabilities based on short-term memory resources, we fail to take into account the majority of capabilities that may be developed.

Complex cognitive tasks require access to large quantities of information [83]. This information is built and crystallized over time by experts and accessed from long-term memory when retrieval cues are perceived. However, retrieval from long-term memory tends to take longer than short-term memory, but experts can achieve memory structures that speed up retrieval to a comparable speed [83]. This means that experts solve complex tasks using slower thinking processes.

Taking into account all that we have seen, speed-based abstract employment tests may not only unknowingly discriminate against experts, but also adult thinking that tends to make more considerations that are of higher quality.

To further illustrate the shortcomings of such methods, research has shown that individuals who received sufficient training in a particular domain were able to use long-term memory as an efficient extension of short-term working memory [83]. For example, one study documented that hundreds of regular college students were able to match the performance of professionals in arbitrary multiplication problems when they used the specific format that they had practiced for hundreds of hours [83].

Since human intelligence encompasses much more than just fluid intelligence and short-term working memory, which are the main components measured by general IQ tests, defining a person's intelligence solely through these methods is superficial. In the worst case, we may witness a repetition of Samuel G. Morton's controversial work from 1839, which quantified brain volume as a measure of 'intelligence' and perpetuated the biases of one race's supposed superiority over others. [84].

Similar to the current usage of intelligence tests, Morton's investigation was not aimed at understanding how the human mind works, but rather at quantifying and ranking intelligence. Morton took a complex and multi-faceted phenomenon and put it through a series of reductions, turning it into a much simpler quantified result [84]. The result is a premature and inaccurate understanding of human intelligence, which is then assumed to be universally applicable across various contexts. The situation is compounded when intelligence rankings result in decreased developmental attention and resources for those who are lower-ranked.

As a response to this, it has been proposed that different types of intelligence exist, each defined as the ability to solve specific problems or create valuable solutions in context-rich situations [85]. For example, there are individuals with savant syndrome who exhibit exceptional abilities in a specialized domain despite significant limitations in other cognitive areas.

- Of the eight intelligences identified, namely linguistic, logical-mathematical, spatial, musical, bodily-kinesthetic, naturalistic, interpersonal, and intrapersonal, only linguistic and logical-mathematical were traditionally valued in schools [86]. Furthermore, the myopic focus on traditional intelligence may lead to the neglect of other important areas. For example, individuals may have high levels of education attainments but continue to lack adequate interpersonal skills or emotional intelligence. As such, an over-emphasis on traditional intelligence could lead us to become blind to the full range and diversity of human intelligence.

Likewise, we can breed blindness towards the 'depth' of human intelligence. For example, intelligence may not necessarily translate into critical thinking, which involves understanding information at a meaningful level, discerning information credibility, evaluating evidence and reasoning, recognizing biases, and solving real-world problems [87]. The bad news is that IQ tests only measure a limited set of cognitive abilities that people need, and these tests do not measure a person's ability to tackle complex real-world problems [87]. The good news is that research findings support the assertion that critical thinking can be taught and transferred [87].

Similarly, it has been found that multiple intelligences (MI) can be taught. A meta-analysis confirms that a substantial number of studies have found that MI interventions led students to outperform non-intervention control groups in academic subjects [85]. However, the same study found that many studies failed to meet the standards for high-quality experimental methodology that would allow for critical appraisal of the interventions' effectiveness, such as ensuring that both the participants and coaches were blind to experimental manipulation. [85]. More research is needed to determine the effectiveness of such interventions.

In MI interventions, coaches may aim to cater to all eight intelligences in the learning process as opposed to categorizing students through multiple-intelligence profiling [88]. One possible reason could be that coaches would want to avoid cultivating unhelpful attributions like 'I am not smart at something.'

Learners of a preferred intelligence can benefit from the learning activities of another intelligence. For example, a learner did not anticipate that intrapersonal reflection would be helpful, but his spatial abilities led him to discover patterns in the ways he enjoyed learning, and that led to more interest [88].

- The strength of MI lies in its ability to engage and cater to the individual's learning needs. For example, story-telling and dramatic narrative can be used to engage one's linguistic, interpersonal, and intrapersonal intelligences, while visualization, hands-on activities, mind-maps, and music may be used to engage one's bodily-kinesthetic and music intelligence [88].

- Neuro-imaging has shown that the same frontal cortex areas were involved in spatial, language, logic, mathematics, and memory tasks [89]. This suggests that our intelligence may not function in terms of multiple intelligences, but instead as a multi-faceted intelligence since the same brain areas are used. However, it was also suggested that the neurons in those brain areas adapt to code information that is relevant to a current task and prune away the irrelevant [89]. This supports the notion that restricting one's intelligence according to multiple intelligence may not promote learning [89]. Instead, an emphasis on all eight intelligences can be beneficial.

Now that we know intelligence is a multi-faceted construct, the question remains, 'is intelligence changeable?' We will answer that question through the lens of IQ, which is often regarded as unchangeable.

In one study, it was found that the IQ scores of urban children declined between the ages of 6 to 11 [90]. Certain factors, namely low birthweight, lower maternal IQ, single motherhood, and lower maternal education, were associated with lower child IQ at 6 years old but not with changes in IQ [90]. Instead, growing up in a disadvantaged community contributed to IQ decline [90]. However, it is important to note that IQ changes were not universally negative, as some children were found to have increased their IQ scores [90].

IQ scores can increase, decrease, or fluctuate greatly over a person's lifespan. Correlations of IQ test scores across ages 2 to 18 showed high correlations when the time interval was small, such as six months, but correlations decreased significantly when the time interval increased, such as from age 3 to 9 [91]. Nonetheless, the correlation of IQ test scores within any three-year period tended to become stronger with increasing age [91].

Nevertheless, the study found that 87% of the children experienced IQ changes of more than 10 points between the ages of 6 to 18, with roughly 9% showing consistent changes of more than 30 IQ points in one direction or the other [91].

Some children also showed significant fluctuations in IQ scores that varied with respect to their disturbing or stabilizing life experiences [91]. The disturbing life experiences included environmental strains like parent-child strains, economic insecurity, parental marital tension, and intra-personal tensions like acute body concerns [91].

Similarly, another study found IQ to be unstable across childhood and adolescence [92]. The study found that 59.5% of participants had IQ fluctuations that were 15 points or more and 7.1% had fluctuations that were more than 30 points [92]. The same study went on to investigate the link between pre-adult IQ and old-age IQ and found that pre-adult fluid intelligence was moderately correlated to old-age fluid intelligence [92]. However, pre-adult scores only accounted for a limited 12% of the variation in old-age scores [92].

As we can see, intelligence is very much changeable. However, one last consideration remains. We should not neglect how intelligence is applied and where it is applied.

Creativity, also known as divergent thinking, is used to generate solutions to unsolved problems. Three intellectual skills are said to be important for creativity: the ability to see problems in new ways and break away from conventional thinking, the analytic skills to determine if an idea is worth pursuing, and practical skills to sell the value of their ideas [93].

These intellectual skills must be accompanied by sufficient knowledge of the current state to move it forward [93]. In addition to this, intrinsic motivation, sensible risk-taking, and persistence during obstacles and ambiguity are crucial [93]. Not to mention, an environment has to be supportive and rewarding towards creativity for it to be displayed [93].

All of these factors seem to suggest that fluid intelligence alone may be insufficient for solving real-world problems. Instead, practical intelligence is needed [93]. This practical intelligence requires various ingredients such as creativity, motivation, sensibility, and perseverance. In other words, holistic development is crucial.

<u>What must Human Beings know about being human?</u>

<u>#6</u>

Why do people drop out of school?

The accumulation of risk factors impacts both cognitive development and school dropout.

One study found that harsh and inconsistent parenting was associated with poor school readiness in terms of cognitive and social development. This, in turn predicted conduct problems, which predicted school social and academic failure [94]. School failure then predicted a lack of parental monitoring, which predicted joining with other at-risk peers. This joining with at-risk peers predicted youth violence [94].

At the same time, students may reject or be rejected by the school [95]. As a result, students can become embarrassed and frustrated by their school failures, and their self-view and self-esteem become impaired [95]. This leads to a downward spiral as students become more disruptive, eventually engaging in delinquency [95]. As such, schools that fail to build student perception of their capacity for academic success or care for their psycho-social well-being may contribute to delinquency.

Moreover, students from schools with a high concentration of student poverty tended to have lower levels of school achievement and attainment [96]. The study suggested that this could be due to lower levels of engagement and aspirations [96]. Furthermore, long-term repercussions can be seen whereby students from high-poverty schools were more likely to be living in poverty later in life [96].

Given that poor school readiness included poor cognitive development, it makes sense to also look into the risk factors for cognitive development.

54

One study noted that the confluence of environmental risks led to greater risks to child intelligence [97]. Children who experienced the most risk factors had an average IQ of 85 compared to an IQ of 120 for children with no risk factors [97]. The risk factors identified included:

- Children being in a disadvantaged minority group [97].

- The head of the household was in low-skilled labor, semi-skilled labor, or unemployment [97].

- Children were in large families with four or more children living at home [97].

- Mother did not complete high school [97]. Here, it is important to note that these findings may not reflect the real causes of poorer cognitive development. Instead, they may reflect the disadvantages experienced by certain groups. For example, the real cause may be the parents' difficulty in being involved in their child's education as they work long hours to support their family.

  - In one study, parents with lower educational attainment were less involved in their children's education [98]. Adolescents whose parents were more involved in their education performed better in school regardless of their parents' education [98]. This involvement included whether parents attended school programs for parents [98]. Furthermore, parental involvement in child education exerted a larger effect on families with fewer resources [98], highlighting the effectiveness of such efforts.

- Risks to poorer cognitive development also included families with an absent spouse that led to lower family social support [97].

- Children experiencing major stressful life events [97].

- High maternal anxiety [97].

- Poor maternal mental health [97].

- Children receiving negative interactions from their parents, characterized by high dissatisfaction, criticism, and hostility, as well as low understanding, enjoyment, and warmth [97].

- The confluence of the above risk factors had an impact on the children's cognitive development, even after accounting for socio-economic levels and inherited IQ [97]. Furthermore, the IQ scores of at-risk children at ages 4 and 13 were highly correlated [97]. Similarly, the risky environments that they were exposed to at ages 4 and 13 were highly correlated [97]. This highlighted that their risky environments persisted, resulting in persisting disadvantages to their cognitive development.

Similarly, in another study, it was found that deficient environments led to a cumulative effect on child intelligence over time [99]. Furthermore, when environments improved, IQ scores also went up [99].

Disadvantageous environments can lead to poor cognitive development through biological effects. For example, early childhood malnutrition was associated with lower intelligence during later childhood [100] [101]. Children who were severely stunted from malnutrition scored much lower on intelligence tests than children who were less stunted [100]. Moreover, early stunting at 6 to 17 months old, persistent stunting, and greater stunting all corresponded with lower intelligence [100].

In a study conducted in a rural village in Indonesia, the prevalence of stunting in young children was observed to be 19% [101]. This was coupled with an underweight prevalence of 15.5% and severe thinness of 3.4% [101]. Once again, malnourished children had the lowest cognitive development scores [101]. Conversely, it was found that psychosocial stimulation, early childhood education, and nutrition positively affected cognitive development [101].

Now that we have seen the risk factors of poorer cognitive development, which was implicated in the pathway to delinquency, let us look at the risk factors for high school dropout. The risk factors are as follows:

- Persons had lackluster grades during first grade [102].

- Low grades during first grade interacted with family poverty to affect the likelihood of graduation [102].

- The child developed aggression during first grade [102].

- There was low parental involvement in the child's education [102].

- There were lenient parental rules with regard to schooling [102]. This could hint at neglectful or permissive parenting.

- Mothers held low hopes and expectations for the adolescents' educational attainment [102]. The mothers' expectations for their children affected the children's own hopes and expectations [102]. There was a heightened risk of dropout when adolescents held low hopes and expectations towards their education attainment [102].

- In terms of academic background, students who had been retained in a grade were 11 times more likely to drop out of school [103]. Furthermore, changing schools increased the risk [103]. Additionally, students who attended schools with high concentrations of grade-retained students were also at higher odds of dropping out [103]. It is conceivable that peer cultures affected the motivation towards school work. This is important because a one-hour increase in homework done per week reduced the probability of dropout by 10% [103].

- In terms of student attitudes, a poor locus of control and self-esteem were risk factors for dropout [103]. Similarly, perceptions that other students viewed them as troublemakers or poor students and perceptions that academic subjects were not going to be useful were risk factors [103]. Conversely, students who believed they were viewed positively by their peers were less likely to drop out [103].

- In terms of the school environment, students who reported having better and more caring teachers were less likely to drop out [103]. This affirms that positive teacher attitudes are important for student achievement. Furthermore, students' perception of their school having a fair discipline policy reduced the risks of school dropout [103]. Since students' behavioral problems predicted school dropout, how teachers handled these behaviors influenced the student outcome [103].

- To make things worse, students who experienced suspension or expulsion were said to be more likely to drop out of school and education [104].

- In another study, the top three reasons reported for dropping out were truancy, failing one or more classes, and getting into trouble with school authorities [105]. All of these indicate a sense of alienation from the school experience. Furthermore, 29.5% cited family problems, 23.5% cited learning problems, 21.5% cited drug and alcohol problems, 12% cited taking on a full-time job, 7.5% ran away from home, and 3.5% cited pregnancy [105]. Notably, among other reasons, some students dropped out because they were thrown out of their homes or beaten up by gangs at school [105].

- A large proportion of dropouts had counseling and treatment history. 73.1% received family counseling, 58.5% were treated for emotional problems, 45.4% were treated for drugs, 29.2% were diagnosed with a learning disability, and 23.8% were diagnosed with attention deficit hyperactivity disorder (ADHD) [105]. 22.3%

were also hospitalized for emotional problems [105]. All of these highlight that many students who dropped out were actually psychologically at-risk and struggled with mental health issues that may have arisen from their family and school environment.

- Furthermore, students who worked more hours in a job were more disengaged and performed poorer at school [106]. They spent less time on homework, paid less attention to class, gave less effort in school, and displayed more school misconduct like copying homework [106]. These adolescents also reported higher rates of delinquency and drug and alcohol use, as well as psychological distress like anxiety and depression and psychosomatic symptoms like stomachaches and headaches [106]. Lastly, they were less involved in family activities and were less monitored by their parents [106].

As can be seen, the risk factors of dropping out do not solely pertain to poor academic achievement. It includes many psychological and social factors. It would be a mistake to conclude that dropouts are simply unintelligent. Instead, a better explanation is that they do not receive the support or development they need. So what then are the repercussions of dropping out?

One study found that persons who dropped out of high school experienced higher rates of unemployment and significantly lower earnings [107]. Furthermore, those who dropped out were 63 times more likely to be incarcerated compared to their college counterparts [107]. Additionally, young female dropouts were six times more likely to become young mothers and almost nine times more likely to become single mothers [107]. A high proportion of these single mothers were said to live in poverty [107]. As we can see, school dropouts may lead to more challenging life trajectories.

It was also found that with each increment in school attendance, there were significant gains in intelligence [108]. Conversely, for each year children missed education, they forwent the beneficial development that school has on their cognitive development [108]. This is not to mention any social and economic benefits created. Furthermore, children who were deprived of school education from a young age had IQ that was comparable to the national average at age 6, but by age 14, their IQ scores were in the mentally retarded area [108].

- In addition, one study found that dropping out of high school had a negative effect on psychological functioning during adulthood [109].

- These effects included derogatory self-evaluations, such as branding the self as a failure, and cognitive disorientation, such as impaired cognitive functioning in response to stress [109]. Furthermore, an individual may display negative psychological reactions when failing to meet a situational demand [109]. They may also be more sensitive to another's opinion, feeling worthless when given criticism [109]. Unsurprisingly, people may also experience unstable self-attitudes, experiencing great shifts in self-feeling when facing failure, success, rejection, and acceptance [109].

Given the negative repercussions of school dropout, how can we prevent it?

In early education, children who liked school participated more in class, achieved more, and avoided school less [110]. This could be the starting point where students like school and continue liking it in the future.

School liking, which may be influenced by child preparedness for school demands, can be confounded with the child's evaluation of their progress and success in school [110].

In other words, their preparedness, positive experience, and sense of progress matter.

<u>Possible Initiatives</u>

- ✓ Some countries provide early developmental programs for disadvantaged children. For example, one such program was designed to facilitate growth in language, motor, social, and cognitive development for economically deprived infants, and it was found to be effective in reducing the effects of psychological and social deprivation on intelligence [111]. However, starting enrichment at a later age did not alter the adverse effects of early deprivation [111]. This highlights the potential importance of the timing of enrichment.

- ✓ Meanwhile, in another program, children from low SES families demonstrated improved cognitive development as well as mastery motivation during follow-ups at one and three years [112]. However, the study did not find effects on language development, socio-emotional development, academic readiness, and social competence despite the curriculum's design to enhance a wide range of outcomes [112]. Thus, programs need to find effective ways to enhance these outcomes.

- ✓ However, even though it was not reflected in this study, behavioral symptoms in children decreased during previous observations [112]. Moreover, parents also improved their knowledge of child development [112]. Coaching was provided to parents to improve their parent-child relationship as well as the quality and quantity of stimulation provided [112].

- ✓ In another study, children with academic-focused parents who attended low-academic preschools did not display academic disadvantage [113]. In contrast, they exhibited a more positive liking towards school [113]. As such, preschools may not need to be academically focused to be effective in fostering academic achievement.

✓ The good news is that preschool prevention programs designed to enhance children's competencies and prevent negative outcomes were generally found to have beneficial cognitive development, socio-emotional development, and parent-family wellness [114]. Some even had effects that persisted until high school [114]. Such programs may be targeted at all children or children from deprived families [114].

✓ Programs with a direct teaching component had the greatest cognitive impacts [114]. Furthermore, longer interventions led to greater gains and having follow-up programs at a later age helped maintain those gains [114].

✓ In one maltreated infant program, a follow-up 15 years later revealed that the adverse outcomes of maltreated children were significantly reduced, which included lower rates of impairment due to alcohol and substance abuse, intergenerational transmission of abuse, or getting into trouble with the law [114].

✓ Furthermore, early developmental programs can be a touchpoint to identify the risk factors faced by an individual. Further resources may then be put together to help a child mitigate those risks. These resources may include supporting parents in building positive mental health and positive parent-child relationship. Given that studies generally found beneficial effects for early developmental programs, we may aim for 100% of children to have access to such resources that may help mitigate the risks they face.

<u>What must Human Beings know about being human?</u>

<u>#7</u>

Can a family environment shape anti-social behavior?

Harsh parenting was found to be a predictor of child anti-social behavior [115]. Instead of convincing a child to adopt a new behavior, coercive parenting leads children to avoid the parent's demand and respond in an aversive manner [115]. Subsequently, the parent is likely to drop the demand due to the child's aversive response [115]. In other words, the disciplining was ineffective.

Long-term exposure to coercive interactions can have detrimental effect on a child's behavior, reinforcing aversive patterns and training them to interact anti-socially [115]. For example, a child may become more likely to reciprocate conflict when scolded by the parent. What follows is a massive social-skills deficit [115]. Consequently, a dysfunctional communication norm perpetuates within the family. Eventually, a child can be deemed as beyond parental control.

A family could provide a socialization setting characterized by high densities of aversive stimuli and reinforcement of conflict escalations [116]. Family members may stop communicating due to negative interactions that stem from various conflicts, such as belittling, discrediting, and prioritizing one's own views over others'. These insensitive actions can persist, leading to the development of avoidant or hostile relationships. Such socialization settings could contribute to the development of aggression.

It was found that parents and children who were in an aggressive relationship were more likely to initiate conflict in response to the other's aversive behavior [116]. They displayed higher levels of aversiveness during conflict, matched the other's aversiveness, had longer conflicts, and were more likely to escalate their behaviors [116].

64

They tried to win with a more aversive behavior and were less likely to de-escalate [116]. These conflicts may then cease due to an aversive behavior, reinforcing the use of higher aversiveness in a subsequent conflict [116].

The situation could eventually escalate to physical violence, including mutual violence. However, despite the dysfunctional outcomes, parents often believed that they used good parenting and blamed the child instead [115].

Furthermore, both aggressive parents and children were observed to be less receptive to soothing [116], which suggests an underdeveloped emotional regulation and problem-solving. In contrast, non-aggressive parents worked to de-escalate their child's aversiveness during a conflict [116].

Dysfunctional communication patterns may go on to affect a child outside of their family. When a child attempts to associate with their peers, their deficits and aggressive repertoire could lead to less reciprocation from non-aggressive peers [117]. Instead, aggressive children were more likely to develop mutual affiliations with other aggressive peers [117]. In addition, children were found to select affiliations based on the positive experience they received [117]. This may mean affiliating with those who are similar or reinforcing [117]. Children who associated frequently with aggressive peers were observed to display more aggressive behaviors over time [117].

Furthermore, the accumulation of risk factors was found to predict adolescents' aggressive and violent behaviors [118]. These risk factors included being a victim or witness of aggression, such as having rumors spread about them or having a history of exposure to neighborhood violence [118]. This was in addition to poorer academic skills, depression, psychoticism, callousness, and a violent media preference during childhood and adolescence [118].

<u>Possible Initiatives</u>

✓ Create behavioral training for parents and children to convert unhealthy communication styles into healthier ones. Foster habits of two-way communication that discuss a child's point of view and the parent's.

- This may include building awareness of sensitive interactions. Individuals can be facilitated to recognize unhealthy needs and compulsions during disagreements. Naturally, the language and emotional management used in peaceful communications can be explored.

- Programs may also provide opportunities to rehearse problem-solving and conflict resolution.

<u>What must Human Beings know about being human?</u>

<u>#8</u>

How is moral behavior developed?

Despite having high levels of educational attainment, some individuals may exhibit low levels of moral development, characterized by underdeveloped moral cognition and internalization.

People may interpret their immoral behaviors as moral because of a need to see themselves as moral and right [119]. In other words, the cognitive dissonance between their positive self-concept and detrimental impact may lead to rationalization, perverse justifications, or whitewashing of consequences. Vile behaviors can be romanticized and deemed as justified, requested, piety, self-defense, or peaceful.

Low levels of moral development could be due to poor moral reasoning. Moral reasoning refers to the logic that people use to make considerations [120]. At low levels of moral reasoning, people may lack awareness of the immorality of their behavior. They may be unable to differentiate between right and wrong due to underdeveloped thinking processes. As such, any behavior that is rewarded and not punished may be regarded as acceptable. Ultimately, impaired moral reasoning may translate into impaired moral judgments.

Moral development requires us to develop a deeper understanding of moral concepts and social reciprocity [120]. Ultimately, this translates into moral awareness and standards set in day-to-day living.

On top of moral reasoning, moral decisions can also be affected by automatic thinking [120]. In other words, moral decision can be made intuitively, with the reasoning constructed afterward [120]. In a fast-moving world where split-second decisions are made, many people may make moral decisions intuitively. This highlights the importance of a dominant moral schema that can be retrieved based on recall cues from long-term working memory.

Furthermore, insufficient working memory in a high-load situation can make moral decision-making difficult [120]. Adequate working memory, on the other hand, allows us to attend to multiple pieces of information and avoid an egocentric bias where we are preoccupied with our own perspective [120].

In addition to working memory, social information processing, such as attention, is also important [120]. This is because we may misinterpret cues, make hostile attributions, and fail to attend to important situational aspects [120]. In other words, our moral sensitivity can be impaired.

Additionally, we may possess an underdeveloped database of adaptive moral mental scripts [120], which contrasts with the adaptive refinement of schemas that is said to enable our moral development [120]. Specifically, moral schemata enable a competent, yet moral response to the demands of a situation.

In contrast, a narcissistic schema may impair moral decisions [120] due to its self-serving focus.

Unsurprisingly, perspective-taking ability may affect moral decisions [120]. It has been proposed that mature moral development is constructed through social perspective-taking [120]. Specifically, higher moral cognitions require us to look beyond our perspectives, think about the inadequacies of our reasoning, and search for more adequate ones [120].

This may necessitate the comprehension and application of abstract concepts, thus making abstract reasoning necessary [120].

Cognitive processes such as flexibility, goal setting, skillful communication, and self-control may also impact moral decisions [120].

These cognitions are conceivably important because they increase our repertoire and enhance our social and executive functioning.

In addition to logical components, affective components such as moral motivation and character can also affect moral decision-making. For instance, we may be motivated to behave morally due to our empathy and recognition of another person's emotions, such as distress [120].

On top of our ability to correctly identify another person's emotions, our emotional regulation, which includes impulse control and goal-directedness when experiencing difficulty and negative emotions, could play an important role in pro-social behavior [120].

Moving further, an affective component that may be less explored is 'needs.' For example, people may prioritize survival over moral behavior. One may also hold Machiavellian views, such as 'life is a zero-sum game' and 'it is better to gain and let others lose' [121].

Furthermore, people may prioritize their love and reciprocity needs [121]. For instance, they may say, 'love me, and I will love you too' [121]. This means operating on an equal exchange basis and may be followed by a focus on belongingness needs [121]. As a result, one may engage in moral behaviors towards in-group members but not towards out-group members.

In addition, people fulfill their need for self-esteem, status, social recognition, and acceptance through their groups [121]. A person's concept of right and wrong is anchored to their group's values [122]. However, a group's values may not always align with societal values. People who are not socialized to societal values may see little obligation to perform quid pro quo with strangers.

This implies that social interactions within life institutions can impact a person's moral behavior. If one is rejected by their peers, that rejection could impair their socialization to societal values and, in turn, their moral behavior.

Thus, without fulfilling the other needs, people may not seek self-actualization [121]. They may not uphold a set of internalized principles that makes up their moral character. A person's moral character is said to comprise three components – moral identity, self-regulation, and a motivational disposition to consider others' interests and needs [123]. When people hold a moral identity, they perform moral behavior because that is 'who they are' or 'who they want to be' [123].

However, a moral identity implies a 'moral self.' The moral self refers to individuals viewing themselves as moral persons [122]. This can be problematic because people seek to protect their moral self and escape self-condemnation during moral failure [122]. As a result, they may avert responsibility, fail to recall moral transgressions, and exclude others from moral treatment [122].

Moreover, the moral self can be extended to a group, meaning a 'moral self' turns into a 'moral us'. For instance, one may seek validation from a friend to confirm their moral superiority over their antagonist. This can create an illusion of righteousness.

The desire to perceive the self as moral can lead to the tendency to search for moral arguments that affirm one's worldview and behavior [122]. Furthermore, people may not revise their initial judgments, even when they fail to find supporting reasons [124]. Instead, they rely on irrational emotions [124]. Such tendencies during moral judgment can cause individuals to detach from reality and ignore the actual impact of their actions.

In one study, participants with prior opinions on a moral subject displayed defense motivation, uncritically accepting evidence that supported their beliefs, but scrutinizing opposing evidence [124]. People may even change their beliefs to avoid the threat of internal contradictions [124], altering their views to maintain that they were right all along.

In addition to internal distortions, moral judgment may be susceptible to social influence [124]. A friend may express a moral judgment against a person and that can be sufficient for us to make a moral judgment against that person [124]. Thus, if we feel a strong identification with our friend, we may adopt the same judgment without giving it enough thought [124]. Such biased conclusions can be due to our desire for a likable impression [124]. This illustrates how social mimicry can distort our moral judgment.

As can be seen, many biases could creep into moral judgment. As such, one may fail to perform moral behaviors even with a moral character. This is on top of any lack of moral reasoning, internalization, emotions, socialization, and identity. Logically, moral development would require us to tend to all of the above.

In a 20-year longitudinal study, sophistication of moral judgment was found to be positively correlated with age, socio-economic status, IQ, and education [125]. Furthermore, moral cognitions were observed to develop along a sequence of stages [125].

These findings support Kohlberg's six-stage cognitive-developmental model for moral judgment. The model proposed that children grow their ability to understand and integrate diverse views and consider more situational factors during a moral conflict [125]. This implies that developmental disadvantages formed by deprived environments could include moral development.

At this point, we know the ingredients needed for moral development. But how do we know if one is developing morally? Kohlberg presents six stages of moral judgment for us to discern so.

Stage 1 is on a 'pre-conventional' level. People follow rules to avoid punishment [125]. Their perspective is egocentric and they do not consider the interests of another [125]. They may not even recognize that others' interests could differ from their own [125]. In other words, they avoid harming others only for their own personal interests.

Moreover, these individuals may view actions from a purely physical point of view [125]. Therefore, non-physical harm, including psychological harm, may not be considered harmful.

Stage 2 is also on a pre-conventional level. People are concerned with individualism and act to meet their interests and needs [125]. However, they let others do the same, acknowledging that others also have their own interests [125].

Here, morality is regarded as a fair and equal exchange [125]. Individuals at this stage may consider anything involving a fair exchange by willing or unwilling parties to be moral, even if it is detrimental, such as buying and selling illicit drugs. Furthermore, individuals may behave morally only if they receive an equivalent benefit.

Stage 3 is on the 'conventional level.' It is about interpersonal expectations and relationships. People at this stage see morality as living up to what people expect from their role as family members or friends [125]. They may also be concerned with how other people feel [125]. However, people at this stage may be motivated by the need to be a 'good' person in their own eyes and the eyes of others [125]. In other words, they are concerned with protecting their moral selves and managing impressions. As we have seen, these motivations are subjected to biases.

Stage 4 remains conventional. It is about a social system. Here, morality is about contributing to a group, institution, or society [125]. It is about upholding laws and fulfilling agreed-upon duties. People behave morally to keep the system or society from breaking down because they recognize *that* would happen 'if everyone did it' [125]. 'It' could refer to crime, anti-social behavior, or even discourtesy. Here, morality shifts from interpersonal motives to one's relation to a system. However, anything that society does not deem immoral may not be regarded as such. In other words, this level of morality assumes that society has achieved the necessary values for moral living.

Stage 5 is 'post-conventional.' It is about social contracts, individual rights, and achieving the greatest good for the greatest number [125]. People perform moral behavior to fulfill their social contract to make laws and abide by them for the welfare of all [125]. At the same time, it is recognized that people uphold a variety of values and opinions relative to their groups, but there are also values and rights that must be upheld in any society, regardless of the majority's opinion [125]. This implies that we are now capable of pursuing a higher moral standard even when no one else is doing it.

Finally, stage 6 is about commitment to ethical principles. This may mean adherence to laws and social agreements, but also standing for what is right if those laws violate ethical universalisms like equal human rights and respect for human dignity [125]. Here, the rational person recognizes morality as 'people are ends in themselves and must be treated as such' [125]. In other words, every person's or group's perspective could be a consideration in a moral decision. Furthermore, the development of each affected person matters.

In the same study, only 18.8% of participants aged 20 to 22 used mainly stage 4 moral judgments for ethical dilemmas [125]. None used stage 5 [125]. A significant 40% used both stage 3 and 4 reasoning, whereas 31.3% used mainly stage 3 reasoning [125]. This reveals that moral reasoning at that age could remain focused on interpersonal expectations and relationships. However, the sophistication of moral judgment improved with age as the proportion of participants who used mainly stages 4 and 5 increased to about 33% from age 24 to 33 and 55% during age 36 [125].

At this point, we have seen how morality develops. However, the question remains, 'what could impair moral development?'

In one experiment, abused and neglected children displayed lower scores on their expressive vocabulary, which was, in turn, correlated to empathy narration, which was one of the measurements for moral development [126].

In the same experiment, children aged 5 were placed into situations where winning without cheating was impossible, and rule violations were needed [126]. Maltreatment, including both abuse and neglect, was found to have a significant effect on cheating behavior [126]. Maltreated children displayed much more cheating behavior than those who were not maltreated [126]. Neglected children displayed the least rule-compatible behavior, while abused children displayed more stealing behavior [126]. A possible explanation for this is that since maltreated children's basic and emotional needs were not met, winning had increased salience, and children were more emotionally reactive towards it [126].

However, in the same experiment, there was no significant difference between maltreated and non-maltreated children in terms of helping and comforting behavior [126]. Similarly, no statistically significant effect on empathy was found for maltreatment [126].

Nonetheless, gender differences were observed, where physically abused girls displayed less guilt and were less likely to give to others [126]. Furthermore, the same study found that the moral emotion of guilt, which could include remorse and apology, was associated with helping behaviors [126]. Taken together, these findings suggest that experiencing maltreatment may reduce feelings of guilt, and thus, reduce helping behaviors, even though the experiment results did not consistently affirm this idea.

In another study of preschool children, it was found that abused children exhibited more aggression and withdrawal towards distressed peers [127]. The term 'distress' in this context included crying, verbal expressions of pain, and requests for assistance or for the person to stop their behavior.

Moreover, the study found that abused children were more likely to cause distress in their peers [127]. This finding supports the notion that abused children may adopt patterns similar to those of their abusive parents. Abusive parents were said to respond to their distressed children with less sympathy, nurturing, and positive interactions [127]. Such a developmental trajectory could be a precursor to later deficits.

In a study of school-age children, it was reported that maltreated children displayed lower pro-social behaviors [128]. Additionally, they scored higher on withdrawal behaviors and received lower ratings from their peers and counselors regarding their social competence [128]. As such, maltreatment and deficits in moral development could potentially affect a child's peer relations and, consequently, their overall adjustment.

In another study, abused children were found to be more emotionally maladjusted and significantly less empathetic [129]. Interestingly, the abused children did not differ from the non-abused group in measures of aggression [129]. However, the lower empathy exhibited by maltreated children suggests that maltreatment may affect various components of moral development.

One study found that incarcerated delinquents scored lower on Kohlberg's moral judgment measures, indicating a retardation in moral development [130]. The same study also investigated anti-social youths who were pre-delinquent, whom the teachers described as aggressive, lacking in impulse control, and showing little forethought in their actions [130]. They were further noted to have emotional dysregulation, poor self-image, and difficulty interacting with their peers [130]. This group demonstrated moral dilemma test scores that were closer to incarcerated delinquents as compared to well-adjusted youths [130].

Nevertheless, past studies have reported that moral judgment is malleable. Youths exposed to moral views at higher stages than their own showed an increase in higher-stage thinking and a decrease in lower-stage thinking [130]. Additionally, discussing and reinforcing higher moral reasoning has been shown to improve moral judgment scores [130].

However, advances in moral reasoning alone may be insufficient for moral behavior, as hinted by neurological findings.

During adolescence, exposure to social stimuli activated brain regions that overlapped with those that were sensitive to reward magnitude [131]. This implies that the mere presence of peers makes risk-taking rewards more salient, as it also activates the same circuitry for non-social rewards [131]. It has been reported that teenagers took double the risks in the presence of peers [131]. Conversely, peer presence had no such effect on adults [131]. In other words, adolescents experience increased sensitivity to socio-emotional stimuli.

This may explain why adolescents were susceptible to anti-social peer influence, and why many instances of risk-taking, such as drinking, delinquency, and dangerous driving occurred in groups [131]. Incidentally, increased sensation seeking has also been found during early adolescence [131].

Cognitive control is the brain system that opposes such risk-taking. Cognitive-control capabilities, such as impulse control, emotional regulation, delay of gratification, and resistance to peer influence, continue to mature into adulthood [131]. During adolescence, the developing cognitive control and judgment may not be strong enough to regulate the risky behavior performed during peer presence and emotional arousal [131].

In addition, neuroimaging has revealed that the dorsal lateral prefrontal cortex, which is important for controlling impulses and weighing decision consequences, is among the latest brain regions to mature [132]. Specifically, adult dimensions were not reached until the early 20s [132].

Furthermore, in another neural study, adolescents displayed deficits in Ventral Striatum (VS) activation during 'gain anticipation' as compared to adults [133]. To put it simply, less VS activation means that adolescents seek more extreme stimuli, i.e., high-risk, high-reward, to compensate for lower VS activity levels [133].

The VS is said to respond to learned cues to motivate efforts to obtain a potential reward [133]. This is in contrast to the mesial frontal cortex, which is said to direct one's energy towards appropriate goals [133]. Thus, if there is low VS activation, a more extreme stimulus with a large enough potential reward is needed to motivate action. This implies that low VS activation may include boredom since cues provide less motivation and anticipated rewards.

Moreover, a VS activation deficit may reflect developmental deficits in attention control, like that of attention deficit hyperactivity disorder [133]. Simply put, less attention and processing may be given to motivational stimuli.

All of these factors may explain why some youths seek strong sensations. One study found strong links between sensation-seeking and risky behaviors, which included pranks, harassment, getting drunk, skipping school, shoplifting, speeding in a motor vehicle, and taking drugs [134].

In particular, risky behavior was correlated with sensation-seeking in terms of 'Activity,' which refers to the desire to do wild things with a group, and 'Outgoingness,' which refers to a desire to be the center of attention [134].

Conversely, risky behavior was negatively correlated with the challenges made by parents and the school towards risky behavior, though correlations for school-made challenges did not reach statistical significance [134]. This indicates that the fewer challenges adolescents received from their social environment, the more they were involved in risk-taking [134]. Interestingly, challenges from friends were found to be related to more risk-taking behavior [134]. This may reflect the desire to stand out and obtain social attention.

Such patterns may have long-term repercussions. For example, adolescent substance use was found to increase the odds of adult substance use [135]. Participants who ever tried smoking in high school were three times as likely to be smoking at age 35 [135]. The odds increased dramatically if participants were heavier smokers during high school [135].

Similarly, participants who drank heavily during high school were three times as likely to be heavy drinkers at age 35 [135]. Participants who used marijuana during high school were eight times as likely to be users at age 35 [135]. Similarly, participants who tried any illicit drug during high school were five times as likely to be using cocaine at age 35 [135]. Furthermore, a history of substance use at 18 years old strongly predicted substance use at age 35 [135]. All these highlight long-term risks.

Thus, if brain neurology, peer influence, and habits could prevent the responsible conduct that denotes possible moral development, how is moral development encouraged instead?

- Parents and peers can influence moral development through their interactional style, moral reasoning level, and ego functioning [136]. Ego functioning refers to one's psychological maturity. Certain combinations of these interrelated factors have been found to facilitate higher rates of moral development [136].

- Surprisingly, peer contexts that challenged one's reasoning were associated with minimal moral development [136]. Informative interactions were also associated with slower moral growth [136]. One explanation could be that a child perceives such interactions to be a lecture or antagonistic criticism, and they respond with defensiveness or aversion.

- Conversely, parental and peer interactions that elicited the other person's opinion and focused on understanding its reasoning were predictive of high rates of moral development [136]. Such interactions, when combined with supportiveness, predicted moral development [136].

- Regarding parent-child interactions, higher levels of moral reasoning were found to be effective at stimulating child moral development [136]. This relationship was not observed within a peer context, possibly due to a lack of disparity in moral reasoning among peers [136].

- Conversely, parents and peers who engage in 'ego-defending' behaviors may not provide stimulating relationships or engage with moral problems in meaningful manners [136]. Ego defending behaviors included rigidity, rationalization, denial, regression, intolerance towards ambiguity, insensitivity to others' feelings and ideas, and mishandling of emotions [136].

- High levels of informative interactions combined with poor ego functioning within peer groups were found to stun moral development [136].

- Parent-child groups with parents who have poor ego functioning displayed interactions characterized by negative affect, devaluation, threats, as well as hostility that interfered with coherent discussion [136].

- Conversely, discussing the child's real-life moral conflicts predicted moral growth [136]. Similarly, discussing hypothetical moral dilemmas with friends also predicted moral development [136].

All of this can lead to neurological development. Persons who demonstrated post-conventional moral reasoning were found to have greater gray matter volume in their ventromedial prefrontal cortex (vmPFC) and subgenual anterior cingulate cortex (sgACC) [137]. This provides initial evidence of brain alterations based on Kohlberg's stages of moral reasoning [137]. The increased gray matter highlights the development of brain abilities that corresponded with the sophistication of moral reasoning.

Other studies have also found that both vmPFC and ACC were activated when one monitored behavioral outcomes, ethically adapted behavior, and experienced moral emotions [137].

Additionally, post-conventional moral reasoning was found to be slightly correlated with moral judgment competence [137]. Moral judgment competence refers to the ability to apply moral values consistently in challenging social situations [137]. Both post-conventional moral reasoning and moral judgment competence were positively associated with the number of years of formal education [137].

Taking all of these into consideration, it is evident that moral judgment is malleable. Just as deprived environments may hinder moral development, interventions can be effective in promoting it.

Possible Initiatives

✓ Parenting courses could include the cultivation of higher moral reasoning and awareness of poor ego functioning. Through role-playing, parents could replace ego-defending interactions with more productive ones. They could learn to seek their child's perspective, understand their reasoning, explain consequences, and clarify why something is right or wrong.

✓ Similarly, children and adolescents could be given opportunities to cultivate moral reasoning within a peer context. They could evaluate risk-taking behaviors and the need to stand out among their peers. This could involve brainstorming moral solutions for moral dilemmas and adverse situations. The goal of these activities would be to enhance moral judgment competence.

<u>What must Human Beings know about being human?</u>

<u>#9</u>

How does moral disengagement work?

As if it were the antithesis to moral development, moral disengagement opposes necessary self-improvement.

Instead of facing up to the consequences of their behavior, people employ mechanisms to disengage from self-sanctions. Validations and rationalizations allow them to live with their unethical actions and continue behaving in that manner [138]. People use moral disengagement to cope with the emotional discomfort that comes with learning about the consequences of their unethical actions [138].

Moral disengagement is a form of cognitive restructuring [139]. Inhumane and detrimental behaviors are considered harmless or even worthy [139]. Moral disengagement is said to encompass four categories: self-exoneration through advantageous comparison, minimizing or displacing one's responsibility, misrepresenting or discounting the detrimental outcome, and victim blaming [139].

People may exonerate themselves by advantageously comparing their detrimental behavior to an equal or greater unethical behavior [138] [139]. For example, one may say, 'I could have done something worse' or 'this is nothing in comparison to what others have done.'

People may also use moral justification and sanitizing language, such as a 'utilitarian' moral justification where they conclude that non-violent options are ineffective for achieving their desired change [139]. This can be accompanied by a second moral justification, where they see their injurious action as a prevention of human suffering, preventing more suffering than the injury caused [139].

- People may also sanitize and sanctify their militant actions while condemning the behaviors of their antagonists [139]. In some cases, they may even claim to be 'carrying out God's will' [139]. This can lead to a sense of moral superiority. Behaviors that were previously considered detrimental are now perceived as acceptable [139]. Furthermore, people may justify aggression as a means of protecting their honor and reputation [140].

The second form of moral disengagement involves minimizing, disavowing, or displacing one's involvement in the harm created [138] [139].

- This is best summed up by the phrase, 'when everyone is responsible, no one really feels responsible' [138]. Blame is spread among other group members, diffusing personal responsibility and making the accountability unclear. This weakens moral control, which is further compounded by anonymity during collective action [139]. In such situations, any harm caused by a group can always be attributed to others [139]. Conversely, moral control is strongest when people acknowledge their role as contributors to the detrimental outcome [139].

- Another common justification for unethical behavior is the idea that 'everyone is doing it' or 'if I do not do it, somebody else will.' This kind of herd mentality can lead to situations where any action becomes acceptable simply because others are doing it, and people fear losing out if they do not participate.

- Individuals may also displace their responsibility onto others. Some of the worst atrocities in World War 2 were committed by people who divested their personal responsibilities and claimed that they were simply carrying out orders [139]. Similarly, people may push the blame onto a few 'bad apples' in the group.

- Some individuals may also argue that the circumstances were beyond their control, claiming they had no choice [138]. This hints at a culture where conformity to harmful behavior is socially rewarding, while moral behavior is punished.

The third form of moral disengagement involves misrepresenting and discounting negative consequences [138]. People disregard or minimize the detrimental effects of their actions [139].

- For instance, people may say, 'my actions did not hurt anybody,' 'they enjoyed it,' or 'it is for your benefit.'

- Selective inattention occurs when people more readily recall the potential benefits of their behavior but not the harm [140]. Similarly, people reject disagreeing evidence but accept evidence that supports their views. Ultimately, this translates into action. People take active efforts to discredit evidence of the harm they create [140].

The fourth form of moral disengagement attributes the blame to victims, dehumanizing and devaluating them [138] [139]. By blaming the victim, unethical behavior becomes excusable or even righteous [138].

- For example, people may say, 'he should not have gotten so drunk.' [138] As such, perpetrators view themselves as faultless victims who are driven to immoral actions.

- Furthermore, people stop regarding others as persons, making it easier to brutalize them [139]. Dehumanized individuals can be seen as undeserving of rights or of lower status.

So why do people engage in moral disengagement? Moral disengagement is often a response to the negative emotions people experience upon learning the harmful consequences of their behavior [138]. More specifically, it causes shame.

Shame is the preoccupation with self-esteem, reputation, and standing with others [138]. Essentially, people engage in moral disengagement to protect their reputation and sense of personal significance.

It is important to note that shame should not be confused with guilt. Guilt is experienced when individuals accept responsibility for the negative outcome and seek to rectify the harm caused [138]. In other words, shame is self-focused, guilt is restitution-focused.

In contrast, shame was found to be positively related to the diffusing and displacing of responsibility, as well as the minimizing and reconstruing of actions [138]. Conversely, guilt was negatively related.

One study found that individuals who were highly prone to moral disengagement, were more easily angered, ruminated on perceived grievances, experienced less guilt, and felt less necessity in making amends for their harmful behavior [140]. These individuals also engaged in higher levels of aggression and delinquent behavior [140].

In contrast, participants who experienced guilt over detrimental actions tended to refrain from aggressive and delinquent behaviors [140].

In addition, those who ruminated were more aggressive in their interpersonal relationships [140]. They were also more transgressive, meaning destructive, verbally abusive, and deceptive [140].

Aggressive and delinquent behaviors were found to be positively correlated with moral disengagements, including the reconstruing of harmful behavior as moral, obscuring responsibility, misrepresenting harmful consequences, and vilifying victims through blame or dehumanization [140].

A direct pathway was found between moral disengagement and delinquent behavior, with an indirect pathway through aggression proneness [140]. Aggression proneness was strongly related to rumination, ease of anger, and less proneness towards prosocial behavior, guilt, and restitution [140].

In contrast, no direct pathway was found between moral disengagement and aggression [140]. However, an indirect path was identified [140]. Moral disengagers were more prone to aggressive thought patterns [140]. In turn, rumination of grievances, punitive retaliation, and proneness to anger lessened restraints towards aggressive behavior [140].

Moral disengagement can be a gradual process where moral self-sanction becomes disengaged from violent conduct [139]. It may begin with pro-social efforts to change social policies or oppose officials who were intent on maintaining an inadequate status quo [139].

Non-violent behaviors, failing to achieve social change, accumulate and confound with hostile confrontations with the authorities [139]. Unconvinced by the authority's stance, disillusionment and alienation set in. People begin to dehumanize the authorities and peaceful actions escalate into violent ones. Thus, individuals who once held pro-social intentions may unknowingly become morally disengaged from the behaviors that are antithetical to the pro-social impacts they desired.

Moral disengagement may also take the form of normalization where people do not perceive or evaluate normalized behaviors. For example, normalization was found to account for alcohol and cigarette use in addition to individual risk factors [141].

In another study, moral disengagement was found to be implicated in the normalization of toxicity in online gaming [142]. Behaviors like verbal abuse were deemed to be within 'acceptable' limits [142]. Furthermore, players who were high in moral disengagement were less likely to perceive online game interactions as toxic [142]. Players did not feel obligated to report toxic behaviors performed onto others, and were reluctant to involve themselves in such matters [142]. Some participants noted, 'I wouldn't care enough to report it' [142].

A possible implication is that as people become more approving of toxic behavior, they become more likely to engage in it [142]. Engaging in the behavior reinforces the belief that such behavior is normal and acceptable [142].

In addition to normalization, being in a group can cause individuals to perform actions that they would not perform when alone. In one study, it was found that being in a group decreased individual self-consciousness [143]. Furthermore, the larger the group, the less self-conscious individuals were, especially when there was a high degree of similarity within the group, and no observation from outsiders [143]. This is problematic because individuals who were less self-conscious exhibited more intense behavior [143]. Additionally, people may become less reliant on their own standards [143].

In other words, people in groups may lose their sense of reason and become disinhibited towards aggression and anti-social behaviors.

Similarly, anonymity can also lead to increased aggression.

In one study, participants played a game that was impossible to win due to other 'players' [144]. However, unbeknownst to them, those 'players' were actually computer manipulations by the experimenter [144]. After the game, participants were given the opportunity to express themselves in a blog about their experience [144].

In those blog posts, participants who were anonymous displayed higher levels of verbal aggression that degraded others [144]. Furthermore, anonymous participants who were exposed to another's aggressive posts had more aggressive posts than those who were not anonymous and not exposed to aggressive models [144].

In sum, we have seen that moral disengagement can occur due to the need to avoid discomfort during the realization of one's own moral failings. This can be done through rationalizations. However, we have also seen that anonymity or deindividuation within a group can unconsciously influence moral disengagement.

<u>Possible Initiatives</u>

✓ Moral education programs could facilitate discussions that critically evaluate the various cognitions and needs that drive moral disengagement. These include sanitization, 'moral' justifications, and the diffusion of responsibility. Additionally, individuals could practice overcoming their discomfort from being wrong and become more receptive to self-improvement.

✓ Programs could also explore the mental fortitude and moral courage required to stand against herd mentality and morally wrong consensus with a group. This may include resisting misaligned incentives.

PART II

Adverse Life-trajectories

<u>What must Human Beings know about being human?</u>

<u>#10</u>

What risk factors accumulate for adverse life-trajectories?

Adverse life-trajectories can begin before birth, as low-quality prenatal environments can lead to long-lasting effects.

<u>Prenatal Risks</u>

In one study, children who were prenatally exposed to cocaine had higher rates of delinquency after accounting for covariates [145]. Similarly, prenatal exposure to methamphetamine was associated with child externalizing problems at five years old [146]. In contrast, marijuana exposure was found to be a risk factor for internalizing problems, but not for depressive symptoms [145]. These risks are compounded by parental substance abuse, which could interfere with competent parenting [146], and parental incarceration resulting from substance abuse, which is also likely to affect child development.

Additionally, prenatal alcohol exposure has been found to be significantly associated with higher levels of behavioral problems among young and old children [147]. Heavy prenatal alcohol exposure, in particular, leads to 'Fetal Alcohol Syndrome' (FAS), which is linked to a devastating array of adverse developmental outcomes [148].

- FAS is one of the leading identifiable causes of mental retardation, with the average IQ of individuals with heavy prenatal exposure being 70 [148]. Additionally, children with FAS have been found to display difficulties in inhibitory control, working memory, and problem-solving, which can be predictive of poorer social skills and greater problem behaviors [148].

- Furthermore, alcohol-exposed children displayed decreased planning, increased rule violations, and increased persistence in incorrect strategies during problem-solving tasks [148].

- Alcohol-exposed children were also found to be impaired in language tests, reading, spelling, arithmetic, and verbal and non-verbal learning that cannot be accounted for by differences in IQ [149]. This was partially supported in another study which found detrimental effects on arithmetic ability to be significant even after controlling for IQ. However, in that study, deficits in reading and spelling were largely explained by IQ [150].

- In the same study, deficits in arithmetic abilities were found to be tied to alcohol dosages, while reading and spelling deficits were tied to drinking amounts that crossed a threshold [150]. Learning retention, on the other hand, seemed to be relatively unaffected [149]. Nonetheless, children with FAS may be at higher risk of academic difficulties.

- Moreover, children with prenatal alcohol exposure also experienced higher rates of Attention Deficit Hyperactivity Disorder (ADHD) [148]. Specifically, children with FAS often displayed difficulty in maintaining attention and inhibiting impulsive responses [148].

- The far-reaching implications of prenatal alcohol exposure extended to lower moral maturity, measured in terms of the sophistication of moral reasoning [151]. In particular, there was lower 'affiliative' reasoning which pertained to an individual helping their family and friends [151]. Although deficits in verbal IQ accounted for significant deficits in overall moral reasoning, the deficits in affiliative moral reasoning were specific to prenatal alcohol exposure [151].

- The same study also found that participants with heavy prenatal alcohol exposure had significantly higher rates of delinquent behaviors, as well as probable conduct disorders measured by problematic behaviors such as stealing, fighting, and lying [151].

So far, we have seen the developmental effects of prenatal alcohol exposure. But what about its impact on life outcomes?

- One study found that prenatally alcohol-exposed youths were disproportionately represented in the juvenile justice system [152]. This highlighted heightened risks of getting into trouble with the law.

- Prenatal maternal drinking was also found to have an effect on offspring alcohol dependence 21 years later, even after controlling for family environment factors [153].

- Lastly, one study found that FAS teenagers had a higher prevalence rate for suicide ideation within a 12-month period [154]. The rate was 35.2%, which was twice the rate of other teenagers [154]. Furthermore, FAS teenagers were almost 5.5 times more likely to make a serious attempt at suicide compared to other teens [154]. All of these suggest life difficulties.

What is little known is that paternal drinking habits may potentially impact fetal development through an effect on the father's sperm genetic material or an accumulation of toxins in the semen [155]. However, the current evidence is mostly circumstantial or based on animal experiments. Preliminary testing showed that the offspring of alcoholic males displayed selective learning and functional impairments [155]. Alcohol exposure during the animal's sexual maturation, followed by an alcohol-free period to restore normal hormonal status, continued to lead to abnormal offspring development [155].

On top of alcohol exposure, prenatal tobacco exposure was found to be associated with an increased likelihood of externalizing problems at ages 4, 9, and 10 [145]. However, studies disagreed on the nature of the link. For example, one study found tobacco exposure to be directly associated with increased problem behavior [156], whereas another suggested that the link was due to confounding factors like familial characteristics [147].

- Maternal smoking, especially heavy smoking, was associated with lower infant birthweight [157]. Prenatal smoking was also associated with fetal deprivation of oxygen and nutrition, and neurological complications [157]. All of this could create risks for future neurodevelopment [157].

- Furthermore, infants of pregnant smokers experienced an increased risk of intrauterine growth restriction (IUGR), which refers to a baby weighing less than 9 out of 10 babies at the same gestational age [158]. IUGR was associated with a six to nine times increase in infant mortality risk [158].

- At the same time, one study found that children born with IUGR had an increased risk of delays in cognitive abilities at two years old [159].

- Furthermore, a study into behavioral development at 7.5 years old found that maternal smoking throughout pregnancy was associated with child ADHD symptoms and internalizing behaviors [160].

The good news is that interventions that helped cease prenatal smoking reduced the number of low-birthweight infants [158]. However, the detrimental effect of smoking was not limited to smoking mothers but also mothers exposed to smoke [158].

Similarly, postnatal smoke exposure poses risks to child development. Various parental factors were found to be associated with child exposure to cigarette smoke. These included household poverty, parental history of ADHD, lower caregiver IQ, lower maternal age, father not living at home, and caregiver hostility and depression [161].

All of these were associated with higher smoke exposure from early childhood to 4 years old [161]. Conversely, having parents who completed college and high school was correlated with lower exposure [161].

A young child's exposure to smoke was, in turn, associated with hyperactivity-impulsivity and conduct problems [161]. This link was substantiated even after accounting for prenatal exposure [161].

In addition, higher levels of hyperactivity-impulsivity were predicted by caregiver depression and complications during pregnancy and delivery [161]. Similarly, conduct problems were predicted by caregiver hostility and lower caregiver IQ [161].

Unfortunately, the effects of tobacco exposure do not stop there. Children who were prenatally and environmentally exposed to tobacco were 1.5 times more likely to experience learning disabilities [162]. Learning disabilities refer to neurobehavioral disorders that affect a person's ability to learn and process information, even with an average IQ [162]. Needless to say, learning disabilities may heighten the risks of school dropout [162].

Although some studies also found that smoking during pregnancy was linked to offspring mental illnesses like bipolar disorder and schizophrenia, one study found that the link was likely due to confounding risks within the family environment [163]. In a sense, pregnancy smoking could indicate a high-risk family environment that is detrimental to the offspring's mental health.

At this point, we have seen that destructive parental habits can lead to adverse development. However, parental mental health also matters in infant development. For example, prenatal maternal anxiety was associated with child externalizing problems, ADHD symptoms, and self-reported anxiety at 8 and 9 years old [164]. This was found to be so even after accounting for postnatal maternal anxiety [164].

<u>Risks within a young children's family</u>

High caregiver stress and psychological symptoms were associated with an almost three times increase in children's risk of developing externalizing problems [146]. A similar association was found in another study. Caregiver psychological distress was associated with child behavioral problems like attention problems, social problems, delinquency, and aggression [145]. Conversely, high-quality home environments, such as those responsive to child developmental and emotional needs, were associated with decreased risk of internalizing and externalizing problems [146].

On top of caregiver psychological distress, child neglect can increase the risk of internalizing and externalizing behaviors [165]. The latter included aggression, antagonism, and rule-breaking behavior [165]. This is on top of any adverse emotional and cognitive development [165]. Furthermore, neglected children were found to face difficulties in identifying emotional facial expressions [165]. This hints at social difficulties.

One study even found the effect size of neglect to be the largest for externalizing behavior [165]. This was in comparison to other maltreatment types like emotional and physical abuse [165].

In turn, externalizing behavior during childhood and adolescence was associated with the development of adult anti-social behavior [165]. As such, neglect could be the pathway to adult violence.

- In parenting theory, neglectful parenting refers to a style that is low in warmth, acceptance, and supervision and control [166]. It is a parenting style where parents are disengaged from child-rearing responsibilities [166]. Parenting styles are important because they have far-reaching effects on a child's psychosocial development, school competence, internalized distress, and problem behaviors [166].

- The same study also found that those with neglectful parents had poorer outcomes across the board when compared to those with authoritative parents who were high in warmth and supervision [166].

- Children who reported neglectful parenting reported poorer psychosocial development, including lower task perseverance, reduced social competence, lower feelings of internal control, and difficulty making decisions independently [166].

- This group also reported poorer school competence, including lower grades, reduced school attachment and satisfaction, and lower academic competence, measured by the ability to complete school homework [166]. Furthermore, neglected children had higher psychological symptoms and were more likely to engage in drug and alcohol use [166], suggesting maladaptive coping.

- Neglected children also reported higher rates of delinquency, including carrying a weapon, getting into trouble with the law, and school misconduct such as cheating and copying homework [166].

In contrast to neglectful parenting, authoritative parenting emphasizes consistency in non-harsh disciplining, inductive reasoning to explain rules, problem-solving, child monitoring, and positive reinforcement of desirable behavior [167]. Such parenting was found to be negatively associated with a child's low self-control, which refers to their efforts to utilize available self-regulation skills [167]. Self-control was measured in terms of impulsivity, ease of frustration, and the desire for quick gratification [167]. These are similar to the poor task perseverance and low feelings of internal control implicated in neglectful parenting.

Low self-control was associated with child delinquency, affiliation with deviant peers, lower affiliation with prosocial peers, and weaker attachment to teachers [167]. Attachment to teachers is crucial because it predicts increased self-control [167].

Improvements in authoritative parenting were associated with increased child affiliation with pro-social peers, while deviant peer affiliation predicted escalations in low self-control [167].

- A closer look at self-control revealed that it can be differentiated into cognitive and attitudinal self-control, which were negatively related to thrill-seeking and delinquency [168].

- Cognitive self-control refers to the ability to consider consequences, while attitudinal self-control involves restraining behavior during temptation [168]. For example, self-control could mean appreciating the costliness of a behavior instead of giving in to carelessness and an inability to delay gratification [168].

- On the other hand, thrill-seeking refers to the degree to which one perceives risky activities as pleasurable or rewarding [168]. Both thrill-seeking and self-control were found to have independent effects on offending [168].

- Specifically, thrill-seeking was strongly related to delinquency [168]. Unfortunately, thrill-seeking was found to have stronger effects than both forms of self-control [168]. Furthermore, the inhibiting effects of self-control on delinquency declined as thrill-seeking increased [168], and at high levels of thrill-seeking, self-control had no effect on delinquency [168].

In sum, parenting can be linked to a child's internalized distress, problem behaviors, school competence, and other developmental areas such as self-control. This has conceivable impacts on child adjustment.

According to a study, teenagers who perceived neglectful parenting and affectionless control had a twofold increase in odds of developing psychiatric disorders during later adolescence [169]. The risk was six times for depressive disorders [169].

Moreover, perceived neglect and affectionless control were positively associated with anxiety, mood disorders, conduct problems, and ADHD scores [169].

In addition to neglectful parenting, permissive parenting is problematic. Permissive parents are lenient, emphasize freedom, and do not require mature behaviors from their children [170]. In other words, they do not set standards or cultivate appropriate behaviors.

- Teenagers with permissive parents were found to be less pro-social and socially responsible [170]. They were also heavier users of illicit drugs and alcohol, less cognitively motivated and competent, less self-regulated, and tended to act out sexually [170]. These behaviors suggest low self-control, as permissive parents fail to guide their children in regulating behaviors [171]. Instead, children may control their parents through coercion and indulge in low self-control and aggressive behaviors [171].

- Moreover, a study found that permissive parenting was associated with child externalizing problems, but only for boys [171]. However, the problematic behaviors may only be symptoms of a deeper problem. This was illustrated in another study which found that permissive parenting was positively associated with a diffuse-avoidance identity style and negatively associated with identity commitment [172], suggesting that children with permissive parents may struggle with their sense of self.

- It was said that adolescents who use a diffuse-avoidant style tend to avoid identity considerations [172]. Moreover, their behaviors may be mainly determined by hedonic cues and situational influences [172], which seems similar to pre-conventional morality. Furthermore, the lack of commitment to a set of values for personal decisions could indicate an underdeveloped moral identity. In contrast, authoritative parenting was found to be associated with identity styles that lead to identity commitment [172].

- The risks of parental permissiveness do not stop there. Perceived parental permissiveness was found to be an independent predictor of narcissistic tendencies [173]. These tendencies included self-grandiosity, fantasies of self-perfection, a sense of entitlement, interpersonal exploitativeness, arrogance, and a lack of empathy [173].

The same study found that *authoritarian* parenting, characterized by harsh control and low warmth and responsiveness to a child's emotional needs, was associated with increased narcissism [173]. In contrast, self-esteem was negatively associated with narcissism [173].

- Intuitively, we can see that parenting that harshly criticizes or debases children for non-compliance is unlikely to be healthy for child development. Authoritarian parenting has been found to be associated with a myriad of negative developmental repercussions.

- Similar to permissive parenting, authoritarian parenting was found to be associated with child externalizing problems [171]. This study measured authoritarian parenting in terms of parental overreaction, and externalizing problems in terms of hyperactivity, emotional symptoms, conduct problems, and peer problems [171].

- Authoritarian parenting can be intrusive, restrictive, and unsupportive. Such parenting has been associated with lower child maturity, resilience, and social consciousness [170]. Children with authoritarian parents also displayed higher internalizing problems and external locus of control [170]. However, this study did not find heightened externalizing problems [170].

- A review noted that authoritarian parenting was implicated with an increased likelihood of child depressive symptoms and co-morbid anxiety and mood disorders [174]. Additionally, authoritarian parenting was also linked to lower child self-confidence and self-esteem [174].

- Similarly, authoritarian parenting has been linked to maladaptive emotional regulation, suicidal tendencies, aggression, and anger outbursts [174]. Children may also engage in self-criticism and self-humiliation [174]. These findings highlight the potential deleterious effects of such parenting on child mental, social, and emotional health.

- Harsh disciplining can lead to child aggression due to the development of maladaptive social information processing, including a hostile attribution bias where children attribute another person's behavior to hostile intentions [175]. Furthermore, a study found that higher levels of harsh discipline were associated with greater information processing difficulties as children pay less attention to relevant social cues [175]. Harsh punishment was also linked to an increased tendency to generate aggressive responses [175].

- In turn, 'information processing deficits', hostile attribution bias, and tendencies to generate aggressive responses were positively related to child aggression [175]. This could be compounded by a positive outcome evaluation for the use of aggression [175]. Additionally, further investigations found that harsh discipline at home was linked to child aggression at school through the pathway of social information processing [175]. To elaborate, school aggression included both proactive and reactive aggression [175]. Proactive aggression involved the use of force to dominate others, whereas reactive aggression involved angry overreactions [175].

- Another study found that harsh parenting had both direct and indirect effects on child school aggression [176]. The indirect link was through the development of poor emotional regulation [176].

- A possible explanation for the link between harsh parenting and child aggression is that harsh parenting includes parental behaviors that are over-reactive, emotionally negative, coercive, and controlling. For instance, if a child misbehaves, parents may react with anger and use methods such as scolding, hitting, or humiliating the child [176]. They may also resort to yelling, derogatory name-calling, and making threats. All of these behaviors suggests that a parent is out of control.

- It was suggested that the link between harsh parenting and child aggression depends on whether disciplining is carried out in an emotionally controlled or emotionally charged manner [176].

- This implies that parents exhibit emotion dysregulation through punitive and aggressive parenting, and this affects the child's own ability to regulate emotions [176]. Additionally, the reciprocal nature of parent-child emotion dysregulation suggests that parents may model dysfunctional emotional responses and fail to teach emotional regulation skills [176]. As a result, a child may carry over the emotional incompetence acquired from their punitive parents to other social contexts, leading to incompetent social behaviors [176]. This implies that such behavior can be transmitted across generations and have long-term effects.

- Affirming this, one study found that aggressive parenting predicted the children's aggressive parenting many years later [177]. Furthermore, the children's aggressive parenting was not predicted by the development of aggressive behavior during adolescence [177]. This supports the notion that children may learn their parents' dysfunctional parenting, but it is unclear if this was due to social learning or dysfunctional emotional responses.

- Genetics may also be a factor. In one study, it was found that children who were genetically predisposed to anti-social behavior had increased risk of receiving negative adoptive parenting [178]. This connection was partially explained by the children's externalizing behaviors [178].

- However, the study found that negative parenting was not associated with an increase in child externalizing behavior in subsequent years, and neither was child externalizing behavior associated with an increase in negative parenting [178]. It is plausible that after the initial factors contributed to the breakdown of the parent-child relationship, genetics and problem behaviors sustained the coercive cycle.

- A twin study found support for the idea that a child's genetically influenced anti-social behavior could evoke a parent's negativity towards the child [179]. However, the relationship between child anti-social behavior and parental negativity was bi-directional [179]. This means that a child's difficult temperament could lead to harsh parenting, but harsh parenting could also increase the child's risks for aggression and anti-social development.

- In the same study, genetics explained slightly more than half the variance of anti-social behavior at age 4 [179]. Non-shared environments explained more than one-third, whereas shared environments seemed to be the least important [179].

- At age 7, genetics seemed to become less important for anti-social behavior, accounting for 40.7% of the variance. In contrast, shared environment accounted for 14.6%, and non-shared environment accounted for 27.9% [179]. The remainder 16.8% was accounted for by parental negativity and child anti-social behavior at age 4 [179]. Similarly, parental negativity and child anti-social behavior at age 4 had an effect on parental negativity at age 7 [179].

- These highlight persisting reciprocal effects of parental negativity and child anti-social behavior on each other, and suggest that the influence of genetics on anti-social behavior decreases with age while the impact of shared and non-shared environments remains significant.

- Zooming in, one study found coercive caregiver-child interactions to be related to future non-compliance towards the caregiver and oppositional defiant behaviors later in school [180]. The conduct problems might then lead to peer rejection and an anti-social developmental trajectory [180].

- So why could coercive interactions lead to future non-compliance and oppositional defiant behaviors?

- Earlier, we saw that coercive interactions constitute ineffective disciplining that reinforces aversive behavior instead. Conversely, for discipline to be effective, it needs to be consistent, administered by an adult who has affective bonds with the child, perceived by the child as 'fair,' be temperamentally and developmentally appropriate, and ultimately lead to self-discipline [181]. For example, inductive discipline may provide reasoning on why a behavior is unacceptable and why a new behavior should be performed. This allows internalization since it makes sense to them.

- Conversely, this implies that ineffective disciplining occurs when a child sees it as an overreaction due to a parent's emotional shortcomings. For example, a parent may nitpick on small and unimportant behaviors, and any non-compliance can be seen as an attack on their authority.

- Then because the parent disciplines a child for their own personal needs, the child may see this as an unwarranted, unfair, and illogical outburst. This damages affective bonding. Furthermore, a child may find it difficult to respect the parent with each humiliation, verbal abuse, threat, and name-calling [181]. It is unsurprising that a child may start to defy the parent instead.

Parenting style matters in moral development. The lowest growth in moral reasoning was found in children with parents who were highly 'informative,' cognitive interfering, and conflictual [182]. 'Informative' interaction refers to opinion sharing, including disagreement [182]. Cognitive interference refers to interactions that prevent a sustained and coherent discussion [182]. Conflictual interactions were those of negative affect, like hostile behavior [182].

- This parenting style resembles an authoritarian parenting style where a parent debases their child's perspectives, prevents discussion, and uses power coercion. This study provides additional evidence that power-coercive parenting leads to moral immaturity.

- Within the study, a second group displayed minimal moral development. This group had parents who were highly operational and informative in their interactions [182]. Operational interactions may explain and clarify but also make competitive requests and critique a child's perspective.

- Operational interactions may not be effective in fostering moral development because they may come across as antagonistic criticism [182]. Similarly, informative interactions can come across as lecturing [182]. Both interaction styles may dismiss the child's perspective, leading to defensiveness. This study highlights the importance of how we deliver inductive disciplining.

- Conversely, children who displayed considerable moral development were those with parents who were supportive, 'representational,' and operated on a higher moral developmental stage [182]. Representational interactions represented or elicited another's reasoning [182]. Supportive interactions were positive and encouraging toward child participation [182].

- In other words, parents who fostered moral development were warm, sought to understand their child's perspective, invited their child's participation, and provided higher moral reasoning. This resembles authoritative parenting.

- A second experiment found that children displayed minimal moral development when parents were highly operational (critical) and interfering and had poor ego functioning [182]. Poor ego functioning refers to defensiveness, rigidity, distortion, insensitivity to others' feelings, self-serving reasoning, denial, and closed-mindedness to others' perspectives [182].

- In contrast, high ego functioning refers to openness, coping, sensitivity, problem-solving, and appropriate emotional expression [182]. This affirmed that highly opinionated, critical, and interfering interactions can be detrimental to moral development when it is accompanied by poor ego functioning.

Conceivable, poor parenting can reach the severity of child maltreatment. Children who were abused or neglected were more likely to become arrested for a violent crime during adolescence [183]. They were also less likely to graduate high school and more likely to become a teen parent or be fired within the past year [183]. In addition, they were more likely to impregnate someone or become pregnant outside of marriage [183].

Childhood maltreatment was associated with adolescent social problems, substance use, and internalizing symptoms such as anxiety and depression [184]. Adolescents, who experienced early maltreatment, experienced almost double the risk of any problem and triple the risk of multiple problems [184]. In fact, 21% experienced three or more problems, as opposed to 7% for those who were not maltreated [184]. The problems did not stop there.

Victims of childhood abuse or neglect experienced an increased risk of psychopathic development [185]. Psychopathic development was found to be a possible contributor to the link between childhood victimization and violence [185]. This was the case even after removing items in the Psychopathy Checklist that could overlap with violence, including the lack of guilt and empathy, poor behavioral controls, early behavioral problems, and criminal versatility [185].

What was leftover included pathological lying, sensation seeking, manipulativeness, parasitic lifestyle, promiscuous sexual behavior, impulsiveness, irresponsibility, and failure to accept responsibility for their actions [185]. These psychopathic traits were in sum higher in victims of childhood abuse or neglect [185].

- Sure, victims of abuse measured higher on psychopathy. But could parents be the ones who transmitted psychopathy?

- The answer is yes. Parental psychopathy was found to be positively associated with authoritarian and permissive parenting [186]. Such parenting was, in turn, positively associated with child psychopathy in all three dimensions, namely grandiosity, callousness, and impulsivity or a need for stimulation [186]. Parental psychopathy was found to have both direct and indirect effects on child psychopathy, with the latter through parenting styles [186].

- On top of parental psychopathy, parental neuroticism, meaning emotional instability, was positively associated with the authoritarian parenting style, but agreeableness was negatively associated instead [186]. On the other hand, permissive parenting was positively associated with neuroticism but negatively with conscientiousness and extraversion [186].

- To clarify the relationships, parental neuroticism indirectly predicted child psychopathic tendencies through permissive parenting [186]. Parental agreeableness and neuroticism indirectly predicted child grandiosity, deceit, impulsivity, and need for stimulation through authoritarian parenting [186]. All of this highlights that parental personality affects parenting and, in turn, child development.

- In contrast, authoritative parenting was positively associated with parental extraversion, agreeableness, conscientiousness, and openness but negatively with neuroticism [186].

Given that poor parenting was implicated in child psychopathy and anti-social behavior, how may such development affect a child later in life?

One study found that two distinct categories of individuals engaged in anti-social behavior. Of the two, the larger group engaged in anti-social behavior only during adolescence [187]. Conversely, there was a smaller group that engaged in anti-social behavior of some sort at every lifestage [187].

It was proposed that life-course persistent anti-social behavior is constructed by a child's neuropsychological problems that interact cumulatively with risky environments [187]. This ultimately leads to a pathological personality [187]. This means that problems arising from poor prenatal care and childhood experiences construct problematic personalities. All this may result in cumulative consequences for major life outcomes.

For example, cumulative consequence was demonstrated by the effect of childhood temper on later occupational status [187]. Child tantrums predicted lower educational attainment and, in turn, poorer occupational outcomes [187]. Specifically, those with childhood tantrums experienced more unemployment [187]. This was on top of increased divorces [187].

Similarly, developmental deficits such as poor self-control, impulsivity, and an inability to delay gratification could increase the risk of teenage parenthood, drug and alcohol addiction, school dropout, and incarceration [187]. Moreover, behavioral problems at school and the failure to acquire literacy or social skills may limit future job options [187]. Consequently, the loss of developmental opportunities in the future could go on to maintain the existing deficits. Add on internalizing problems such as depression and anxiety and individuals may find themselves stuck in an endless rut, a debilitating outcome that prevents the actualization of their positive potential.

<u>What must Human Beings know about being human?</u>

<u>#11</u>

Could the challenges faced by parents lead to vulnerable child environments?

Harsh disciplining and environmental adversity, such as socio-economic deprivation and stressful life events, have been linked to child emotional and behavioral problems [188]. The stressful events included the death of a family member, changes in financial situation, parents losing their job, parental divorce or separation, and parental depression [188].

Children who experienced socio-economic disadvantage and harsh disciplining exhibited the highest levels of conduct problems [188]. While this study found a small negative correlation between poverty and harsh disciplining, other studies have found harsh parenting to be socio-economically patterned [188]. One possible reason for the inconsistency in findings could be the self-reporting of parenting behaviors, which may be influenced by the desire to maintain a favorable image [188].

Nonetheless, the study found that harsh disciplining exacerbated the negative effects of adverse life events, increasing the internalizing and externalizing problems of children exposed to high levels of environmental adversity [188].

However, harsh disciplining did not explain why stressed and economically deprived children had more externalizing and internalizing problems [188]. This is in contrast to some studies which found that harsh disciplining mediated the effects of environmental adversity [188]. In other words, it is unclear if environmental adversity and harsh parenting could have cumulative effects or if environmental adversity could lead to harsh parenting and, in turn, emotional and behavioral problems.

In another study, parental financial hardship was measured in terms of lower income, unstable work, income loss, and debt [189]. Financial hardship influenced the parents' economic pressure, which included their difficulties making ends meet [189]. Economic pressure, in turn, influenced the parents' depressed mood, which was, in turn, associated with increased marital conflict, characterized by hostility, reciprocal negativity, rejection, and coercion [189].

The study found that marital conflict was negatively associated with nurturing and involved parenting [189]. Nurturing parenting, which involves warmth, low hostility, sufficient age-appropriate monitoring, and consistent disciplining, was found to be associated with positive child adjustment, including better school performance, social adjustment with teachers and peers, sense of control, self-esteem, and self-efficacy [189]. It was also found to be negatively associated with child adjustment problems such as hostility, aggression, anti-social behavior, depressed feelings, and anger [189]. This affirms that authoritative parenting promotes pro-social development and inhibits anti-social behaviors and attitudes [189].

All in all, financial difficulties lead to more depressed parents, more marital conflict, and less nurturing and involved parenting. This results in poorer child adjustment. A child may also develop internalizing and externalizing problems.

Similarly, marital conflict may also affect an infant. A study found that marital conflict was associated with fewer positive, sensitive, and achievement-encouraging parenting [190]. This was accompanied by poorer parental attitudes [190].

To clarify, poorer parental attitudes include lower levels of child acceptance, less value placed on the parenting role compared to other adult roles, and viewing the time spent with the baby as lower priority [190]. Additionally, parents may not perceive themselves as significant for child development [190]. All of these hinder the formation of a secure parent-infant attachment, which is said to be important for infant emotional adjustment [190].

Infants of parents with chronic conflict during the prenatal and postnatal period displayed more disoriented behavior during parental presence, indicating a disorganized attachment [190]. Moreover, marital conflict predicted disorganized attachment in a way that could not be explained by parenting behaviors [190].

It was proposed that frequent and unresolved marital conflicts create scary environments for an infant. Frightening or frightened parents become unapproachable to an infant who seeks comfort. As such, a child does not develop a coherent strategy for alleviating personal distress. This results in a disorganized-disoriented attachment, said to be linked to later behavioral problems [190].

Given marital conflict's implications, it is important we ask, 'what causes marital conflict?'

The same study found that parental psychological maturity was negatively associated with marital conflict [190]. Marital conflict was measured not only by the amount of conflict but also the amount of negative emotions [190]. This was in addition to a lack of conflict negotiation, egalitarian problem-solving, and responsibility for one's own behavior [190].

In other words, parents with poor ego-functioning may be at higher risk of marital conflict, which can ultimately lead to divorce (which has its own set of repercussions). All of this suggests that child development is best achieved when parents can cope well and have healthy spousal relationships.

Unsurprisingly, divorce was also found to be a risk factor in child development. In the years leading up to a marriage breakdown, children may spend many years in an unsupportive and conflict-ridden environment [191]. Parenting patterns during this period included an early disengagement of fathers, unreliable parenting, authoritarian demands, and anger towards children [191]. Children, on the other hand, displayed under-controlled and impulsive behaviors during the pre-divorce, divorce, and post-divorce periods [191].

In one study, some children from divorced and remarried families were found to be maladapted, displaying irritability, social withdrawal, aggressiveness, and insecurity [191]. These children typically came from homes with high levels of negative affect and conflict, as well as neglectful and authoritarian parenting [191]. In contrast, some children were caring and competent. These children tended to have warm and supportive mothers, whether in a remarried family or mother custody [191].

Even ten years after their parents' divorce, a significant number of children, who became adults still experienced vivid memories of the family breakdown and its traumatic events [191].

Many of these children remained troubled, drifting, and underachieving [191]. Most of them also experienced anxiety towards love and marriage [191]. However, many also became strongly committed to the ideals of lasting marriage and fidelity [191].

But even with that said, adults who experienced parental divorce in their childhood were more likely to experience poorer psychological well-being compared to those from intact families, as well as being at higher risk of divorce themselves [191]. This suggest that the effects of divorce may persist across generations. The implications of poor psychological maturity and ego functioning in handling parenting and marriage responsibilities are highlighted by all of these findings.

As with marital conflict, couples facing financial difficulties, such as difficulty meeting ends meet, were found to be at a higher risk of divorce [192]. However, financial stress was only found to be responsible to a small extent [192].

The same study also investigated whether the reverse would be true – specifically, whether spouses who were busy with work would be at higher risk of divorce. It was found that couples who interacted less were at a higher risk of divorce, but the effect was marginal [192]. Other factors may be at play.

For example, another study found that high workload was related to negative workplace emotions, which, in turn, predicted negative emotions at home [193]. Negative emotions at work were found to mediate the link between one's workload and emotions at home [193]. However, positive emotions at work can also spill over into one's home life [193]. But workplace effects do not stop there.

High workload was linked to perceptions of 'work-family conflict' [193], for example, family time can be taken up by work. In turn, work-family conflict predicted lower social participation at home [193]. This was the case despite controlling for the lower time spent at home. In other words, employees socially withdraw from their families after work. This has conceivable repercussions to familial relationships.

Taken together, parental stress, deficient parental development, and marital conflict create risks to child development through parenting that is less nurturing and involved. However, such risks may not exist alone, as they could combine with a child's personal risks.

To illustrate, one study found that children with difficult temperaments and high conflict homes were almost four times as likely to manifest internalizing problems compared to those with non-difficult temperament and low conflict at home [194]. This was the same for externalizing problems [194].

118

To further elaborate, predictors of later internalizing and externalizing problems included family conflict, child temperament, interactions between conflict and child temperament, and prior externalizing problems [194].

Similarly, a review highlighted that children with early externalizing problems and experienced risk factors such as negative parenting and familial stress, could be at risk for continuing problems [195]. This risk may also be compounded by a child's temperament, poor impulse control, poor emotional regulation, hyperactivity, and various cognitive deficits [195]. We have already seen that some of these risks may arise due to harmful prenatal behaviors.

In sum, a parent's challenging situation, poor parenting, poor prenatal care can combined with deficient child development, leading to deleterious effects on a child's well-being and appropriate behavior.

<u>What must Human Beings know about being human?</u>

<u>#12</u>

Can a neighborhood or school develop one's aggression?

Within a study, African American children from low-income single-parent families displayed the most aggression [196]. However, this was only true for those in neighborhoods of low socio-economic status (SES) [196]. In contrast, a middle-SES neighborhood acted as a protective factor, reducing aggression in children from high-risk families [196].

On the other hand, 'White' children from low-income single-parent families living in middle-SES neighborhoods were more likely to be peer-rejected compared to those in low-SES neighborhoods [196].

Thus, neighborhoods can act both as a protective factor and a risk factor. Systematic disadvantages and neighborhood cultures may play a role in the development of aggression.

One study investigated neighborhood risk and found that adolescents' frequency of fighting was associated with their exposure to violence and personal victimization within the community [197]. This was in addition to harsh disciplining and depression symptoms [197]. To clarify, exposure to violence and personal victimization accounted for a small amount of variation (7.6%) in fighting frequency [197].

Moreover, adolescents' involvement in gang fights was linked to their anticipation of lower socioeconomic status [197]. Similarly, gang fight involvement was associated with higher levels of depressive symptoms, lower sense of life purpose, and more feelings of hopelessness [197]. Again, exposure to violence and victimization accounted for a small amount of variation (11.5%) in gang fighting [197].

In another study, it was found that socioeconomic status was negatively related to perceived neighborhood danger [198]. Perceived neighborhood danger included the frequency of fights, beatings, robberies, as well as the noticed prevalence of threatening aspects in the neighborhood, such as drug selling, drug usage, public drinking, gang fights, and people taking advantage of one another [198].

Perceived danger, in turn, was positively associated with positive beliefs about aggression [198]. These beliefs pertained to youth endorsement of aggression, such as the idea that 'beating someone teaches them a good lesson.' Both perceived danger and positive aggression beliefs were positively linked to actual aggression [198].

Similarly, restrictive and harsh disciplining was associated with positive aggression beliefs [198]. However, poor parental monitoring was specifically linked to actual aggression [198].

Another study reported similar results, finding that poverty predicted children's stress and aggression supporting beliefs, which, in turn, predicted child aggression [199]. In other words, impoverished children had more accepting beliefs towards aggression and experienced more stress from life events and neighborhood violence [199]. These stressors and beliefs partially explain the link between poverty and aggression [199].

The study further investigated poverty and found that community economic status interacted with individual economic status to relate to aggression [199]. However, only individual economic status was a weak but direct predictor of aggression [199].

Among aggression-supporting beliefs, aggression can be seen as an effective method to obtain social status and rewards. In addition, social status insecurity was associated with popularity goals to a larger extent than social preference goals [200].

The difference between popularity goals and social preference goals is that people with popularity goals seek to be included and held in a certain peer status, whereas people with social preference goals want to be well-liked, accepted, and perceived as good people [200].

However, neither goal is particularly healthy as both lead to behavior driven by how one wants to be viewed by others. Despite this, the two goals can lead to vastly different outcomes.

For instance, popularity goals were found to be positively associated with self-reported and peer-nominated aggression, but negatively with pro-sociality [200].

Social preference goals were the opposite. They were positively associated with self-reported and peer-nominated pro-social behavior, but negatively with aggression [200]. However, it is also possible for people to become 'doormats' and people pleasers if they prioritize social preference goals too much.

In this context, aggression included both overt and relational aggression. Overt aggression encompassed name-calling and saying mean things, on top of physical aggression [200]. On the other hand, relational aggression referred to excluding and ignoring others, as well as threatening to stop liking someone unless they comply with their demands [200].

Conversely, pro-social behavior included how frequently people cooperated and shared with others, cheered others up, and communicated that they cared about others [200].

Similarly, another study reported that social status insecurity was associated with popularity-motivated aggression [201]. This was even more among adolescents who scored high on callousness [201]. The definition of aggression in this study included cyber aggression, physical aggression, and relational aggression [201].

124

Social status insecurity was positively associated with callousness but negatively associated with popularity-motivated pro-social behaviors [201]. In other words, a strong desire for social status may be accompanied by a lack of empathy, guilt, or concern for misconduct, bearing some resemblance to a psychopathic construct.

Similar to popularity goals and social-preference goals, one study looked into status goals and affection goals [202]. Status goals included wanting others to admire and respect them and listen to what they say [202]. The measurement would go on to subtract submissive goals, such as not 'doing something foolish' or 'wanting others to get angry with them' [202].

In contrast, affection goals included feelings of being accepted and being close to others [202].

At a younger age, status goals were found to be associated with peer-reported aggression [202]. However, by middle adolescence, status goals were only associated with aggression when affection goals were low [202]. Moreover, both status and affection goals became increasingly important as people aged [202]. This implies that if individuals do not value a good relationship with others but only desire admiration and respect, they may be more likely to engage in aggression.

Children may also satisfy their desire for admiration by imitating the behaviors of older peers. Similarly, teens may engage in delinquent behavior to prove that they have outgrown their childhood status and are now capable of independence and more [187].

Past research has reported that proving one's 'maturity' and 'autonomy' were strong motives for offending [187]. Some people may relish the feeling of being ahead of their peers, while others may compensate for their status loss, such as from being left behind in their academics, by seeking admiration from others. All of these are speculations regarding the possible psychologies that may underlie status-motivated aggression.

Having established that neighborhood factors can influence aggression through aggression-supporting beliefs and the use of aggression to gain status, the question arises: 'could culture also play a role in aggression?'

A study comparing children from two different cultures found that culture may influence aggressive behavior [203]. In a 'conflict dilemma', children from one culture demonstrated higher levels of aggression, anger, avoidance, and under-regulation of emotion, but also more prosocial and affiliative behavior [203]. Furthermore, in a 'challenging situations' task, children from that culture were more prone to report that anger would be the emotion they experience, as opposed to other emotions [203].

Although this study suggested that different levels of aggression in societies could be attributed to differences in cultural values, the evidence is neither conclusive nor generalizable due to methodology limitations. Therefore, this finding should be taken with a heavy pinch of salt.

Nevertheless, this study highlighted the potential importance of examining cultural scripts that pertain to how children talk, feel, and respond in challenging situations.

It has been proposed that children who display aggressive behavior have learned aggressive scripts early in life [204]. These scripts can be picked up through observation or enactment [204]. Once these scripts are acquired, they can be recalled when a child experiences environmental cues, such as goal blocking, which the child attributes to another's actions [204]. The more these scripts are rehearsed, the more likely they would be recalled [204]. Additionally, the child may experience a conditioned emotional arousal [204].

But before acting out a script, a child may evaluate it based on past reinforcement and their current situation to see if it would achieve a desired goal [204]. If aggression has allowed or allows a child to achieve a desired goal, they may evaluate an aggressive script as acceptable or desirable. This could be the case if the child's environment condones or rewards their aggression.

Over time, these aggressive scripts can form enduring schemas that persist into adulthood and are resistant to change [204]. This is particularly true if a child is unable to generate alternative scripts [204]. As time goes on, a child may continue to acquire more aggressive scripts [204]. Together, this suggests that a culture with high levels of aggression is likely to perpetuate it.

School cultures may be no different. The prevalence of violence in schools was reported in a US survey conducted during the 1996-1997 school year, which revealed numerous incidents such as physical fights, rapes, sexual batteries, and robberies, totaling thousands or even hundreds of thousands, depending on the type of violence [205].

Furthermore, the absence of positive interaction norms in school environments may contribute to increased aggression among students. For instance, one study found that a high level of aggression in an elementary school classroom increased the risk of male students being highly aggressive when transitioning to middle school [206].

In this study, child aggression included rule-breaking, breaking things, fighting, harming others, lying, teasing classmates, taking others' property, and yelling at others [206].

A study that examined peer-group dynamics found that students who associated with peers with similar levels of bullying and fighting exhibited inter-group differences in their levels of aggression [207]. The study also revealed that the level of aggression within a peer group predicted individual bullying and fighting behavior over time, indicating that peer-group aggression influenced an individual's aggression over time [207]. These findings demonstrate that classroom aggression levels could contribute to individual aggression.

In addition, another study found that aggression levels of incoming students predicted the subsequent level of classroom aggression and classroom climate quality [208].

Classroom climate refers to the effectiveness of the teacher's classroom management, which includes responsiveness to students' needs and feelings, quality of student engagement, and emotional supportiveness as opposed to being critical and negative [208]. In other words, initial levels of student aggression could result in teachers' difficulties in creating a positive classroom climate and effective learning environment.

Furthermore, classroom aggression levels and climate quality independently influenced changes in student aggression as students transitioned from kindergarten to second grade [208]. To elaborate, a low-quality classroom climate marked by student disengagement and negative teacher behaviors predicted subsequent child aggressive-disruptive behavior [208]. In contrast, high-quality climates marked by supportive teacher behavior helped reduce it [208].

It has been suggested that classroom aggression may encourage individual aggression through social synchrony, which can take the form of aggressive responses, and peer contagion such as provocation [208]. For instance, a child may be teased if they do not appear aggressive or use 'tough' language, which can result in the performance of aggression to fit in socially.

It was said that supportive teacher interactions can enhance a child's self-regulation and conflict management [208]. Notably, supportive teaching resembles the style of authoritative parenting, which involves responding sensitively to a child's needs as opposed to being critical and controlling.

One study examined *teachers'* perceptions of negative teacher behaviors and suggested that certain behaviors could shape student aggression. These behaviors included discriminating against certain students, insulting students who asked more questions, and showing an inability to understand students' feelings and learning difficulties [209]. Additionally, teachers were reported to make insulting remarks against students' performance and family background, display favoritism and grudges, and use abusive language [209]. It is not surprising that such negative behavior can lead students to dislike their teachers, as these teachers are hardly exemplary or savory role models.

In contrast, a study found that teacher support and positive peer affiliation were related to less individual aggression [210]. In other words, when teachers are helpful, encouraging, and concerned, and students feel well-liked by their classmates, these positive interactions could reduce individual aggression. However, the link between these factors and reduced aggression was indirect.

Specifically, before being linked to reduced aggression, teacher support and peer affiliation directly influenced the students' positive attitude towards authority [210]. This, in turn, was associated with avoiding a non-conforming social reputation [210]. On the other hand, a negative attitude towards authority and a non-conforming social reputation were directly linked to school aggression [210].

Negative attitudes towards authority included perceptions that it was acceptable to disobey teachers if there were no punishments. It also included perceptions of injustice, where students felt that teachers would only take care of students with good grades [210]. These attitudes were linked to a non-conforming social reputation, including self-views as a bully or tough guy [210]. These findings highlight that social support at school can influence individual aggression.

As children become alienated from authority figures and perceive bias rather than impartiality from them, they may begin to distrust and lose confidence in the system's ability to provide meaningful protection and justice [211]. Feeling excluded from the protection or benevolence of authority, some children may turn to delinquency and develop a dangerous reputation for self-protection [211].

This can also occur in cases where there were no effective interventions, such as when children experience abuse from their guardians [211]. Children may see the law as unavailable or ineffective, leading to cynicism towards authority [211].

Not only were negative views towards authority figures like teachers, police, and the law linked to one another, but negative views towards the law and the police were associated with non-compliance [211]. As such, low-quality relationships between a child and authority figures may contribute to law flouting.

Even in kindergarten, low-quality teacher-child relationships were found to predict later behavioral problems [212]. The conflict between kindergarten teachers and children was associated with poorer academic outcomes and more disciplinary infractions during elementary school [212]. Interestingly, the most common disciplinary infraction was defiance towards school authority [212].

The association between negative teacher-child relationships and later disciplinary problems was strongest for children with the most behavior problems during kindergarten [212]. However, while the teacher-child relationship was a predictor, other factors were also likely at play. Negative teacher-child relationships only accounted for a small amount of variance, and future child behavior was largely mediated by earlier behaviors [212].

In addition, chronically rejected children displayed higher levels of aggression than those who were rejected once [213]. Those who were rejected once displayed more aggressive behavior than those who were never rejected [213].

Furthermore, increased chronic rejection has been associated with an increased stability in 'acting-out' behaviors over time, such as aggression, disruptiveness, and attention-seeking [213]. Additionally, children who exhibited high levels of initial externalizing behavior and experienced chronic peer rejection tended to have the greatest stability in externalizing problems [213].

Higher absenteeism was also observed among children who experienced peer rejection [213], highlighting the potential impact of peer rejection on child behavior and school engagement. Additionally, rejected children may miss out on crucial opportunities to learn and practice social skills [213]. This leads to a potential downward spiral.

While it may be tempting to assume that only the relational aspects of school culture contribute to aggression, this is a mistaken belief. Children's ability status can also play a part.

Perhaps the most controversial school policy is grouping students by their ability level. This practice aims to tailor teaching to students' learning needs, but it remains highly debated. One meta-analysis of past meta-analyses found that 'between-class' ability grouping had a negligible effect on academic achievement, regardless of ability level [214]. However, a mini-meta analysis of randomized studies showed a small positive effect for between-class ability grouping [214].

At the same time, 'within-class' ability grouping had a small to moderate positive effect on academic achievement [214]. However, the findings varied greatly for randomized studies [214]. Even so, grouping gifted students into special programs had moderately positive effects [214].

Now, considering that ability grouping has the potential to yield a small positive effect, why is it still a controversial topic?

This is because ability grouping could lead to negative non-academic effects. In one review, some studies found 'between-class' ability grouping to be beneficial to the school well-being of well-performing students, but detrimental to the school well-being of weaker students [215]. School well-being here included attitudes towards school, teachers, peers, and school-life [215]. This was in addition to feeling safe at school, which includes not being bullied [215].

A possible explanation for poorer well-being is the loss of status [215]. Students may feel like failures [215]. One study found evidence that ability grouping resulted in polarizing attitudes of strong and weak students, dividing them into pro-school and anti-school [215]. However, poorer school well-being could also be the result of teachers using increased criticism towards lower-track students [215]. Furthermore, lower-track students were often stereotyped by teachers, being labeled as slow, difficult, or dumb [215].

At the same time, the academic self-concept of both stronger and weaker students can be adversely impacted [215]. High-ability students may feel insecure comparing themselves with equally strong or stronger classmates within the high-ability class [215].

Students in lower-track classes may suffer a negative academic self-concept immediately after being placed in a lower-track, comparing themselves with those in high-ability classes [215]. However, one study found that low-track students had a more positive self-concept than high-track students three years later [215]. A possible explanation may be that weaker students eventually felt better from comparing themselves to equally weak or weaker classmates [215].

'Within-class' ability groupings were also problematic. One study found that children in the bottom brackets displayed increased emotional problems and hyperactivity [216]. This was despite controlling for several individual and family factors that were associated with emotional and behavioral problems [216]. Now, how do all these tie in with aggression?

One study found that students' aggression could be predicted by their attitude towards school and students' self-confidence regarding school subjects [217]. We have already seen that these predictors were linked to ability grouping, though it may not exclusively be the case.

In addition, student aggression was linked to a negative school climate, such as a climate that includes frequent bullying [217].

In particular, students, who felt safer at school, evaluated the school climate as more positive, and felt more confident regarding school subjects, reported lower levels of aggression [217]. Again, these factors were implicated in ability grouping.

All of this was in line with past research which found that aggression was related to low school connectedness and negative attitudes towards school and school subjects [217].

In the worst case, school aggression can take the form of school violence. School violence can be child perpetrated or teacher perpetrated, and includes physical and psychological injury, bullying, threats, exploitation, and the use of weapons [218].

Violence risks accumulate at multiple levels, including at the individual, family, peer group, school, and community levels, where severe and chronic exposure is likely to increase the risk proportionately [218].

Early warning signs of school violence included social withdrawal, low school interest, poor academic performance, patterns of impulsivity and intimidation, intolerance for differences, prejudicial attitudes, and uncontrolled anger [218]. This was on top of feelings of isolation, rejection, and being picked on [218].

However, there is no useful profile of students who engage in targeted school violence, and school violence is rarely perpetrated impulsively [218]. Thus, using early warning signs to label students is not only faulty but prejudicial. It could be helpful to improve the environment instead.

Separately, the safe school initiative study found that many school shooters had difficulty coping with significant losses and personal failures [218]. Many felt bullied and persecuted, and many considered or attempted suicide [218]. These highlight severe maladjustment.

It was suggested that school environment and curriculum could be conducive towards school violence if they promoted student competition that comes with a corresponding shame for the 'losers' or a 'dog eat dog' worldview [218].

It was conceptualized that such environments could exacerbate situations where peer marginalization had led to blocked personhood [218].

Blocked personhood refers to situations where self-assertion is ineffective or blocked, and ridicule and humiliation have become the norm. Over time, people cannot restore their basic sense of personal significance, and they see violence as their final recourse [218].

At that time, severely maladjusted persons may begin to view other persons, not just their bullies, as the source of their agonies, as their antagonists can be popular individuals who enjoy social recognition and acceptance within the school. We have already seen that people may perpetrate aggression for their popularity goals.

This was affirmed in one study, which found that bullies were among the most popular students in school, receiving more peer popularity on average than others [219]. This highlighted that bullying might not merely be a phenomenon that occurred between a bully and victim but also those who condoned or rewarded it.

In sum, aggression can be influenced by the neighborhood climate, classroom culture, peer rejection, bullying, and even ability grouping. All of these suggest that an individual's school and neighborhood environment can indeed promote the development of aggression.

<u>What must Human Beings know about being human?</u>

<u>#13</u>

Can aggressive and anti-social 'personalities' change?

Let us begin by looking at the surface. There is evidence for both continuity and discontinuity of early maladjustment and problem behavior.

In one study, a significant portion of children and adolescents who had behavioral and emotional problems did not have persisting problems during adulthood, although some did [220]. About 29% to 41% of participants displayed deviant levels of problems during the follow-up 14 years later [220]. Thus even though childhood maladjustment and problem behavior posed risks, problematic development was not guaranteed.

So what could have contributed to persisting problems?

One study found that increased difficult temperaments in adolescence were associated with increased childhood behavior problems [221], suggesting that adolescent problems may be rooted in childhood problems [221] and that difficult temperaments may play a role in maintaining persisting problems.

At the same time, increased difficult temperaments in adolescence were associated with increased adolescent use of cigarettes, alcohol, and drugs [221]. Furthermore, adolescents with the highest number of difficult temperaments had the highest incidence of substance use [221]. However, difficult temperament was also associated with lower perceived family support, increased depressive symptoms, and delinquent behavior [221].

138

In other words, adolescents with the most difficult temperaments perceived their families as the least supportive and manifested more internalizing and externalizing problems [221].

While the direction of casuality was not established in this study, the correlates suggest that co-morbid environmental factors could help explain the maintenance of problems. Moreover, the measured temperaments were said to be associated with mental health, and social and cognitive competence [221], all of which could affect one's ability to thrive in their life institutions.

One study found that difficult childhood temperament was linked to personality in young adulthood and adult outcomes [222]. Similar to the previous study, children with difficult temperaments displayed more externalizing problems during adolescence and signs of internalizing problems [222]. But that is not all.

An 'under-controlled' child temperament was linked to young adult personality traits of aggression, lower self-control, and greater alienation [222]. In other words, children who were irritable, impulsive, emotionally reactive, avoiding of difficult tasks, resisting of adult direction, and had low goal persistence, grew up to display personality traits of willingness to hurt others for self-advantage, recklessness, and indignation, meaning feelings of being mistreated and believing themselves to be targets of false rumors [222].

Under-controlled children were involved in increased conflicted relationships in adulthood, marked by less intimacy and trust [222]. They also had less social support, including material support, mentoring, companionship, and emotional support [222]. Additionally, they were more likely than well-adjusted children to become diagnosed with a psychiatric disorder and become alcohol dependent [222]. Unsurprisingly, they were also more likely to have made suicide attempts [222]. However, the risks of difficult childhood temperament did not stop there.

Under-controlled children were 1.5 times more likely to be unemployed and 2.5 times more likely to be fired from a job [222]. This suggests that a persistent and ineffective interpersonal style could be brought to the workplace. As such, not only were children with difficult temperaments at more risk of poor familial relationships, but also greater difficulties at work.

Under-controlled children were also more likely to get into trouble with the law, perform more illegal and anti-social activities, and live a life of crime [222]. Thus, early temperament and personality could evolve anti-socially. This begs the question, is personality changeable?

One study revealed that personality traits have propensities for both change and consistency over time [223]. According to a prior meta-analysis, personality correlations with a preceding age became stronger as one aged, eventually plateauing at about 0.7 during old age [223]. However, the proportion of variance explained did not surpass 50% until age 50 [223]. This suggests that personality changes can occur even after early adulthood [223].

Some studies also found support for personality growth, where disinhibition, negative emotionality, and psychoticism decreased, and conscientiousness and agreeableness increased [223]. This is said to reflect psychological maturation [223].

The same study also observed that negative personality traits have the propensity to change over time [223]. Specifically, negative traits decreased as one aged [223]. These traits included malignant egotism, callous hostility, impulsiveness, irritability, sensation seeking, and anti-social values which comprises opposition to authority and skepticism towards society [223].

To elaborate, the study defined malignant egotism as a personality trait characterized by a belief of self-superiority and willingness to behave badly, while callous hostility refers to a trait of ruthlessness and insensitivity to the suffering of others [223].

Further investigations have revealed that juvenile delinquents who received court sentences tended to display higher levels of negative personality traits and increased personality continuity [223]. This may be due to the deprived environments available to them. For example, individuals with anti-social tendencies may affiliate with other anti-social individuals [223]. In other words, personality traits may remain consistent because of a consistently low-quality environment. Similarly, it may be possible for personality change to occur if parents or other caregivers provide support and encouragement to help a child overcome a difficult temperament.

The influence of environment on personality has been affirmed by a twins study that found participants' personality differences to be roughly 41% genetic, 26% shared environment, and 32% non-shared environment [224]. These findings were reported to be consistent with previous studies [224].

Given that personality could change for the better, what then are the implications?

A study has shown that there is a link between personality and relationship happiness [225]. Specifically, the study found that relationship satisfaction was predicted by one's personality traits and their partner's. The relevant personality traits included low negative emotionality, high positive emotionality, and high constraint, which encompasses self-control and harm avoidance [225]. Additionally, the study found that the partner's personality traits had an additive effect on relationship outcomes [225]. In other words, one's personality and that of their partner can impact how happy one perceives their relationship to be [225].

In addition, the quality of a relationship, indicated by trust, emotional intimacy, balance of power, respect, fairness, and open communication, has been found to be strongly related to relationship satisfaction [225]. These findings suggest that successfully resolving conflicts and maintaining healthy communications are crucial for maintaining relationship satisfaction. Interestingly, the study found no evidence to support the notion that partners need to be similar in personality to have a happy relationship [225].

As you may have noticed, we have previously explored how marriages fail and how said failure affects child development. By adding in personality to the equation, we have now seen how relationships can succeed instead. It logically follows that we should examine how parenting can contribute to positive child development. All of these constitute improvements to child environment that may help positive personality formation or changes.

(From here, we will look at adjustment and behavioral outcomes rather than personality outcomes, because interventions to change 'personalities' seem intrusive and deterministic.)

Compared to children who received other parenting styles, children who received authoritative parenting, characterized by healthy levels of control, responsiveness, and supportiveness, displayed the most positive developmental outcomes [170]. These outcomes included higher social consciousness, maturity, resilience, self-esteem, cognitive competence, cognitive motivation, self-regulation, pro-sociality, social responsibility, as well as lower internalizing and externalizing problems [170]. All of these indicate that children who receive authoritative parenting tend to be well-adjusted [170].

- Personality may not be the only factor that maintains problem behavior. The parents' hostility and lack of warmth towards adolescents and children predicted adolescents' alcohol problems, drug use, delinquency, and coping through alcohol use and emotional outbursts [226]. Higher frequencies of parental fighting also predicted adolescents' coping through alcohol and outbursts [226]. This highlights maladaptive coping strategies. Furthermore, parental values matter to children's values. Permissive parental views towards alcohol and drug use predicted adolescents' alcohol and drug use [226].

Interventions that sought to improve parent-child interactions through the improvement of parenting behavior tended to be effective in improving child problem behaviors [227]. These programs may cultivate psychological resources and management strategies to provide appropriate consequences for child misbehavior, and reward for pro-social behavior [227]. Furthermore, parents improved their parental warmth and self-efficacy, and decreased their hostility [227]. All of these can be important for child development.

Similarly, a divorce intervention sought to cultivate non-coercive disciplining, problem-solving, child monitoring, child skill encouragement, and positive involvement in child schooling and prosocial behavior [228]. The intervention was found to be effective in decreasing coercive parenting, negative reciprocity, and reinforcement of negative child behavior [228].

While parents in the study exhibited a decline in positive involvement similar to that of the control group, they also displayed more problem-solving abilities and a slower decline in involvement [228]. Nonetheless, the study found that participants continued to exhibit higher levels of positive involvement than the control group [228].

Moreover, the divorce intervention was found to predict effective parenting, which, in turn, was associated with better school adjustment, including lower levels of externalizing behavior and higher levels of prosocial behavior [228]. Similarly, the effective parenting predicted reduced child maladjustment in terms of depressed moods and peer relationship problems [228].

In a separate study, child social skills training was found to be an effective intervention for improving social behavior [229]. The curriculum included communication skills, emotional coping, empathy, and social problem-solving [229]. Additionally, the training was found to be effective in reducing child aggression [229]. Furthermore, based on a review of prior research, improving social competence may reduce the risk of delinquency [229].

A meta-analysis affirmed these findings, revealing that child social skills training had a small positive effect in preventing the development of aggression [230]. This was also the case for anti-social, delinquent, and oppositional development [230]. In particular, children who exhibited problem behaviors benefited the most from preventive programs [230]. However, the small effect suggests that other efforts are needed in conjunction.

In one study, high-quality emotional and instructional support from teachers significantly impacted the students' social competence and self-control [231]. A high-quality classroom here included a climate that was characterized by teachers' sensitivity to students' emotional needs, classroom positivity, and the absence of over-control or a hostile and punitive tone [231].

This was accompanied by an instructional climate where teachers effectively managed child behavior and provided feedback regarding the child's work and behavior [231]. Such instructional climate was focused on child mastery, concept development, understanding, and persistence [231].

Results further suggested that children will display better social competence with increasing levels of teacher emotional support and instructional feedback [231]. Furthermore, children in such environments displayed increased positive behaviors with their peers [231].

Conversely, low-quality classrooms were confounded with functional risks, such as lower sustained attention, higher externalizing behavior, and poorer social skills and academic competence [231]. As a result, children in low-quality classrooms displayed even poorer social competence and self-control [231]. These findings suggest that high-quality teacher support, in addition to social skills training, can foster child social competence.

So far, we have seen that preventive measures such as parental training and child social skills development could reduce anti-social development. But what can we do to help those who are anti-social?

In one program, aggressive incarcerated juveniles were trained to remediate their social problem-solving skills and modify their aggression-supporting beliefs [232]. This program was found to have a positive effect on six out of the seven social problem-solving skills [232].

The six skills included attending to non-hostile cues when defining a social problem, setting non-hostile goals, gathering additional information, increasing the number of solutions generated, having an effective second-best solution towards a goal-directed and non-violent outcome, and lastly, the number of consequences considered [232]. The seventh which could not be substantiated was the 'effectiveness of the best solution' [232]. But on the whole, incarcerated juveniles who went through the training displayed greater social problem-solving skills compared to those who did not [232].

Similarly, a positive effect was found for four out of the five aggression-supporting beliefs. These were: aggression is legitimate, aggression increases self-esteem, aggression avoids negative image, and victims deserve the aggression [232]. The fifth that could not substantiate was 'victims do not suffer' [232]. However, on the whole, participants were less likely to endorse the four aggression-supporting beliefs than the control groups [232].

Furthermore, significant decreases in three behavior categories were observed [232]. These were: aggressive behavior, impulsive behavior, and inflexible behavior, which means narrow-mindedness when tackling problems [232]. This outcome highlights the use of alternative solutions and increased cognitive self-control.

In a further analysis that considered all twelve social-cognitive measures, the belief that 'aggression is a legitimate response' remained the only significant predictor of post-test aggression [232]. This hints that addressing the social-cognitive measures ultimately reduced aggression by refuting aggression as a legitimate response. But the effects did not stop here.

In addition to decreased aggression, the participants were also less likely than those in the control groups to recidivate, though statistical significance could not be established [232]. Further analysis revealed that four out of the twelve social-cognitive predictors had a significant effect on recidivism [232]. The four were: social problem definition, goal selection, aggression as a legitimate response, and victims deserve aggression [232].

Despite the positive effects of the program, it is important to note that the post-release environments for juvenile offenders may not reinforce the newly learned cognitions [232]. Consequently, offenders may revert to their prior cognitions and social behaviors [232].

Lastly, a separate study suggested that parental training could be an effective intervention in reducing juvenile offending amongst chronically offending delinquents [233]. However, despite a faster decline in 'non-status' offenses, neither the delinquents' aversive behaviors (such as destructiveness, humiliation, and negativism), nor the parents' aversive behaviors (such as humiliation, threats, and yelling) showed a significant decrease [233]. As such, it would be premature to conclude that the training program had a direct impact on juvenile recidivism, as was suggested by the study.

146

Possible Initiatives

✓ Hospitals can use assessments to evaluate parental risks to the fetus and child and provide educational touchpoints to raise parents' awareness of habits that may expose their child to prenatal and postnatal risks. Parental change programs can also be implemented to promote safe environments for children. These programs progressively educate on effective parenting, disciplining, and building better ego functioning to prevent over-reactive, punitive, and abusive interactions.

✓ In school, students can be provided with opportunities to build their social skills, which can lead to benefits such as reduced aggression and more positive interactions with others.

- In one study, social skills were found to be associated with psychological well-being [234]. This link was mediated by high-quality friendships [234]. In other words, social skills may help students create positive friendships and experiences.

- However, social competence and high-quality friendship features such as support, could be culture-specific [234]. As such, cultivating social skills may require cultivating intercultural considerations.

- Thus, as individuals embrace high-quality relationship behaviors, it can pave the way for schools to foster a positive culture.

✓ Schools may also develop the social information processing abilities of students through debunking aggression as a legitimate response or a means for status, building attention to non-hostile cues, and expanding the repertoire of non-aggressive responses, such as social problem-solving.

✓ Lastly, schools would want to replace all punitive and discriminative teacher behaviors with supportive and effective ones. This may require teachers to build their emotion management skills. Ultimately, it is desirable for every student to encounter a supportive learning environment, regardless of their personality and temperament. Every student should have the opportunities to pick up the skills they need to thrive in life institutions.

<u>What must Human Beings know about being human?</u>

<u>#14</u>

How does ADHD create susceptibility within risky environments?

Attention Deficit Hyperactivity Disorder, commonly known as ADHD, can present co-morbid risks when an individual is exposed to adverse environments, such as their family, school, and peers.

One study on the prevalence of ADHD reported that 85.8% of participants experienced no clinical ADHD problems of inattention, hyperactivity, and impulsivity during their childhood [235]. 7.5% reported subthreshold childhood symptoms, and 6.6% reported full childhood symptoms [235].

The prevalence of adult ADHD was found to be about 4.4%, and this group consisted entirely of persons who exhibited childhood symptoms [235]. Within the 'low-risk' group who exhibited subthreshold childhood symptoms, the prevalence of adult ADHD was only 7.3% [235]. Conversely, the high-risk group with full childhood symptoms had an adult prevalence of 84.8% [235]. However, there was also a middle-risk group where adult prevalence was 36.6% [235].

These findings suggest that ADHD symptoms could decrease in severity as individuals transition into adulthood. This was affirmed by a meta-analysis which found that the persistence rate of full criteria ADHD at 25 years old was approximately 15%, while ADHD in partial remission was roughly 40-60% [236].

ADHD is the neuropsychological impairment of inhibition towards a currently or previously reinforced response [237]. Traditionally, ADHD has been regarded by its symptoms of impulsivity, hyperactivity, and poor sustained attention [237].

However, ADHD impairment is believed to lead to secondary impairments in four neuropsychological functions, namely, an individual's *working memory* to utilize information to direct a response, *self-regulation* of emotions to delay response during emotionally provocative events such as gratification and temptation, allowance of time for *internalized speech*, which is an internal discussion of alternatives to exert control over behavior, and lastly, *reconstitution* where event information is distributed to other information processing systems for the construction of new and novel responses [237].

As a result of the secondary impairments of ADHD, individuals may encounter cognitive and behavioral deficits, such as a diminished ability to self-direct internally [237]. This implies that it may be difficult for individuals with ADHD to inhibit a response, even when feedback indicates that it is ineffective or maladaptive [237].

Additionally, ADHD may be accompanied by emotional reactivity. Studies have described irritability, hostility, low frustration tolerance, and emotional hyper-responsiveness as common emotional characteristics associated with ADHD [237]. The impaired self-regulation may also be accompanied by difficulties in regulating motivation and sustaining effort [237], which can potentially result in delayed growth.

In addition to impaired self-regulation, individuals with ADHD may also exhibit impaired internalization which can manifest as non-compliance. Some studies have found that children with ADHD were less compliant with their mother's directions [237]. Consequently, parents employ coercive methods, which are ineffective, to demand compliance. However, the repercussions of impaired internalized speech may not end here.

It has been suggested that impaired internalized speech could lead to delays in moral development due to a less-developed moral reasoning [237]. Although research has found that moral reasoning was less developed in children with ADHD or hyperactivity-impulsivity, it is unclear if this was due to deficient internalization [237]. Nevertheless, this finding seems to align with the earlier moral developmental model, which regards internalization as a salient component.

Taken together, children with ADHD may be more susceptible to negative reinforcement within a coercive family cycle. They may also be more susceptible to an unsupportive peer or school environment. In other words, they may face heightened risk within negative environments. This risk, undiscovered, or worse, misattributed to a child's temperament or innate character, becomes exacerbated within life institutions that do not have the correct knowledge to promote positive development.

True enough, long-term outcomes tended to be worse for those with untreated ADHD compared to non-ADHD persons [238].

Poorer outcomes for untreated ADHD included anti-social behavior, peer rejection, drug use, other addiction behavior such as tobacco use, and poorer academic achievement, such as failing grades [238]. Some individuals also experienced poorer employment, self-esteem, and driving outcomes [238]. In contrast, ADHD treatment tended to improve each outcome [238].

Moreover, a study found that individuals with ADHD had higher risks of co-morbid disorders during adulthood [235]. These disorders included mood disorders, depression, bipolar disorder, anxiety disorder, substance use disorders, and intermittent explosive disorder [235].

People with intermittent explosive disorder may display repeated episodes of impulsive, aggressive, or angry outbursts that are out of proportion with their situations [239]. These episodes may include road rage, or throwing and breaking items [239]. Logically, intermittent explosive disorder could increase the risk of impaired relationships and getting into trouble at home, school, or work [239]. As such, co-morbid disorders may add to the risks of adverse adult outcomes.

A review observed that ADHD was linked to risk-taking behaviors across multiple domains [240]. For example, childhood ADHD was consistently linked to risky adult driving, such as driving under the influence of alcohol or without a license [240]. Drivers with ADHD were also more likely to engage in driving-related risk-taking behavior [240].

The prevalence of ADHD was also found to increase by five-fold in youth prison populations and ten-fold in adult prison populations [240], highlighting an increased risk of getting into trouble with the law.

ADHD has also been linked to earlier sexual activity, a higher number of sex partners, more sex outside of relationships, more sexually transmitted diseases, and more teenage pregnancies [240].

The risks associated with ADHD extended to problem gambling and food-related risk-taking behaviors, such as overeating [240]. Additionally, a link has been found between ADHD and obesity [240].

A possible explanation for increased risk-taking could be sensation-seeking. ADHD was repeatedly found to be positively related to sensation-seeking [240].

- A study found a negative correlation between high sensation-seeking and risk appraisal [241]. Specifically, high sensation seekers viewed activities as less risky compared to low sensation seekers [241]. Individuals who scored high in sensation seeking and appraised the risks as low were more likely to engage in risky behavior [241]. However, the strongest predictor of risk-taking was the individual's estimate of the number of peers engaging in the same behavior [241]. Nonetheless, sensation-seeking was the second strongest predictor of risky behavior [241].

One study investigated into whether there was a link between ADHD and violence. In a study of adult offenders of violent offenses, childhood ADHD and persisting ADHD were found to be positively associated with reactive violence, which referred to violence that is committed where there was a prior provocation and the perpetrators displayed affective symptoms when committing violence [242]. The same study found ADHD to be negatively related to proactive violence, which was said to be linked to psychopathic traits [242].

In other words, violence linked to ADHD could be mistaken for instrumental violence, which may be used proactively and psychopathically to achieve a desired goal such as status. However, this does not mean that a proneness to reactive violence would preclude the use of proactive violence.

One study proposed that the developmental course of ADHD can be extremely heterogeneous due to the related neurobiological processing mechanisms of co-morbid disorders, which include depressive and anxiety disorders, antisocial personality disorder, and borderline-personality disorder [243].

Anti-social personality disorder include symptoms such as low frustration tolerance, problems abiding by social norms, and aggressive behavior due to a lack of adaptive problem-solving strategies [243]. Borderline-personality disorder symptoms include a lack of adaptive problem-solving strategies, inappropriate and uncontrollable anger, and unstable emotions [243].

A possible developmental pathway for individuals with ADHD could involve the disorder being overlooked due to co-morbid disorders, leading to rejection by caregivers and peers [243]. As a result, children with ADHD may experience school anxiety and perform poorly in academics. This may eventually lead to school reluctance [243]. In adolescence, delinquent behavior may emerge, influenced by peers and a general resignation toward learning [243]. These adolescents may then turn to substance abuse as a coping mechanism [243]. Without proper intervention from poorly equipped life institutions, the accumulation of developmental deficits and unattended ADHD may lead to the onset of Anti-social and borderline-personality disorders, further exacerbating problems in various areas of life such as work, home, and relationships.

Misunderstandings by teachers towards children with ADHD, such as interpreting an inability to sustain attention and effort as a lack of academic interest, may lead to harsh judgments that take a toll on the student's sense of potential [244]. Unsurprisingly, students with ADHD were at significantly higher risk of high school dropout and grade retention [245].

On top of lower educational attainment, hyperactive children had significantly poorer job outcomes [246]. They were more likely to have been fired from a job, from a larger percentage of their jobs, and employers rated them as having more symptoms of ADHD and oppositional defiant disorder, which predicted the likelihood of dismissal [246].

The same study also discovered that individuals with ADHD had fewer close friends during adulthood [246]. Although they also had fewer social acquaintances, this relationship did not reach statistical significance [246]. These results suggest that individuals with ADHD may have fewer supportive ties.

A possible explanation is that the behaviors of ADHD children could negatively affect their supportive ties. For instance, a study found that siblings felt victimized by their ADHD sibling's aggressive actions, even in the absence of oppositional defiant disorder [247].

Siblings in the same study reported that their family overlooked or disbelieved the severity of their victimization [247], which suggests that the ADHD sibling's aggression was negatively reinforced due to a lack of compelling consequences. Additionally, siblings may cope through avoidance or retaliatory aggression [247], further reinforcing the aggressive behavior. These dynamics can also lead to siblings feeling unloved by their parents [247].

The study also found that both siblings and parents identified 'disruption due to ADHD symptoms' as the most significant family problem, while children with ADHD identified 'other people,' including their family, teachers, and peers, as the most significant problem [247]. Furthermore, many ADHD siblings reportedly used self-justifications for their aggressive behavior [247].

Given the risk of adverse developmental trajectories and the deleterious effects on caregivers' mental well-being, preventing ADHD may be a logical solution on top of equipping life institutions with coping and developmental resources. As such, it is important that we understand how ADHD is formed.

In one review, it was suggested that the risk of ADHD was largely influenced by genetics, although not completely [248]. Environmental factors have also been implicated, such as exposure to toxins like maternal consumption of mercury-contaminated fish and exposure to polychlorinated biphenyls found in paints [248].

A study of monozygotic twins provided evidence that environmental factors also contribute to the risk of developing ADHD [249]. Since monozygotic twins tended to have identical genomes, differences in development were more likely due to environmental factors [249]. The study further differentiable the twins into two groups: discordant and concordant twins [249]. Discordant twins had one twin affected by ADHD, whereas the other was not, while concordant twins had both twins either affected or unaffected. By comparing environmental differences experienced within discordant twin pairs and between high and low-attention problem concordant twins, risk factors for ADHD were identified [249]. These risk factors included low birthweight and maternal pregnancy smoking [249].

Similar to the findings of this study, the earlier-mentioned review reported that some studies found significant associations between prenatal alcohol-use and child ADHD, but some did not [248].

Just as poor parental habits could increase ADHD risks, good parental habits could help reduce it. One study found that positive parenting could reduce a child's hyperactivity-impulsivity and inattention [250]. This included restlessness, difficulty waiting for one's turn, distractibility, and the inability to persist and concentrate for more than a few moments [250]. However, it is too early to conclude that positive parenting has an effect on clinical levels of ADHD, especially since many environmental risks are biological. A robust investigation is needed.

With these limitations in mind, positive parenting within the study was measured by quality guidance, supportive presence, child acceptance, effective limit-setting, respect for child autonomy, and low hostility, which encompasses anger, criticism, and rejection [250].

The same study found that positive parenting along with the child's temperament of inhibitory control predicted lower hyperactivity-impulsivity and inattention [250]. Here, inhibitory control refers to the suppression of an inappropriate but dominant response for an appropriate but subdominant response. This supports the notion that appropriate parental involvement, warmth, and encouragement could help with ADHD symptoms.

Further analysis revealed that 'vantage sensitivity' could explain the relationship between positive parenting and lower ADHD symptoms. Vantage sensitivity refers to certain individuals reaping increased benefits from positive experiences. But how so?

Specifically, positive parenting predicted lower ADHD symptoms only when a child's inhibitory control was high [250]. In comparison, children with low inhibitory control were observed to have higher

ADHD symptoms regardless of parenting practices [250]. This suggests two implications.

Firstly, if ADHD does lead to a secondary impairment of child inhibition, as suggested by previous evidence, positive parenting could be ineffective in reducing ADHD symptoms. Secondly, combining positive parenting with strategies to foster child inhibition could be an effective approach to reducing ADHD symptoms. However, more research is needed to investigate this.

<u>Possible Initiatives</u>

✓ Prenatal programs can raise awareness of the behavioral causes of ADHD and support parents in changing harmful habits such as tobacco use, drug use, and alcohol consumption, potentially preventing the behavioral causes of ADHD.

✓ Schools can educate teachers and parents to avoid misattributions of child behavior and promote the use of positive disciplining that supports the growth of a child's inhibitory control. This can facilitate developmentally beneficial interactions and prevent environmental factors, such as peer rejection and delinquency, that may contribute to ADHD co-morbidity.

<u>What must Human Beings know about being human?</u>

<u>#15</u>

The Dark Reality of Abuse

In 2017, there were approximately 674,000 child and adolescent victims of abuse and neglect in the United States alone, with 1,720 of them dying as a result [251].

The majority of these victims did not have prior contact with child protection services within the past three years, indicating fresh occurrences of abuse. It is also possible that the actual prevalence of child abuse is much higher, as the reported numbers are based on cases that were brought to the attention of child protection services. Moreover, forms of abuse such as emotional abuse may go undetected or unrecognized.

Given the widespread adult illiteracy regarding proper care for children and adolescents, it is necessary to examine the risk factors associated with abuse.

On a national level, four caregiver risk factors were observed: 12.1% of victims had an alcohol-abusing caregiver, 30.8% had a drug-abusing one, 14.9% had a caregiver in financial distress, and 27.2% had a caregiver at risk of domestic violence, either as the perpetrator or victim [251].

The factors involved in child maltreatment may also reflect enduring vulnerability. These factors include biological factors, parental history of being maltreated, and 'transient' factors such as marital problems, job loss, and child disciplining issues [252]. Conversely, there may be enduring protective factors such as parental history of receiving good parenting, and transient buffers such as improvement in financial condition and marital harmony [252].

However, other factors may also interact such as families having low socioeconomic status and being isolated from community support. Additionally, cultural beliefs and values on a macro-system level, such as the widespread acceptance of physical punishment, can contribute to the problem [252]. All of these factors may combine to create maltreating parents who are depressed, lacking in social support, and have weak impulse control when aroused or stressed [252].

Another study found that child maltreatment and the parents' alcohol and drug problems were two distinct but often interrelated conditions that co-occurred about one-third of the time [253]. However, having alcohol and drug problems does not automatically make someone a child abuser. Rather, when these issues co-occur, they suggest a broader global parental dysfunction [253].

The same study suggested that the assessment of the parents' risk factors should include their problem-solving capacities, readiness for change, and their cognitive, emotional, and social functioning [253].

This may be a good time to clarify what constitutes maltreatment. Child maltreatment includes a wide range of conditions such as physical abuse, emotional abuse (e.g., saying hurtful and insulting things), sexual abuse, (e.g., being made to watch or do sexual things), emotional neglect (e.g., the family is not a source of support), and physical neglect (e.g., children wearing dirty clothes) [253]. All of these suggest that the children's basic, socio-emotional, and developmental needs are not tended to or may even be violated. As a result, abuse can have pervasive impact on a person's being.

This impact may be long-term as childhood abuse can lead to intergenerational transmission. One study found that parents with a childhood history of abuse or neglect were twice as likely to be reported to child protection services for child maltreatment [254].

In contrast, self-reported perpetration by abused parents did not reach statistical significance, except for neglect [254]. Additionally, their self-reports were not more likely than non-abused parents' to report their perpetration of child physical or sexual abuse [254]. These findings do not eliminate the possibility of abusers having biases of self-censorship, denial, or whitewashing.

However, children of parents who experienced childhood abuse were significantly more likely to report being victims of neglect or child sexual abuse [254]. Although this study did not find evidence for the intergenerational transmission of physical abuse, it did support an increased risk for neglect and sexual abuse [254].

So what kind of development could lead to abusive behavior? It would be a mistake to assume that every abusive individual is one who is coping poorly with a disadvantaged or stressful situation. One study investigated a much-unexplored direction by exploring the links between narcissism, empathy, and abuse.

Physically and emotionally abusive parents, as compared to non-abusive foster parents, were less able to see from another person's perspective [255]. They showed less warmth, compassion, and concern for others, yet displayed an increased tendency to experience distress during challenging interpersonal situations, losing control [255]. All of this suggests poorer performance in empathy aspects.

Abusive parents were further found to differ from non-abusive foster parents on measures of overt narcissism [255]. Overt narcissism here refers to self-aggrandizing and exploitative behavior [255].

To elaborate, abusive parents differed from non-abusive parents in terms of authority, exhibitionism, superiority, and entitlement [255]. It is interesting to note that abusive parents had low levels of self-superiority and authority, indicating low confidence [255], which is counter-stereotypic for narcissism. However, they displayed high levels of exhibitionism, meaning a lack of impulse control, and high levels of entitlement, displaying hostility, intolerance for others, and a need for power [255].

Further analysis revealed an inverse relationship between perspective-taking and the need for power, control, dominance, and a lack of impulse control [255]. These findings suggest that empathy and narcissism may not be compatible.

Given the mixed results for overt narcissism, it has been suggested that covert narcissism may be a better predictor. While some narcissists may appear self-aggrandizing and exploitative, others may display covert narcissism, characterized by a proneness to belittlement, delusions of persecution, and hypersensitivity [255]. Individuals with covert narcissism may have their feelings easily hurt by the slighting remarks of others [255], and as a result, take those remarks very personally. In the same study, it was found that abusive parents exhibited significantly higher levels of covert narcissism [255].

The study also identified a possible scenario of covert narcissism in abusive parents. These parents may expect their child to be responsible for the parents' happiness and emotional needs [255], which can be challenging for the child to fulfill as they are expected to live up to an adult role that even adults may find challenging. Moreover, a narcissist's lack of empathy and difficulty recognizing another's needs, feelings, and subjective experiences can worsen the situation [255]. Even when these needs and feelings are recognized, they may be disparaged as a weakness [255], further complicating the parents' ability to understand their child's behavior or deal with it rationally [255].

Abusive parents may view a child's behavior hyper-sensitively, perceiving it as misbehavior, an affront to their authority, a personal insult, a wounding, a source of humiliation, and a loss of control and authority [255]. Consequently, abusive individuals may view themselves as the victims rather than the aggressors. Moreover, such behavior violates their sense of entitlement [255], which is the expectation that others should comply with their expectations [255]. This implies that anyone who does not is seen as a disobedient troublemaker.

These slights, real or imagined, can lead abusive parents to experience a deeply felt emotional disequilibrium, which prompts an urgent attempt to re-establish equilibrium [255]. Unfortunately, this attempt may disregard the feelings of others, and parents may resort to using force, including physical or emotional abuse, to demand entitled compliance [255].

What we have just seen is a narcissist's 'self-centeredness' [255]. Rather than wishing deliberate harm onto others, the narcissist's self-centeredness is motivated by a preoccupation to prove their worth, ease pain, and feel good. It is a preoccupation so intense that it precludes the consideration of others' feelings and perspectives [255].

The self-centeredness of a narcissist, as described above, may not be limited to physical and emotional abuse. In the original context, Gilgun used such self-centeredness to describe sexual abuse perpetrators [255]. Other studies have also mentioned narcissism in the context of sex abusers who exercised their patriarchal 'privilege' or 'entitlement' to bed their daughters [255].

As can be seen, abusive behaviors may result from dysfunctional or delusional personalities, even if substance abuse or poor coping contributes to their occurrence. Moreover, abusive behaviors may be intergenerationally transmitted, with a possible explanation being that a narcissist with impaired empathy impairs a child's empathy development through abusive behavior.

This was investigated in a study, which observed that abused toddlers reacted to another toddler's distress with threats, physical attacks, fear, and anger, instead of concern and empathy like non-abused toddlers [256]. Such behaviors could resemble a hypersensitive parent who views a child's crying and distress as a personal rejection or non-compliance and responds abusively.

Similarly, another study observed that abused children exhibited lower levels of empathy and greater emotional maladjustment than non-abused children [257]. These findings support the idea that abusive behavior may be part of a cycle of abuse. Alternatively, it could be that parental abuse stems from a lack of preparedness and competence for parenthood.

Abusive parents may provide inadequate care for their infants from the very beginning. For instance, a study found that mothers of abused, neglected, and mistreated infants were significantly younger than non-abusive mothers [258]. Moreover, a disproportionate number of these mothers were single and lacked familial support [258].

However, the abusive and non-abusive groups did not show significant differences in the measures of impulsivity, anxiousness, hostility, and suspicion [258]. This suggests that aggression traits were not predictive of the quality of care that mothers had provided for their infants [258].

This is significant because the quality of mother-infant interactions predicted later maltreatment and neglect [258]. The study observed that many abusive mothers lacked the skills to care for their children and manage their own lives [258]. Additionally, abusive mothers displayed disengagement from the mother-infant relationship and misunderstood their child and the nature of child-rearing [258].

In some cases, abusive mothers also reported receiving intimate partner violence [258]. This suggests that child maltreatment may be a co-morbidity that accompanied abusive spouses or partners.

- It was argued that intimate partner violence is used to maintain control over one's partner or wrestle for control in a mutually controlling relationship [259]. Furthermore, it has been suggested that intimate violence could be supported by a sense of entitlement, a patriarchal culture, or a gender asymmetry that views intimate violence by *women* as appropriate and 'feminine' [259].

- In one study, it was suggested that an abusive partner may exhibit narcissistic traits. These individuals may have a fragile self-esteem that makes any rejection devastating [260]. Furthermore, they may prioritize their own needs over their partner's and demand that their partner comply with their directives [260]. Despite this, they may hold an inflated sexual esteem and consider themselves to be skilled lovers [260]. This is because insecure narcissists have a constant need for validation, reinforcement, and ego-stroking [260].

- For instance, some men may prove their masculinity by asserting their dominance over their partner, whom they view as their property and thus are entitled to do whatever they wish without their partner's consent [260]. This may be one way in which abusive relationships can manifest.

- Moreover, controlling behaviors within intimate violence may often involve emotional abuse [259]. It is possible that abuse gradually alters an abused person's self-views, relationship views, and perceptions of their place in this world [259]. Consequently, abusive behaviors can result in a wide range of negative consequences for the abused individual.

Abused children may experience adverse emotional development, as evidenced by increased fearfulness, anger, and sadness during mother-child interactions [261]. Moreover, maltreated children displayed less accuracy in recognizing emotions but were hypersensitive towards detecting anger [261]. This suggests deficits in social information-processing and it can be accompanied by increased distractibility and poor concentration [261].

Additionally, attention deficits, anger recognition, and maladaptive social information processing interact, possibly leading to increased negativity and aggressive reactivity [261].

In one study, it was found that 80% of maltreated children exhibited either an under-controlled or over-controlled emotional regulation pattern [261]. Additionally, maltreated children were observed to experience delays in their theory of mind development [261]. To refresh, theory of mind refers to an individual's understanding that others may hold different perspectives from their own [261]. This understanding implies that people may not have access to the same information as we do or feel the same way as we do.

-   Considering that maltreated individuals often exhibited dysfunctional emotion regulation and an impaired theory of mind, it is possible that maltreated individuals may struggle with their relationships. In fact, it was reported that chronically maltreated children may experience repeated rejections throughout their childhood and adolescence [261]. Consequently, maltreatment can lead to maladjustment later in life.

One study found that experiencing childhood maltreatment, including sexual abuse, emotional abuse, and emotional neglect, was associated with a multi-fold risk of suicide during adulthood [262]. This risk was the highest when the abuse was complex and repeated [262]. Furthermore, this risk was not mediated by participant characteristics such as psychiatric diagnoses and mental health conditions [262].

At the same time, childhood maltreatment could lead to maladaptive behavior. In one study, self-reported childhood abuse and neglect were significantly related to lower educational attainment and increased substance abuse, psychological distress, and use of avoidant coping during adulthood [263]. Here, avoidant coping was measured by denial, as well as behavioral and mental disengagement [263].

- After a more detailed analysis, it was found that the relationship between childhood trauma and alcohol and drug abuse was partially explained by lower educational attainment and the use of avoidant coping strategies [263]. Additionally, lower educational attainment was directly linked to increased substance use and avoidant coping [263]. Moreover, using more avoidant coping strategies was directly linked to increased substance use and psychological distress [263].

- As can be seen, maltreatment can exert influence through maladaptations, leading to increased vulnerability. It has been suggested that childhood trauma may increase the risks of adult re-victimization [263].

Chronic maltreatment has been linked to increased risks of having one or more problematic child outcomes, which included mental health diagnoses, suicide attempts, requiring healthcare for head injuries or sexually transmitted diseases, violent offending, and substance use [264].

Similarly, chronic maltreatment during childhood and adolescence has been linked to adverse adult outcomes such as maltreatment perpetration, substance use, and mental health treatment [264]. However, after accounting for problematic childhood outcomes, the association between chronic maltreatment and two adult outcomes, namely substance use and mental health treatment, was reduced [264]. This suggests that these adult problems may be some form of continuation of childhood outcomes.

A study investigated the association between childhood victimization and mental health outcomes in adulthood. The results showed that adults who experienced abuse and neglect during childhood had more symptoms of antisocial personality disorder, such as truancy, physical cruelty, and potentially criminal acts [265]. Adults who experienced childhood maltreatment also had more symptoms of persistent depressive disorder, which can include poor concentration and feelings of hopelessness [265]. Notably, subsequent stressful events were identified as a possible link between childhood maltreatment and the development of mental disorders later in life [265]. Moreover, adults who experienced childhood maltreatment reported more stressful life events over their lifetime [265], which may reflect a larger disadvantage that includes a lack of social and family support.

The link between child maltreatment and antisocial personality disorder aligns with the findings of another study, which revealed that individuals who experienced childhood abuse and neglect had a higher likelihood of having an arrest record for a violent or non-traffic offense [266]. These findings suggest that the inter-generational cycle of violence may extend beyond the perpetration of maltreatment by adults.

Cumulative risk may have cumulative effects, as child maltreatment can interact with other transient or enduring influences. A study found that communities with high and stable levels of violence had higher rates of child maltreatment, and both maltreatment and community violence had independent and additive effects on a child's poorer functioning [267].

- To elaborate, maltreated children had higher levels of externalizing and internalizing behaviors [267]. Additionally, children who witnessed or experienced community violence had lower self-esteem and more traumatic stress and depressive symptoms [267]. Traumatic stress symptoms included anxious or intrusive thoughts and sleep problems [267].

- Combining the two, maltreated children who were also exposed to high levels of community violence had even higher levels of externalizing behaviors, internalizing behaviors, traumatic stress, and depressive symptoms [267].

- In addition to the impact on social and emotional functioning, childhood maltreatment can also have adverse effects on cognitive development. According to a study, adults who were abused or neglected during childhood had significantly lower IQ scores, and lower reading ability scores that averaged at a sixth-grade level [268].

- Even after controlling for socioeconomic differences, childhood physical abuse and neglect predicted IQ [268]. At the same time, neglect predicted reading ability [268]. Conversely, sexual abuse was not a significant predictor of IQ or reading ability [268].

- Furthermore, after controlling for increased truancy rates, suspension, expulsion, and lower years of school completion, abused and neglected persons scored lower on reading ability [268].

One study looked implicitly into maltreatment as part of a wider ecosystem of violence and found that men and women who were victims of any type of violence by the age of 16, such as home violence, community violence, or sexual assault, were more likely to drop out of high school [269]. Furthermore, women who were victims of all three types of violence completed less education than women who suffered fewer types [269]. The same was observed for men, but the finding did not reach statistical significance.

In summary, we have seen that maltreatment can have significant and long-lasting effects on a person's social, emotional, cognitive, and behavioral functioning. Furthermore, outcomes such as arrest records and school dropouts have been associated with childhood maltreatment. Additionally, chronicity, community violence, and the number of violence typologies can further exacerbate these negative outcomes. However, there may be yet another factor that worsens the impact of childhood maltreatment.

A study that investigated into sexual abuse found that there was an elevated risk across different psychopathologies when there was attempted or completed sexual intercourse, abuse by a relative, use of force or threat, and when victims received a negative response when reporting the abuse [270]. The psychopathologies included major depressive disorder, anxiety disorder, panic disorder, drug dependence, and multiple disorders [270]. To put it simply, the circumstances during the abuse and its aftermath may aggravate.

- To elaborate, if victims received a negative response from the people they reported the abuse to, meaning the person did not believe them, did not support them, or instead punished them, psychopathology risks increased [270]. As such, perpetrators of secondary victimization also posed increased psychopathological risks to victims. This highlights the harm of condoning or downplaying abuse.

- In contrast, if the act of telling someone effectively stopped the abuse, psychopathology risk was reduced [270]. As such, the response of those whom the abuse is reported to matters! This includes the response from a non-abusing parent.

- This can be juxtaposed with abuse that is perpetrated by a relative, meaning those in positions of fiduciary trust. Given that parents fall under this category, examining their role may help explain why abuse from these persons can be aggravating.

- To begin, parents hold the role of buffering an infant's stress [271]. There could be risks of biological changes if parents are not available to perform that role.

- One review informed that maltreated children often display dysregulation in the hypothalamic-pituitary-adrenal (HPA) axis, which coordinates adaptive responses to stressors [272]. Specifically, the hypothalamus stimulates the anterior pituitary and, in turn, the adrenal cortex [272]. This leads to cortisol production, which regulates the body's energy during a stress response [272].

- Although the activation of the stress system is considered adaptive, atypical cortisol levels due to HPA dysregulation can be problematic. For example, physical abuse and neglect were found to be associated with lower morning cortisol levels [272]. In turn, lower morning cortisol levels and atypical afternoon cortisol levels were associated with lower levels of pro-social behavior and higher levels of not only aggression but also externalizing problems, depression, and internalizing symptoms [272].

- As can be seen, HPA dysregulation that is linked to child maltreatment can be associated with various cognitive and behavioral problems. Such dysregulation may persist into adulthood and have implications for later mental and physical health [272].

- These findings suggest that a relative's abuse can be particularly aggravating because the individuals who are supposed to help a child regulate stress are not only absent, but also the source of stress.

Here, we can come full circle. One study found that emotional dysregulation contributed independently to a child's bully and victim status [273]. Furthermore, emotional dysregulation mediated the link between child maltreatment and bullying or victimization [273].

Children are said to be emotionally dysregulated if they respond with hyperarousal or emotional constriction within a neutral or friendly context [273]. Emotional constriction may promote instrumental aggression due to impaired empathy and emotional responsiveness [273].

- In a study on youth offenders, it was found that empathy was a differentiating deficit between offenders and non-incarcerated peers

172

[274]. Youth offenders responded with less frequent and less intense empathy and also reported lower levels of perspective-taking [274]. Unsurprisingly, the levels of empathy predicted delinquency [274].

- At the same time, the responses of the two groups were cognitively differentiable [274]. Non-incarcerated peers tended to respond based on what the other person is feeling [274]. In contrast, youth offenders tended to respond based on their own experiences, saying things like, 'I felt angry when his mother was yelling at him because I had been treated in the same way' [274]. In other words, youth offenders' responses tended to be based on an association with their own experiences [274], rather than an empathetic understanding of another person's emotions.

- In addition, there were different levels of anger, social maladjustment, and alienation between the two groups [274]. Youth offenders were quicker to anger, more anti-authority, and more distrusting of people than their non-incarcerated peers [274]. Furthermore, the study noted that 84% of the youth offenders reported experiencing some form of abuse during their upbringing [274].

- These findings support the notion that child maltreatment may be linked to anti-social outcomes, possibly due to deficient or maladaptive development.

One study investigated a different aspect of maltreatment effects and found that experiencing punitive parenting and abusive behavior like yelling and slapping at age nine was indirectly associated with more shame-proneness [275]. This was through the pathway of parental rejection at age fifteen [275].

Both shame-proneness and parental rejection were found to be associated with increased child depression symptoms at age seventeen

[275]. Parental rejection encompasses parents humiliating or shaming their child, acting as though they are ashamed of their child, and yelling at their mistakes [275].

At the same time, child maltreatment at age nine was linked to lower parental warmth at age fifteen and higher delinquency at age seventeen [275]. In contrast, higher parental warmth was associated with more guilt-proneness and less delinquency [275]. Conversely, parental rejection was associated with lower guilt and, in turn, higher delinquency [275]. These findings suggest that maltreatment could be part of a broader spectrum of poor parenting behaviors that may also contribute to anti-social outcomes.

A study conducted on young offenders revealed that shame was a predictor of higher recidivism, whereas guilt was a predictor of lower recidivism [276]. Moreover, it was suggested that shame might pose a significant personal threat, which may prompt strategies like denying responsibility or injury to avoid critical self-evaluation [276]. As can be seen, there could be a multitude of risks involved.

One review added another risk factor, estimating that 60% of male study participants who engaged in marital violence came from a violent family background [277]. Specifically, these men witnessed inter-parental violence or experienced child abuse or unduly harsh disciplining [277]. This percentage was three times higher than that observed in men who did not exhibit violent behavior in their martial relationships.

- The link between family-of-origin violence and future relationship violence was affirmed in another study. The study found that family-of-origin violence, whether in the form of child abuse or witnessing violence between parents, was positively associated with perpetration and victimization in subsequent relationships [278]. This included psychological abuse, such as dominance, isolation, threats, and emotional and verbal abuse [278].

- Although the associations mentioned were generally modest, odds ratio analysis revealed that individuals who experienced mother-to-self violence were twice as likely to perpetrate relationship violence [278]. Nonetheless, there were no uniform patterns for specific family violence.

Similar to the increased risk of marital violence, child maltreatment may increase risks for elderly abuse. In one study, childhood abuse, measured by physical hurt, screaming, insults, and threats, was positively associated with elderly abuse [279].

The World Health Organization reported according to a 2017 review that one in six elderly persons was subjected to some form of abuse [280]. Elderly abuse can take the form of physical, emotional, and sexual abuse, as well as financial abuse, neglect, abandonment, or any action that leads to the elderly person's loss of dignity [280].

According to a review, the risk factors for elderly abuse included the abuser's physical and mental health problems, substance abuse, dependency on the victim, intolerant attitudes, lack of empathy, and viewing the victim as a source of stress [281].

Moreover, abusers may display hypercritical attitudes, poor impulse control, reluctance towards caregiving, and relationship issues with others [281]. Lastly, a lack of social support may also increase the risk of perpetration [281].

On the other hand, the victim's risk factors included the victim's physical and mental health problems, substance abuse, social isolation, as well as poor relationships with the abuser [281]. Though dependence on the abuser was not a predominant cause of abuse, it was still linked to victimization [281]. Additionally, attitudes such as self-blame, stoicism, or a desire to protect the perpetrator can also make the victim more vulnerable [281]. Furthermore, victims may tolerate their abusers due to their fear of reprisal [281].

In contrast, few victims were said to employ problem-solving and instead rely on withdrawal or terminating contact with the abuser [281].

Having seen the risk factors, it is important to note that elderly abuse, neglect, and abandonment can significantly impact not only the elderly person's mental and physical well-being but also their lifestyle. For instance, it was reported that some elderly individuals in South Korea no longer had contact with their children and they struggled with poverty and the lack of economic opportunity, even turning to prostitution for their livelihood [282].

At this juncture, we can see that the impact of abuse may be a profound one – one that deeply permeates into the thoughts, behaviors, and outcomes of those who interact within society. Such is the enduring nature of the scars and traumas inflicted upon society.

This poses one last question. We know that breaking the chains of abuse at every possible point is important, but can we overcome the effects of abuse?

One study investigated the prevalence of resilience outcomes in children who had contact with child protection services and found that 14% consistently displayed social competence during all three studied time-periods, 22% displayed resilience in their school achievement, while 19% were resilient in their mental health [283]. However, it is important to note that in this context, resilience does not necessarily mean excelling, rather, it means not operating at a disadvantage.

In this study, mental health measurements included a child's externalizing behaviors, such as rule-breaking, aggressiveness, and hot-temper, as well as internalizing behaviors, such as depression and anxiety [283]. Additionally, these measurements included self-esteem, substance use, and Post-Traumatic Stress symptoms, which include intrusive thoughts and avoidance of painful feelings [283].

At the same time, social competence was rated by caregivers and teachers, taking into account a child's cooperation, responsibility, and self-control [283].

Although 11% to 14% of the children were resilient in all three domains at any given time period, only 2% were consistently resilient in all three periods [283]. 7% never reached a resilient outcome in any domain [283]. These findings suggest that even though resilient outcomes are achievable, additional resources may be needed to support maltreated children.

One review identified protective factors that may contribute to resilient outcomes. At the family-level, a stable caregiving environment and supportive caregivers were found to be protective factors [284]. At the community-level, normal peer relationships, positive relationships with adults, and access to non-familial support, such as from counselors, were also identified as protective factors [284].

Individual factors associated with resilience included having an internal locus of control, positive self-esteem, mastery over impulses, resourcefulness, and optimism towards the future [284]. Additionally, individuals may overcome their trauma-related beliefs, such as self-blame and powerlessness [284], which further emphasizes the importance of enhancing the children's life skills.

In a separate study, it was found that 44.5% of child abuse victims did not experience any mental health problems during their 30 years of adulthood [285]. Furthermore, when compared to a random group, this abuse-resilient group displayed lower rates of criminality, relationship instability, and difficulties in personality functioning [285]. This means that this group exhibited effective functioning in their work, intimate relationships, friendships, social interactions, day-to-day coping, and negotiations [285], as opposed to pervasive failures in these domains.

In the same study, it was found that resilience rates were higher among adults who had at least one very caring parent [285]. Additionally, resilience was strongly related to having normal peer adolescent relationships, high-quality adult friendships, as well as stable and supportive adult love relationships [285].

In other words, high-quality relationships across the abused children's childhood, adolescence, and adulthood were important for their psychological well-being [285]. The stability of these environments may also be important.

Furthermore, it is probable that a positive early environment is important. After all, the presence of psychiatric disorders during adolescence differentiated the resilient and non-resilient groups [285]. This indicated adult continuity of difficulties for the non-resilient group [285].

Ultimately, fostering high-quality relationships across the lifespan may require the mitigation of developmental risks that are associated with maltreatment. As such, it may be important to maintain an ongoing process of improvement for an individual's competencies in forming and maintaining supportive relationships, from which one can also benefit [285]. Such environments and skills have the potential to break the intergenerational cycle of abuse.

For example, in one study, it was found that abused mothers who provided adequate childcare and broke the cycle of abuse were significantly more likely to have received emotional support from a non-abusive adult during their childhood [286]. They were also more likely to have had an intact, non-abusive, stable, and emotionally supportive partner relationship [286]. Furthermore, they were more likely to have participated in therapy [286].

178

In terms of personal experiences and characteristics, mothers who continued the abuse cycle experienced higher life stress, anxiety, and depression [286]. These mothers also had higher aggression and dependency, but these personality findings were not consistent over time [286].

But most importantly, this study has shown that the cycle of abuse can indeed be broken with the right adult support and high-quality relationships. Combine this with the right skills to form and maintain these relationships, victims can break the intergenerational transmission of abuse and violence, which can take the form of peer bullying, intimate partner violence, or elderly abuse. In other words, victims can say NO to the destructive developmental path that their abusers had chosen for them.

<u>Possible Initiatives</u>

✓ Individuals can be held legally responsible to report detected abuses within their life institutions. Moreover, a coalition of institutions could be trained to recognize and detect a myriad of abuses, with direct mechanisms in place to report misconduct to regulatory bodies with the necessary power and resources for effective intervention. Watch groups may also monitor institutional risks based on the institution's track record, opacity, and power structure to prevent the covering up of misdeeds. Ultimately, institutions must gain clear understanding of what constitutes abusive behaviors and adopt a zero-tolerance stance towards them.

✓ At the same time, outreach programs can provide developmental resources to both the abused individuals and, mandatorily, to the abusers. These programs can facilitate cognitive development, emotional regulation, inhibitory control, social skills, and perspective-taking.

✓ Some programs could focus on maltreatment prevention. Here, parents may gain awareness of realistic child capabilities and learn to challenge faulty interpretations. They may also receive training on how to overcome unhealthy emotional needs and abusive stress responses.

<u>What must Human Beings know about being human?</u>

<u>#16</u>

Psychopathy, a possible consequence of maltreatment

Psychopathy is a personality disorder characterized by traits from four categories [287].

The four categories are *affective*, defined as callousness and a lack of empathy; *behavioral instability*, defined as impulsiveness and a lack of behavioral control; *social deviancy*, defined as delinquency and criminal versatility; and lastly, *interpersonal*, defined as grandiosity and boldness [287].

You may notice that psychopathy is made up of traits like the lack of behavioral control and empathy that we have explored within other risky developmental pathways.

A meta-analysis of 47 studies revealed a moderate association between psychopathy and child maltreatment [287]. However, it may be important to note that sexual abuse only had a small link [287]. Of course, this is not to say psychopathy would only develop where there is child maltreatment. Similarly, it would be a mistake to conclude that child maltreatment inevitably leads to psychopathy.

Continuing from where we left off, the study recounted an incident where a victim of child maltreatment, who was also a victim of bullying during elementary school, switched from being a victim to a bully after he realized from hitting another school kid that he too had the power to become a bully [287].

The recounted incident was shared by a 35-year-old violent offender who had a long and versatile criminal history, ranging from multiple intimate partner assaults to embezzlement from employers, all while

182

taking pride in his ability to manipulate others [287]. This suggests an internalization of maladaptive narratives, possibly developed as a coping mechanism for a harsh environment.

Resembling this, the affective aspect of psychopathy (callousness and lack of empathy) was reported to be associated with a reduced psycho-physiological response to negative emotional stimuli [287]. This 'disassociation' could be a coping mechanism developed in response to a personal history of traumatic interpersonal experiences [287].

It has also been proposed that 'complex trauma,' which refers to early trauma and stressors, can compromise an individual's secure attachment with their caregivers [287]. This can cause an organism to enter a 'survival' mode, resulting in changes to mechanisms such as self-regulation, attention, and learning [287]. Additionally, it has been suggested that a narcissistic grandiosity may be used as a defense mechanism against betrayal trauma [287]. Said grandiosity could have similarities to that of psychopathy [287].

Past research has also shown that victimization within the family predicted *Factor 1 Psychopathy*, which pertains to the affective and interpersonal aspects [287]. In contrast, negative school experiences and other forms of societal adversity predicted *Factor 2 Psychopathy*, which involves behavioral disinhibition and anti-social behavior [287]. However, the consistency of these findings across different studies has been mixed [287]. In the present meta-analysis, child maltreatment was found to have a stronger association with behavioral disinhibition and anti-social behavior [287].

It has been reported that psychopaths were twenty to twenty-five times more likely than non-psychopaths to be incarcerated, and four to eight times more likely to recidivate [288]. Despite male psychopaths making up only 1% of the adult male population, they constituted 15% to 25% of the prison population in North America [288]. Moreover, it was suggested that the only mental disorders that were more common than psychopathy were those related to drug and alcohol abuse, depression, and post-traumatic stress disorder [288].

As if things could not get any worse, psychopaths were reported to resist most forms of treatment [288]. Furthermore, psychopathy can be comorbid with other disorders. In one study, factors of psychopathy were found to positively correlate with various DSM-IV Personality Disorder scores [289].

- Specifically, the Interpersonal factor scores of psychopathy, i.e., grandiosity and deceit, were positively correlated with narcissistic personality scores [289].

- Affective factor scores, i.e., the lack of remorse, empathy, or acceptance of responsibility, were positively associated with adult anti-social and schizoid scores [289]. To clarify, Schizoid Personality Disorder includes a pervasive detachment from social relationships, restricted emotional expression within interpersonal settings, and an indifference to praise and criticism from others [290].

- Conversely, adult anti-social scores describe criminal and aggressive behaviors that do not meet the full criteria for an Antisocial Personality Disorder, but are serious enough to warrant clinical attention [290]. The criteria for an Antisocial Personality Disorder includes pervasive disregard for and violation of others' rights since the age of 15, with individuals needing to be at least 18 years old to receive a diagnosis [290].

- Delving further, individuals with narcissistic or schizoid traits may be particularly prone to explosive anger outbursts during stressful situations [290]. This is an associated feature of intermittent explosive disorder [290]. All of this suggests further potential co-morbidity.

- Similarly, 'lifestyle' factor scores of psychopathy, i.e., impulsivity, irresponsibility, and lacking goals, were positively associated with 'histrionic' scores, borderline scores, and adult anti-social scores [289].

- Clinical descriptions of Histrionic Personality Disorder include a pervasive and excessive need for attention as well as a dependency within relationships [290]. Meanwhile, clinical criteria for Borderline Personality Disorder include frantic efforts to avoid real or imagined abandonment, a persistently unstable self-image, potentially self-damaging impulsivity, and inappropriate anger expression [290].

- Unsurprisingly, Anti-social scores of psychopathy, i.e., poor behavioral control and anti-social behavior, were positively associated with conduct disorder and adult anti-social scores [289].

- Conduct disorder, while similar to antisocial personality disorder, includes physical cruelty to people and animals, property destruction, deceitfulness, and functional impairments in social, academic, and occupational domains [290]. Individuals with conduct disorder may exhibit little empathy, guilt, and concern for the well-being and feelings of others [290]. This can be accompanied by poor frustration tolerance and misinterpretation of other's intentions as hostile and threatening [290].

The implications of psychopathy development could extend beyond co-morbid disorders. For instance, individuals with a history of heroin and amphetamine use and drug dependence were found to have significantly higher total psychopathy scores [289].

Similarly, total psychopathy scores were significantly higher for participants with convictions, prison sentences, homelessness, psychiatric hospital admission, attempted suicide, and perpetration of interpersonal violence within the past five years [289]. While these findings cannot be generalized to all individuals with such histories, it highlights the wide range of adverse outcomes that can be associated with psychopathy.

The same study also found a negative relationship between verbal intelligence and psychopathic traits, specifically the *anti-social* factors and *lifestyle* factors, i.e., impulsivity and irresponsibility [289]. This finding supports a previous study [289]. However, the study did not support previous findings that found the *interpersonal* factor, i.e., grandiosity and deceit, to be positively associated with verbal IQ, creativity, and analytic thinking [289].

One meta-analysis did find a small, significant, negative relationship between intelligence and total psychopathy, as well as a small positive relationship between the interpersonal factor and certain IQ measures [291]. However, it is worth noting that incarcerated persons were overrepresented in this meta-analysis, which could suggest that lower IQ may be linked to incarceration rather than psychopathy. Therefore, this link may not be generalizable to non-incarcerated psychopathic populations.

Given that psychopathy has been implicated in poorer intelligence and life outcomes, these findings challenge the age-old stereotype that psychopaths are inherently evil persons who only seek to harm others through 'clever' machinations for personal gain. Neurological findings also seem to challenge this notion.

FMRI data has shown that psychopaths displayed abnormal and persistently decreased neural activity in the paralimbic brain regions [288]. These regions contain important structures associated with moral reasoning, affective memory, and inhibition [288], which could conceivably affect learning and long-term working memory, thus impacting one's intelligence.

In an fMRI study on reinforcement learning, offenders with antisocial personality disorder and psychopathy displayed greater activation of the posterior cingulate cortex (PCC) region during the 'punished reversal error' situation compared to a 'rewarded correct response' situation [292]. Non-offenders and those without psychopathy did not exhibit this pattern [292].

To clarify, 'punished reversal error' refers to a situation whereby an individual is punished for a decision that was previously considered 'correct' and rewarded [292]. For instance, if committing a crime was once a dominant and rewarding behavior but is later punished, this can be considered a 'punished reversal error.' In other words, the 'reversal' refers to a change in what is considered correct.

Conversely, a 'rewarded correct response' refers to an individual being rewarded for performing an initial behavior and a new behavior after the old behavior was deemed incorrect [292].

Normally, the PCC would *decrease* activation in response to punishment, signaling a behavioral error and a need to adapt one's behavior [292]. In this study, offenders with psychopathy displayed greater activation to punishment and decreased activation to a 'rewarded correct response' [292]. As such, the offenders displayed an abnormal response to punishment and the reward for correcting a response.

At the same time, offenders with psychopathy showed increased activation of the anterior insula in response to punished reversal errors compared to non-offenders [292]. The anterior insula is involved in motivation, reward, pain avoidance, and tracking the salience of actions with regard to an outcome, for example recognizing an error [292], and possibly how a behavior leads to an outcome.

Putting the two together, the abnormal activations in the PCC and anterior insula indicate an altered information processing system [292].

Specifically, there may be dysfunction in the weighing of reward and punishment, which is responsible for reinforcement learning [292]. In other words, people with psychopathy may experience differences in reinforcement learning, which can result in impaired adaptive decision-making and an inability to assess consequences.

Furthermore, offenders with psychopathy were found to have less activation in the superior temporal gyrus in response to reward information compared to non-offenders [292]. The superior temporal gyrus is reported to be involved in subjective value [292]. The lower activation suggests that offenders with psychopathy have lower sensitivity to reward information from 'correct responses.'

Putting the three together, the diminished neurological activation of persons with psychopathy towards rewarded correct response, and the increased activation towards punishment during behavior replacement, imply impaired behavioral correction. This may explain why persons with psychopathy are resistant to behavioral change and at increased risk for recidivism.

Contrary to the traditional notion that offenders with psychopathy are insensitive to reward and punishment, it is possible that they have atypical information processing instead.

As such, it was suggested that interventions may need to work on modifying a psychopath's 'subjective value' and re-focusing their attention instead [292].

One study zoomed in on the persistence of behavior for people with psychopathy. Offenders with psychopathy tended to persist in their behaviors even when circumstances become increasingly likely to punish them than reward them [293].

In the study, the offenders would win 5 cents if they got a J, Q, K, or A poker card and lose 5 cents if they got a 'number' card. They were then given immediate feedback to see if they had won or lost each time they played a card. However, the probability of losing was actually increasing by 10% for every 10 cards played, starting from an initial 10% loss probability [293].

Within this condition, it was found that offenders with psychopathy played almost 50% more cards and, as a result, lost more money [293]. The mean number of cards played was 89.6 for offenders and 62.8 for non-offenders, indicating that offenders with psychopathy continued to play cards even at highly disadvantageous probabilities of 90 to 100%. They failed to notice the increases in punishment probability, and failed to adjust their dominant responses [293].

A second group repeated the conditions but received cumulative feedback on the cards that appeared, giving them feedback on their history of winning or losing. In this condition, the mean number of cards played by offenders decreased to 80.8 [293]. However, the results failed to reach sufficient statistical significance.

Finally, a third group was given both cumulative feedback and a five-second wait time between plays to improve their use of the information. Both offenders with psychopathy and non-offenders played a comparably low number of cards, with a mean of 48.4 and 48.3, respectively [293]. This result reached statistical significance.

As can be seen, offenders with psychopathy tended to persist in their behaviors even when faced with punishment. However, providing them with cumulative feedback on their performance and sufficient time to use that information, resulted in a decrease in behavior persistence, as evidenced by their comparable performance to non-offenders.

However, in addition to deficient adaptation, individuals with psychopathy may also have a weaker ability to recognize distress. To investigate this, one review examined the neural activities associated with psychopathic-like deficits in emotionality, such as callousness and an inability to respond to others' distress.

It was said that the Anterior Cingulate Cortex (ACC) serves to receive peripheral information and generate neural signals when distress cues are heightened [294]. ACC was shown to activate during emotional pain, whether physical or social, and whether the pain was experienced by oneself or others [294].

The review found that in one study, people high in psychopathy had weaker ACC activation during an emotional memory task [294]. Similarly, another study found weaker ACC activation during a task that suggested internal conflict [294]. These findings indicate a less active empathy-related neuro-circuitry. Specifically, distress cues may not cross the required threshold to indicate that there is a conflict or a need to adjust behavior [294]. As such, a stress response may fail to trigger in the implicated brain regions [294].

It has been reported that individuals with high levels of callous-unemotional traits often exhibited reduced amygdala activation [294]. The amygdala is involved in enhancing the learning and memory for emotional events, which can influence future decisions [294]. Therefore, individuals with reduced amygdala activation may exhibit difficulties in emotion-related decision-making due to impaired learning [294].

Furthermore, individuals with reduced amygdala activation in response to their own distress may also experience difficulty processing the distress of others [294]. It has been suggested that individuals with low arousal towards others' distress may also experience low arousal towards their own [294]. This is consistent with the fact that offenders with psychopathy tend to persist in behaviors that are punished.

Given the atypical and non-adaptive development associated with psychopathy, is it possible for individuals to develop strategies to manage their heightened risks of adverse outcomes? The answer is yes, it is possible.

One study investigated non-incarcerated individuals with psychopathic traits and found a positive association between gray matter density in the ventrolateral prefrontal cortex (VLPFC) and psychopathic traits [295]. The VLPFC is known for its role in regulating emotions and aggressive and impulsive behavior [295]. This finding suggests that individuals with psychopathic traits can indeed develop inhibitory and self-regulation mechanisms to compensate for the deficits associated with psychopathy.

However, experiment limitations prevent a strong conclusion from being drawn. Specifically, the participants were not narrowed down to non-incarcerated individuals with high levels of psychopathic traits. This may be due to difficulties in finding such individuals since inhibition presumably opposes the impulsiveness factor.

In other words, individuals who achieved high levels of self-regulation may not exhibit high levels of psychopathy. Therefore, it may be beneficial to examine programs that aim to cultivate inhibition in incarcerated individuals with psychopathic traits. By doing so, we can assess if such programs could lead to a decrease in recidivism.

<u>What must Human Beings know about being human?</u>

<u>#17</u>

What is a relationship style conducive to well-being?

It was documented in John Bowlby's 1973 book, Attachment and loss, that young children's separations from their mothers had repercussions [296]. This conclusion was based on observations of how young children behaved when they were away from their mothers and later returned home to her [296]. The observations suggested that maternal deprivation was traumatic [296].

In addition, children and adults, who experienced a parental loss or long separation, or had grounds to fear one during childhood or adolescence, experienced difficulties in forming and maintaining affection bonds with their parental figures, partners, and children [296].

A potential explanation for this phenomenon could be the development of an anxious attachment. Anxious attachment can result from a parent's threat of abandonment [296]. In other words, when parents say things like, 'I will leave you behind if you do not come,' it can be extremely detrimental to a child's development.

In a 1968 study, it was documented that no less than 27% of the parents studied used threats of abandonment as a means of discipline [296]. This suggests a widespread lack of understanding of the impact such threats can have on children's development.

In reality, threats of abandonment may be much more traumatic than it seems. In one recount, a father accused his child of stealing money from his pockets, and when the child denied doing so, the father said that he would punish the child for lying. The child eventually lied that he stole the money in order to escape being beaten [296]. But things only got worse. His father drove him to a home that was run by the authorities to give up the child there, only rescinding that intention when the father deemed him to be suitably sorry [296]. A week later, the same child refused to go to school as he experienced intense fear and anxiety [296].

In another account, a parent placed the blame on the child when the other parent used threats of abandonment and severe bodily harm towards the child [296]. In other words, the child was held responsible for the parent's use of threats. Once again, the child reported experiencing intense fear and anxiety during a different situation. However, the repercussions may not end there.

Apart from the fear and anxiety related to abandonment, separation can also evoke feelings of anger. In a study on child responses to a separation scenario, children growing up in a stable family expressed distress and concern two to three times more often than anger and blame [296]. In contrast, children who experienced long and repeated separations or family rejections expressed just as many angry and blaming responses as distress and concern [296].

Such anger and blaming could manifest as an 'insecure' attachment style in future relationships. It was said that separation and rejection not only arouse a person's hostile thoughts and actions but also increase their fear of further rejection or losing an attachment figure [296]. The result may be a combination of intense possessiveness, anxiety, and anger [296].

Ultimately, parent-child interactions lead children to form a model that pertains to how they view themselves and their parents [296]. These 'self-representations' and recollections of early experiences with their parents would go on to be associated with 'attachment styles' that correspond with the various levels of anxiety and avoidance [297].

Specifically, four interpersonal styles emerged based on the combinations of anxiety and avoidance [297]. They were –

1) Secure attachment, which is characterized by low anxiety and avoidance.

2) Preoccupied attachment, which is made up of high anxiety and low avoidance.

3) Dismissive attachment, which is characterized by low anxiety and high avoidance. People avoid close relationships due to a sense of self-sufficiency.

4) And lastly, Fearful attachment, which is made up of high anxiety and high avoidance. People with this attachment avoid close relationships due to fear of mistreatment and rejection.

In other words, these attachment mechanisms that reflect mental representations of the self, others, and relationships can influence later lifespan relationships [297].

Simply put, people who hold a negative mental model about others may hold a dismissive or fearful attachment style; thus, they avoid others [297]. In contrast, people who view themselves negatively may be more anxious and hold a preoccupied or fearful attachment style [297].

It was further found that increased attachment insecurity, meaning higher anxiety and avoidance, was related to a more hostile and submissive interpersonal style [297]. In addition, people with a less secure attachment style reported more negative relationships during adulthood, marked by less support and more conflict [297].

Conversely, people who hold positive self-models, such as having a secure or dismissing attachment, may be more autonomous and resourceful [297]. In contrast, people with a positive 'other-model', such as secure and preoccupied attachment, may be more empathic and communal [297].

As such, a secure attachment that reflects both a positive self-model and other-model may bring the best of both worlds.

Affirming this, greater attachment security was associated with a more affiliative, extroverted, and less neurotic interpersonal style [297]. Furthermore, greater attachment security was associated with higher perceived social support during adulthood [297]. This hints at better social functioning.

In line with theory, attachment security was found to be related to adult self-representations and recollections of interactions with parents and between parents [297].

To elaborate, an insecure attachment was associated with hostile self-representations and recollections of hostile interactions with parents and between parents [297]. Furthermore, people with insecure attachments recalled less affiliative interactions with parents [297].

Investigating further, the avoidance and anxiety that makes up an insecure attachment were negatively associated with the active and reactive love given by parents to their children and between parents [297]. This provides evidence that secure attachment is built by the warmth and care that parents provide to their children and to one another.

A secure attachment could provide additional benefits to child development. According to a review, sensitive and responsive caregiving, which is associated with secure attachment, could play a vital role in buffering the cortisol levels of infants and young children [298].

In one of the studies reviewed, preschool children with the highest cortisol levels were described to have the poorest effortful control and self-regulation [298]. It is possible that impairments caused by high cortisol levels can have adverse effects on the necessary brain development for competent cognitive and emotional functioning [298].

The developmental differences between those with secure attachment and those with insecure attachment were observed in one of the reviewed studies. 18 month-old infants who were securely attached to a physically present parent and exposed to unfamiliar events did not exhibit elevated cortisol, whereas those with insecure attachment did [298]. The lack of buffering of stress in insecure relationships may be attributed to intrusive parental behavior [298].

In a different experiment involving unfamiliar events, infants with fearful attachment, also known as disoriented attachment, which is typically observed in abused or neglected children, exhibited higher cortisol levels [298].

Thus far, we have seen that children with secure and insecure attachments exhibited different behaviors during unfamiliar situations when a parent was present. Let us now examine what happened when the parents were absent.

In general, infants were able to use a substitute caregiver who was warm and sensitive to buffer cortisol responses during temporary separations from parents [298]. However, they showed a significant cortisol increase when the substitute caregiver was cold and distant [298].

Furthermore, children who were more negative tended to be the ones who had elevated cortisol from having a cold and distant substitute caregiver [298]. Children were also more likely to have elevated cortisol if they received poorer quality care [298].

In another study, instead of using cortisol levels as an indicator of stress response, the study used what is known as high-frequency heart rate variability (HRV) [299]. In past studies, modest reductions in HRV in response to stress or emotional stimuli were associated with adaptive functioning, including social competence and resilience [299]. Conversely, excessive reactivity or a lack of HRV regulation was associated with emotional dysregulation [299].

Children aged 9 to 11 participated in the study, and it was found that children with a more secure attachment experienced more positive affect when preparing for a socially stressful task of giving a speech, and they displayed greater recovery of positive affect after the task [299]. However, secure attachments did not predict emotional regulation or changes to negative emotions [299].

Conversely, children with avoidant attachment, also known as dismissive attachment, experienced less negative reactivity after the stressful event [299]. This was in line with theory that states that avoidant children may display patterns of emotional suppression due to rejection avoidance [299]. However, avoidant attachment did not predict emotional regulation or positive emotions [299].

In contrast, 'ambivalent' children, meaning those with preoccupied attachment, displayed less emotional regulation during the speech and more negative emotions after, but also more decline in negative emotions later on [299]. However, there was also less of a rise in emotional regulation [299]. In other words, the decline in negative emotions may be due to an unknown factor. While these findings were not aligned with the study's hypothesis, theory suggests that ambivalent children experience heightened emotions due to their patterns of seeking caregiver attention [299].

As can be seen, attachment patterns could affect emotional reactivity, recovery, and regulation during later childhood. While secure attachment did not predict emotional regulation, children with secure attachment displayed a baseline HRV that was indicative of better adaptive functioning and resilience under stress [299]. These findings suggest that secure attachment could have benefits beyond emotional regulation.

In a longitudinal study, toddlers who had secure attachment were rated by teachers to be more socially competent during grade 1 [300]. This social competence, in turn, predicted more adolescence friendships that were close and authentic, which in turn, predicted more positive experiences within their adult intimate relationships [300]. Both partners in these relationships reported positive experiences, which were accompanied by fewer reciprocal negative emotions during their collaborations and conflict resolutions [300].

The link between secure attachment and positive adult relationships was found to be mediated by social competence during grade 1 and high-quality friendships during adolescence [300]. These findings suggest that early experiences shape later relationships and that positive experiences, learning, and attachment patterns accumulate over time.

During adulthood, those who become parents have the potential to influence their children's attachment patterns. Supporting this notion, a meta-analysis found a moderately strong association between the parents' attachment patterns and their children's [301]. For instance, the parents' dismissive attachment was moderately associated with the children's avoidance patterns [301]. Overall, the correspondence between a parent's attachment and an infant's was a substantial 75% when splitting based on a secure and insecure classification [301]. This suggests that broader classifications based on secure and insecure attachment classifications may be more effective in predicting attachment patterns compared to predictions of specific attachment patterns.

To elaborate, it was found that the secure attachment of parents, meaning the parents had a coherent and supportive childhood, was incompatible with the insecure attachment of their infant [301]. Furthermore, a parent's secure attachment can be influenced by sensitive parenting, which can in turn, influence the attachment style of their own children [301].

In contrast, a meta-analysis found that maltreated children were more likely than non-maltreated children to have an insecure attachment [302].

Infants with maltreating parents may develop fearful attachment because the parent, who may be their only source of comfort, frightens the infant through unpredictable and abusive behaviors [303]. In addition, infants displayed 'disorganized' and contradictory behavior, which included freezing and excessive distress during separation with parents, but also indifference upon their return [303]. Thus, these infants were described as having a 'disorganized' attachment due to their lack of a coherent attachment strategy.

The same study also found that children with maltreating parents had a two to three-fold risk of developing disorganized attachment [303]. The same risk was observed for children with parents who abused alcohol or drugs [303].

Similarly, there was a positive association between frightening parental behavior and disorganized attachment, although this was only examined within two studies [303]. Additionally, insensitive parenting was found to have a small association with child disorganization [303]. These findings suggest that harsh and authoritarian parenting may lead to disorganized attachment. Furthermore, disorganized attachment was found to predict externalizing behavior later in school [303].

Poor parental mental health may pose challenges in providing the necessary sensitive care to children. A reviewed study found that maternal depression played a mediating role in the association between maternal and child attachment insecurity [304].

However, a second study found that maternal depression had a direct relationship with infant attachment security [304]. Specifically, lower levels of depression were associated with increased infant attachment security [304].

In a third study, it was found that the association between maternal depression and child attachment was *moderated* by the parent's secure or insecure attachment state of mind [304]. (Moderated means strengthened or weakened based on the secure or insecure state of mind.) All of these findings suggest that parental mental health is likely a crucial factor in attachment transmission.

Thus far, we have seen that attachment patterns can be transmitted across generations. However, the question remains: can a secure attachment style become insecure? And most importantly, can an insecure attachment style become secure?

One study shed light on this matter. Among a sample of children who were at-risk for poor developmental outcomes, attachment during infancy was predominantly secure at a rate of 59.6% [305]. To clarify, the at-risk children here included those whose mothers were young and single, had unplanned pregnancies, did not complete high school, and lived in poverty [305]. However, by adulthood, a predominant 59.6% of the sample exhibited insecure-dismissive attachment [305]. So, what could have happened?

The study found that infants who had a secure attachment but transitioned into insecure adult attachment had mothers who were more often depressed [305]. On the other hand, participants who had an insecure attachment as an infant and adult, were more likely to have experienced child maltreatment [305].

The traffic, however, was not one-way, as some participants with insecure infant attachment transitioned into secure adult attachment [305]. Specifically, those who transitioned from an insecure infant attachment had a higher level of family functioning during adolescence [305]. These findings suggest that attachment patterns can be influenced by difficult life experiences, but also transformed by positive environments.

Ultimately, an individual's attachment style influences the individual's relationship behavior. We also know that a secure attachment style tends to be conducive to high-quality relationships. This relationship quality may then predict life satisfaction [306]. However, what are the actual behaviors that are implicated in high quality and low-quality relationships?

One study found that criticism and intrusions were negatively associated with relationship quality [306]. Specifically, criticism and intrusions referred to experiences where individuals felt criticized or intruded upon when asked about their home, health, finances, social activities, and future plans [306]. However, this finding should be interpreted with caution because self-reported feelings may overlap with problematic personalities. For example, a hypersensitive narcissist may interpret a child's actions as criticism. Therefore, although this study focused on the perspective of the person experiencing criticism and intrusiveness, it does not preclude the possibility that an individual's own behavior may also play a role in the quality of the relationship.

This possibility was illustrated in another study which found that older adults who experienced negative interactions in one social relationship tended to encounter negative interactions within other relationships [307]. Specifically, negative interactions with children, relatives, and friends were moderately inter-correlated [307]. Similarly, married adults who had negative interactions with their spouses tended to have interpersonal problems with their children, relatives, and friends [307]. Furthermore, negative interactions tended to persist over the years, highlighting ongoing problems within the relationships [307]. Older adults with higher levels of depressive symptoms also encountered more negative interactions [307].

To clarify, negative interactions included social encounters that were criticizing, disapproving, competing, intruding, and lacking in reciprocity [307].

As can be seen, individuals can contribute to creating a network of negative relations. One study asserted that if an individual's social exchanges are often negative, they can be damaging to emotional well-being instead [308].

In this study, positive and negative exchanges were measured by emotional support, instrumental support, and informational support [308].

Emotional support was considered positive when others expressed warmth, sympathy, and care [308]. Instrumental support was considered positive when people helped one another, including providing material aid [308]. On the other hand, informational support was considered positive when one received helpful advice and information [308].

Mirroring the three domains of positive social exchanges, negative social exchanges included the emotional domain of receiving criticism and a lack of sympathy or care from others [308]. Likewise, the instrumental domain was considered negative when others demanded excessive help or failed to provide aid [308]. For instance, people may only contact us when they need our help. Lastly, negative behavior in the informational domain included receiving intrusive and bad advice [308].

Unsurprisingly, positive social exchanges predicted positive emotional states, and negative social exchanges predicted negative ones [308]. The bad news is that a follow-up three months later revealed that negative exchanges predicted less positive emotional states and more negative emotional states [308]. On the other hand, positive exchanges did not predict emotional states during the follow-up [308]. This means that negative exchanges may have stronger and more lasting consequences than positive ones [308]. However, this does not mean that positive social exchanges do not have impact.

In fact, a study found that high-quality family relationships protected adolescents from the detrimental effects of stressful events [309]. Adolescents with high-quality relationships with their parents did not display increased externalizing problems, whereas those with average or poor relationships did [309].

Within the study, high-quality family relationships were characterized by emotional bonding, supportiveness, non-coercive disciplining, safety in expressing opinions, high-quality communications, and child-monitoring [309].

Besides family support, peer support can also have an impact on an individual's adjustment. A study examining adolescent relationship narratives found that both family and peer relationships could function as sources of distress and support [310].

In addition to conflict with parents, one's concerns about peer acceptance, judgments, and approval were common sources of stress [310]. Furthermore, fears regarding others' approval can prevent help-seeking [310]. However, at the same time, adolescents also valued emotional support the most [310]. The emotional support they valued was measured by empathic responses, feeling that others were concerned, and that they were not invisible [310].

However, social support can backfire, for instance, when others trivialize what is happening to support seekers [310].

In one investigation on depression support, stigmatizing responses were the most common disadvantage cited for support-seeking [311]. Participants reported being told by their family and friends to 'get over it' [311]. Moreover, participants were denied the validity of their experiences and were instead ridiculed, blamed, and criticized [311].

Participants were also deemed as selfish, weak, attention-seeking, and self-pitying [311].

The second most common disadvantage cited was inappropriate support [311]. Specifically, there was a lack of interest, emotional understanding, and confidentiality [311].

Other disadvantages included people treating the support-seekers differently, providing heaps of useless advice, and people lacking knowledge and expertise, including the lack of comprehension towards depression [311]. Nearly 40% of the participants reported experiencing at least one disadvantage when seeking social support [311]. However, despite the possible disadvantages of social support, not having any could have its own repercussions.

One review noted that perceived social isolation, also known as loneliness, was implicated in poorer cognitive performance, increased depressive cognition, increased attention to negative social stimuli, and increased memory of negative social events [312]. Loneliness was also highlighted as a risk factor for faster cognitive decline as individuals aged, as well as clinical Alzheimer's, a form of dementia [312]. All of these can be the possible repercussions of not having supportive relationships.

It is important to note that loneliness was found to be more closely related to the quality of social interactions rather than the quantity [312]. As such, positive social exchanges are likely crucial not only for a person's adjustment but also for their development. If it could not get any more obvious, people who fail to care for another person's social experience damage the mental health of said persons. However, the good news is that we now know the positive relationship behaviors to perform and the negative ones to avoid.

PART III

Demystifying the Human Condition

<u>What must Human Beings know about being human?</u>

<u>#18</u>

What Increases the Risks of Poor Mental Health?

A 2017 study on the global burden of disease estimated that more than 200 million people worldwide were experiencing a depressive disorder [313].

This accounts for more than 2% of the entire world's population! And we are only talking about one type of psychological disorder among many!

In a sample of English-speaking residents in the United States, it was estimated that the lifetime prevalence of psychological disorders was 46.4% for one disorder, 27.7% for two or more disorders, and 17.3% for three or more [314].

Psychological disorders often coexisted with one another [315]. For example, the co-occurrence of depressive and anxiety disorders increased the risk of suicide ideation, more so than when depression occurred alone [315].

Furthermore, individuals with multiple anxiety disorders were more likely to experience inadequate social support [315]. This suggests that social support may be affected when an individual experiences psychological disorders.

Contrary to common belief, psychological disorders can emerge early in life. According to a World Health Order survey with approximately 85,000 participants, the median age for the onset of impulse control disorders was 7 to 15 years old, depending on the country. For mood disorders, the median age was 29 to 43 years old, for substance use disorders, it was 18 to 29 years, and for generalized anxiety disorder and post-traumatic stress disorder, it was 24 to 50 years old [316]. It is worth noting that mood disorders included major depressive disorder, while impulse control disorders encompassed intermittent explosive disorder, oppositional defiant disorder, and conduct disorder [316].

Given the high prevalence and early onset of mental health issues, it is apparent that underlying societal problems and negative social structures must be addressed. Improving the quality of lifespan institutions could help prevent both initial onset and subsequent disorders. However, before we can make progress in this direction, it is crucial to understand how environmental factors contribute to the increased risk of poor mental health.

In one study, lifetime exposure to adversity, measured by stressful life events, traumas, and witnessed violence, was associated with an increased risk of subsequent development of depressive and anxiety disorder [317]. This association remained significant even after controlling for childhood conduct disorder, ADHD, PTSD, and prior substance dependence [317]. Moreover, both distal and recent events independently contributed to the risk of depression and anxiety [317], highlighting that effects of stressful life events can accumulate over time.

In the same study, stressful life events that were associated with depressive and anxiety disorders included abandonment by parents, separation from parents, parental divorce, parental unemployment, abuse from caregivers, coercion to perform sexual acts, witnessing violence and abuse, and physical abuse from an intimate partner or any person [317]. Many of these risk factors suggest adversities within the family.

Moreover, peer rejection has been linked to poorer mental health. For instance, perceived peer rejection has been found to be associated with depressive symptoms [318].

On the other hand, positive family environments and social support can protect against the development of mental disorders in children who face stressful situations. For example, a review of 32 studies found that half of those studies supported the idea that social support could have buffering effects [318]. Additionally, 61% of 28 studies found evidence that family environments could be protective against mental disorders [318]. These studies examined family characteristics such as cohesion, parenting style, and attachment patterns [318].

Moreover, 15 out of 16 studies supported the hypothesis that family processes contribute to the link between poverty and psychological symptoms [318]. These family processes included harsh and inconsistent disciplining, lack of warmth, and poor parent-child relationships [318]. Other exacerbating factors included inadequate supervision, lack of school involvement, and lack of support [318]. We have already explored all of these factors.

One study also found that suicide victims were more likely to have been exposed to higher family stressors [319]. Suicide victims experienced higher rates of family histories where first-degree relatives had major depression, alcohol abuse, drug abuse, or any affective disorder [319]. Suicide victims were also more likely to have experienced physical abuse, conflict with parents, or had an unstable place of residence [319].

Furthermore, within family constellations where adolescents did not live with both biological parents, parents showed higher rates of mental disorders and substance abuse [319]. Parental mental disorders also mediated the link between family constellation and suicide risk [319]. However, an unstable family could also be part of a larger pattern that some children experience.

Multiple lifetime exit events, such as the death of family members and close friends, parental divorce, and removal from parents, have been linked to the onset of anxiety and depression in school-age children and adolescents [320].

212

In addition, family and peer factors were found to exert independent effects on anxiety and depression [321]. To elaborate, family factors included the mothers' distress and lack of confidants [321]. On the other hand, peer factors included adolescents lacking high-quality friendships and social achievements, defined as achievements that result in social esteem [321].

According to a study, interpersonal stressors were a common precipitant of adolescent suicide [322]. These stressors can include conflicts and separations with significant others, such as boyfriends or girlfriends [322]. In fact, the study found that approximately 62% of adolescent suicide precipitants were related to separation, conflict, and other interpersonal problems [322].

Other common precipitants of adolescent suicide included family discord, school or work problems, as well as disciplinary or legal difficulties [322]. These findings are consistent with a previous study that found adolescent suicide to be frequently precipitated by a rejection, humiliation, or disciplinary crisis [322].

A review noted that some studies found depression to be linked to a higher density of negative life events that were *dependent* on the depression, particularly so in the interpersonal domain [323]. However, some studies also found an increased rate of stressful events that was independent of depression [323]. In other words, there is a possibility of a compounding effect where negative life events and depression can feed into each other, making the situation even more challenging to manage.

However, some studies did not find depressive symptoms to be a predictor of subsequent stressful events [323]. Therefore, given the mixed findings, the notion that depression creates stressful life events remains a possibility.

A review that investigated into the relationship between stressful events, depression, and personal cognitions, noted that certain vulnerable cognitions, such as hopelessness, self-criticism, and negative social self-esteem, predicted higher levels of interpersonal stress [323]. Similarly, an avoidant coping style and excessive reassurance-seeking were also found to predict higher levels of interpersonal stress [323]. Interpersonal stress was, in turn, found to be a predictor of depressive symptoms, and one study also found that interpersonal stress served as a mediator between initial and subsequent depressive symptoms [323].

One study also asserted that vulnerable cognitions, such as negative perceptions of the self, the world, and the future, may play an important role in the onset and continuity of depression [324]. Specifically, low self-esteem cognitions such as 'I am no good,' and rigid perfectionistic beliefs such as 'I cannot be happy unless people admire me,' were linked to depression symptoms [324]. This was in addition to a negative attributional style that regarded each event to be caused by the self, meaning *internal*, have long-lasting consequences, meaning *stable*, and has negative implications to other parts of life, meaning *global* [324].

An additive model as well as a 'weakest link' model for the above cognitions predicted and accounted for large amounts of variance for depression [324]. The 'weakest link' means that a person's most maladaptive score on a specific cognition was the best predictor for depression risk [324]. These models did not interact with life stress levels [324].

Additionally, a study found a link between unfavorable social comparisons and depression [325]. This link was exacerbated by the perceived importance of the compared dimension in attracting the attention and interest of others [325]. The dimensions that were deemed important included intelligence, social skills, artistic ability, physical attraction, and emotional stability [325]. These dimensions make up three types of self-worth: social, personality, and ability self-worth

214

[325]. These social and self-evaluative aspects of self-worth suggest the existence of social and self-evaluative aspects of depression.

Affirming this, a study found evidence that depression can be differentiated into 'Anaclitic' and 'Introjective' depression [326]. Anaclitic depression is characterized by interpersonal concerns, such as neediness, loneliness, fears of abandonment, and hypersensitivity to rejection [326]. In contrast, introjective depression is characterized by achievement concerns, such as self-criticism and poor self-evaluation [326].

In addition, anaclitic depression was predicted by preoccupied attachment, characterized by feelings of dependence, seeking others' acceptance to bolster self-worth, and a negative self-view but positive view of others [326]. This link was partially mediated by social perfectionism, which involves the need for social approval, a hypersensitivity to criticism, and the avoidance of negative evaluation from others [326].

In contrast, people with introjective depression may compulsively strive for achievement, including unrealistic goals that perpetuate failure experiences [326].

Introjective depression was predicted by the fearful-avoidance attachment, which involves a negative view of the self and others, a fear of intimacy, reluctance to depend on others, difficulty trusting others, and low self-worth [326]. This link was partially mediated by social perfectionism and self-oriented perfectionism which refer to self-imposed unrealistic standards [326].

These findings suggest that maladaptive perfectionism may accompany insecure attachment, and both may be linked to depression. In contrast, individuals who reported low levels of anaclitic and introjective depression tended to have greater attachment security [326].

With all that is said, specific circumstances may also pose increased risks for depression.

One study with pregnant participants found that high levels of depressive symptoms were associated with negative life events, inadequate social support, and chronic stressors such as poor housing conditions and financial difficulties in meeting basic needs [327].

Another review noted mixed evidence regarding a link between single motherhood and depression [328]. Nevertheless, it is conceivable that single parents may experience increased financial strains and poorer social support, suggesting a potential indirect link.

The review also noted that several studies found low-quality marital relationships to be a predictor of postnatal depression [328]. The same review conducted its own analysis and affirmed that an unsupportive intimate partner relationship is a risk factor for postnatal depression [328].

One study delved deeper and found that women, who were victims of intimate partner violence during pregnancy, were more likely to exhibit depression symptoms during their child's early childhood [329]. In turn, maternal depression predicted the children's depressive symptoms during adolescence [329]. This association was found to have a separate indirect path through physical punishment of children at age 5 and victimization by peer bullying at age 9 [329]. However, these correlations were small. Nonetheless, these findings highlight that intimate partner violence may have long-term effects.

A study conducted in Ethiopia revealed that risk factors for intimate partner violence included women's lack of decision-making autonomy, partners' alcohol consumption, and community norms that tolerate intimate partner violence [330].

In another study, dysfunctional communication patterns were found to be associated with intimate partner violence [331]. In particular, contempt was associated with one's violence perpetration as well as the partner's [331]. This type of contempt included sarcasm, eye-rolling, insults, mocking, name-calling, and facial expressions of disgust, all of which demonstrate a lack of respect for the partner [331].

Furthermore, anger, which included commands to stop a partner from violating their autonomy, was found to be associated with one's violence perpetration [331]. The same study found a high correspondence between the couples' anger, contempt, and violence [331].

On top of dysfunctional communication patterns, conflicts within intimate partner relationships may reflect a bias that was carried over from childhood.

In one study on sibling conflicts, children perceived their opponents' transgressions as more severe than their own and reported a greater number of opponent-perpetrated conflict actions [332]. Additionally, they justified and denied their own transgressions more frequently [332], viewing themselves as less blameworthy and more as the aggrieved victim.

It has been suggested that children may behave in such manners to maintain a positive self-view [332]. Moreover, in a previous study, adolescents reported that their opponents started 90% of their conflicts [332], indicating that a similar bias has persisted. If such bias could be seen during adolescence, could this also be the case during adulthood?

In one study, adult participants who took on the role of a transgressor downplayed the consequences, narrating a negative incident as an isolated event with no lasting implications [333]. On the other hand, those who took on the role of 'victims' narrated incidents in the context of long-term harm and grievances, and were more likely to view the 'perpetrators' as unjustified and immoral [333].

In the same study, perpetrators tended to view their offending or provoking behavior as meaningful and comprehensible [333]. In contrast, victims saw the perpetrator's behavior as gratuitous or incomprehensible [333]. Perpetrators often believed that their victims were inappropriately or excessively angry [333]. Additionally, perpetrators frequently portrayed the victim as having done something to provoke the incident [333]. This evidence supported the hypothesis that perpetrators perceive only a single incident and regard the victim's angry response as an unjustified overreaction [333].

As a result, perpetrators may see themselves as victims and may be unaware of the consequences of their actions. Evidence suggests the existence of an adult bias similar to that of a child, and such mentalities may form the basis of intimate partner violence, which we know increases the risk of parental depression. Parental depression, in turn, may lead to further repercussions.

One study found that maternal and paternal depression during the prenatal and postnatal periods predicted emotional and conduct problems in young children [334]. The link between parental depression and child problems was partially mediated by marital conflict during these periods [334]. However, both parental depression and marital conflict remained strong independent predictors of child problems [334].

In another study, maternal depressive symptoms were positively associated with child externalizing behavior but not internalizing behavior [335]. However, higher levels of positive child involvement by the father were associated with a decrease in both internalizing and externalizing problems [335]. This highlights the protective effect of positive paternal involvement.

Positive involvement was measured by how often a father discussed important decisions with a child, listened to a child's side of the argument, and how close a child felt to the father [335]. In this way, a spouse can compensate if depression impairs a partner's parenting.

However, a stressful maternal environment can also pose other risks to child development.

For example, maternal stress has been found to be associated with an increased risk of low birthweight delivery [336]. Maternal stress can include financial, emotional, traumatic, or spouse-related events [336].

Furthermore, maternal stress interacted with a disadvantaged neighborhood, characterized by high poverty and low education, to affect low birthweight outcomes [336]. Specifically, those in the most disadvantaged neighborhoods had a higher risk of low birthweight delivery, but those who experienced stress in favorable neighborhoods did not [336].

One review further suggested that racism can be a distinct source of maternal prenatal stress [337]. Racism includes not only individual experiences but structural racism, which refers to the differential access to goods, services, and opportunities [337].

Two studies provided preliminary evidence that maternal prenatal exposure to racism is a risk factor for low birthweight [337].

Preterm delivery and low birthweight were the leading causes of infant mortality [337]. Moreover, children born preterm or with low birthweight were more likely to exhibit cognitive deficits [337], performing poorer on measures of intelligence and academic achievement and were less likely to graduate from high school [337].

In one study of extremely low birthweight infants, 46.8% were reported to have behavioral problems at 30 to 36 months old [338]. Additionally,

20.4% displayed deficits in socio-emotional competence [338], which were associated with low scores in psychomotor and mental development [338]. In this study, socio-emotional competence encompassed empathy, prosocial peer relations, and mastery motivation [338].

All of these factors may contribute to a vicious cycle in which disadvantageous conditions persist across generations. One possible indicator is that mothers who were low birthweight infants had a higher risk of delivering children who were also low birthweight [337]. However, more investigation is needed to clarify the reasons for this association.

Given that stress is linked to low birthweight delivery, mental conditions could potentially affect birth outcomes. In one meta-analysis, five out of the eleven studies found maternal prenatal depression to be significantly associated with low birthweight delivery [339]. However, six studies did not find such an association [339]. Given these mixed findings, depression may instead be an indicator of the stressors that may be the actual causes, or perhaps the depression itself led to the stressful events.

- However, the study also suggested that prenatal depression may promote adverse birth outcomes through the dysregulation of the hypothalamic-pituitary-adrenocortical (HPA) axis, which leads to dysregulated stress hormones such as the cortisol [339]. The resulting biological changes can restrict oxygen and nutrients to the fetus [339].

In addition to depression and stress, mothers may also experience the risk factors of prenatal anxiety. These factors included unwanted pregnancy, as well as low self-esteem, marital satisfaction, and perceived social support [340]. These factors were further found to mediate the link between prenatal anxiety and postnatal depression [340].

220

Prenatal exposure to elevated maternal cortisol, pregnancy-specific anxiety, as well as maternal stress and depression during pregnancy, has been linked to increased child anxiety at ages 6 to 9 [341]. Previous research has suggested that maternal cortisol may pass through the placenta and affect the fetal nervous system, impacting the fetal's emotional and cognitive functioning [341]. Therefore, the link between maternal distress and child anxiety may have biological pathways.

Additionally, the study also proposed that fetal exposure to maternal depression could have epigenetic effects [341]. For instance, child anxiety could be a result of changes in gene expression.

Maternal prenatal anxiety has also been associated with poorer cognitive development in infants [342]. Postnatal depression and parental stimulation partially mediated the link between prenatal anxiety and child cognitive development [342].

As we have seen, depression can lead to developmental risks for one's offspring. But what about the individual who experiences depression?

Preliminary evidence suggests that recurring major depression may cause the atrophy of the hippocampus gray matter volumes that was not a result of overall brain atrophy [343]. While the study could not rule out the possibility that the loss of hippocampus volume preceded the development of depression, the loss was correlated with the lifetime accumulation of depression duration [343]. This hippocampal damage was said to combine with cortisol dysregulation, possibly leading to subsequent vulnerability towards depression [343]. The result is a downward spiral of depression and hippocampal damage.

Depression may be accompanied by maladaptive coping strategies. In a study involving female adolescents and adults, adolescents at high risk of depression reported higher levels of maladaptive coping [344]. Similarly, depressed adults reported higher levels of rumination and lower levels of adaptive coping [344].

Measurements of adolescent maladaptive coping included involuntary rumination, intrusive thoughts, emotional arousal, and involuntary disengagement through numbing and escape [344].

In contrast, adaptive coping included 'primary control' strategies such as problem-solving, emotional regulation, and emotional expression [344]. For instance, individuals may attempt to change the problem or fix the situation in various ways [344].

Adaptive coping also includes 'secondary control' strategies such as cognitive restructuring, positive thinking, and acceptance [344]. For example, individuals may adapt to the problem or tell themselves that things will be alright [344].

As levels of primary and secondary control decreased, higher levels of maladaptive coping were associated with higher levels of depressive symptoms [344].

Adult adaptive coping was measured in a similar manner. It included problem-solving coping, such as concentrating efforts to do something about the problem, and planning, such as coming up with a strategy [344]. This was in addition to cognitive restructuring coping, which included positive reinterpretation, growth (such as looking for something good in what is happening), and emotional processing (meaning taking time to figure out one's own feelings) [344].

Similar to adolescents, adult maladaptive coping was measured by rumination, with higher levels of rumination being associated with higher levels of depressive symptoms [344]. In contrast, higher levels of problem-solving and cognitive restructuring were associated with lower levels of depressive symptoms [344].

Rumination can be defined as persevering and fixated thinking that does not lead to problem-solving [345]. Brooding rumination, which is the tendency to perseverate on negative actions and situations, was found to be associated with increased suicide risks [345]. However, rumination cannot be simplistically regarded as a maladaptive coping style.

To start with, rumination is a normal response that follows stressful and traumatic experiences [346]. Rumination can be both intrusive and deliberate.

Intrusive rumination involves unintentional, unwanted, and uncontrollable images or thoughts about a stressful event [346]. A recount of intrusive rumination could be, 'thoughts about the event kept me from concentrating' [346]. Intrusive rumination can become chronic and lead to post-traumatic stress [346].

Deliberate rumination, on the other hand, may involve attempts to make sense of events [346]. This type of rumination includes constructive thinking, such as, 'I thought about whether I learned anything from this' [346]. As such, it may be possible for deliberate rumination to lead to post-traumatic growth.

The same study found that immediate intrusive rumination after a negative event was associated with regret, hopelessness, sadness, and 'threat evaluation' [346].

Threat evaluation refers to the discrepancy between an individual's situational meaning and global meaning [346]. Global meaning includes an individual's worldview, such as their belief that the world is benevolent and meaningful and that they, as a person, is worthy [346]. This threat from a situation to an individual's worldview, self-view, and ideal world can be accompanied by fear and hopelessness [346].

However, intrusive rumination may not stop immediately after the event. Intrusive rumination was positively associated with chronic intrusive rumination that persisted beyond a year [346]. Chronic intrusive rumination, in turn, was negatively related to finding meaning [346].

However, one may also find a negative meaning that leads to feelings of disgust or depression [346]. After all, not everyone can answer, 'why did this happen?' or 'Why me?' It may even be unfair to ask victims to find positive meanings to their ordeals.

On the other hand, regret was associated with immediate deliberate rumination, whereas threat evaluation did not directly lead to deliberate rumination [346]. However, immediate intrusive rumination was weakly associated with deliberate rumination later on [346]. This highlights that discomfort can trigger feelings towards a need for change. The study proposed that people who regretted their actions during a stressful event may become motivated to make the best use of that experience and seek to better handle a future event or prevent it entirely [346]. Deliberate rumination was associated with finding meaning [346].

In theory, meaning-making could lead to better adjustment if it reduces the discrepancies between event and global meaning [347]. However, until it does so, meaning-making may be related to distress instead [347]. In one review, a handful of studies found that meaning-making was related to higher distress [347]. However, many studies have also found meaning-making to be related to positive outcomes such as growth, successful coping, identity development, and lower levels of depression [347].

One study, however, reported that those who never searched for meaning were better adjusted than those who searched but did not find meaning [347]. Similarly, a few studies have reported that those who were not searching had better adjustment than those who were searching [347].

As can be seen, different outcomes may depend on the type of rumination and the meaning-making process. This may also be true for the many forms of stressful events. In the study on intrusive and deliberate rumination, 28.5% of the stressful events pertained to relationships, including being bullied at school, falling out with a teacher, and relationship rupture [346]. Another 9.6% of the events pertained to family events, such as abuse, parental divorce, or separation [346].

Rumination can take the form of angry thoughts. In one study, high levels of hostile rumination were found to be associated with violent behaviors [348]. Furthermore, hostile rumination was associated with irritability, which correlated with violent conduct and verbal aggression [348].

Additionally, adolescents who were more irritable and increased in irritability, became more ruminative two years later [348]. Those who increased in hostile rumination also became more irritable over time [348]. Such ruminations could be made up of emotional reactivity and hostile attributions.

With all that is said, it is worth noting that rumination is not the only form of maladaptive coping.

To illustrate, a study found that the more types of problem behaviors adolescents exhibited, the more likely suicidal thoughts turned into action [349]. The problem behaviors included violent behavior, binge drinking, disturbed eating behavior, regular smoking, drug use, and risky sexual behaviors, such as having four or more sex partners [349].

In addition to maladaptive coping, maladaptive schemata may complicate the situation.

In an Iranian study, early maladaptive schemata, measured by Young's Schema Questionnaire, were significantly associated with internet addiction, defined as the excessive use of the internet leading to emotional, mental, social, academic, or professional damage [350].

The identified maladaptive schemata are as follows [350]:

1) Emotional deprivation, meaning one expects that their need for affection would never be met [351].

2) Abandonment, meaning one perceives that significant others are unable to provide emotional support [351].

3) Mistrust or abuse, meaning one expects that others would be abusive, humiliating, or manipulative [351].

4) Social isolation or alienation, meaning one believes that they are isolated because of their socially undesirable features, like being ugly [351].

5) Fault or shame, meaning one believes that they are defective and fundamentally unlovable [351].

6) Failure to achieve, meaning one believes that they are inadequate compared to others and that it is their destiny to fail in achievements like school or career [351].

7) Dependence, meaning one is unable to competently manage their day-to-day responsibilities [351].

8) Vulnerability to harm and illness, meaning one has exaggerated fears that various disasters will strike at any time [351].

9) Enmeshment, meaning one cannot survive without another's constant support [351].

10) Subjugation, meaning one's self-belief that their desire is unimportant compared to that of others [351].

11) Sacrifice, meaning one holds exaggerated responsibility or duty to others [351].

12) Emotional inhibition, meaning one believes that emotional expression would lead to negative consequences [351].

13) Unrelenting standards, meaning one holds themselves to unrealistic and impossibly high standards [351].

14) Entitlement, meaning one believes that they should act without regard for others [351].

15) And lastly, insufficient self-control or discipline, meaning one believes that self-discipline is unimportant and that their emotions and impulses do not require restraint [351].

These maladaptive schemata were also found to be moderately and positively associated with depression and anxiety, and negatively with self-esteem [351]. These schemata may originate from early experiences with caregivers and form a central part of an individual's self-concept [351].

Overall, these findings suggests that maladaptive behavior may exist within a complex interplay of internal and environmental issues.

To add on, one study found that poor social self-esteem and family-home self-esteem were predictors of internet addiction [352]. Similarly, poor self-efficacy was associated with increased internet addiction behaviors [353].

In summary, the social environment can have negative impacts on a person's mental health, and this impact may be potentially transmitted to future generations. Mental health may also be exacerbated by maladaptive coping and schemata, including rumination, which is a normal response to traumatic experiences. Depending on the issue, self-esteem and self-efficacy may also be impacted.

Ultimately, it would be helpful to address each aspect that is implicated in this complex web of issue, as we have been doing throughout this book.

<u>Possible Initiatives</u>

✓ Schools and parental programs can promote awareness and practice of positive social interactions, which contribute to thriving relationships and mental well-being. These interactions include emotionally supportive behaviors that show warmth, empathy, and care.

✓ Logically, programs can also educate participants to identify negative social behavior that are criticizing, competing, intruding, and lacking in reciprocity. Programs may go one step further to develop the participants' adaptive-coping knowledge and competence, which may incidentally replace negative social behavior. It also makes sense to teach participants to spot and intercept unhelpful ruminations.

✓ Additionally, participants may be guided to deeply examine their maladaptive schemata and discover adaptive ones. This could help them to prevent maladaptive behavior.

✓ Medical institutions may form a touchpoint to identify individuals who face risk factors of prenatal and postnatal depression, and refer them to resources, support, and interventions that may enhance their personal wellness and parenting. This can be done with the goal of helping vulnerable parents achieve a sense of control during pregnancy, childbirth, and parenting.

- In a study, higher sense of control was found to predict lower symptoms of depression and anxiety in both fathers and mothers [354].

- Sense of control refers to a general belief that one can master and influence their own life, as opposed to feeling powerless, where a person believes that their life is determined by external forces [354].

- It is important to distinguish sense of control from concepts such as locus of control, self-efficacy, autonomy, and helplessness [354]. During parenthood transition, a change in sense of control, rather than enduring control, was found to be most important with regard to depressive symptoms [354].

✓ Ultimately, the goal of promoting awareness, knowledge, and adaptive behavior is to transform families, schools, and workplaces into supportive institutions rather than environments of hostilities, failed relationships, and mental health deterioration.

<u>What must Human Beings know about being human?</u>

<u>#19</u>

Self-Esteem or Narcissism? Where is the line drawn?

From a young age, children receive cues from their parents regarding their lovability and capability. This affects their global self-esteem [355].

At the same time, young children detect that their behaviors evoke a reaction from others [355]. However, their perspective-taking skills are limited [355]. Despite this, children sought positive responses for their successes and attempted to avoid negative ones for their failures [355].

It was said that child abuse leads to hypervigilance toward others' reactions [355]. This interferes with a victim's ability to attend to their own needs, thoughts, and desires [355]. Maltreated children also reported less internal-state language, such as language that pertains to their negative feelings [355]. These children also narrated a more negative and less coherent self-representation [355].

Additionally, without parents who help them co-construct a positive and coherent self-narrative, these children may lack both a descriptive vocabulary to define themselves and a meaningful personal narrative [355]. In this manner, a child may not even have a sense of self [355].

In addition, intrusive parents may demand their child to comply with their expectations [355]. This results in a child presenting a false outer self that does not reflect their true inner experience [355]. Similarly, abusive behavior and coercion can lead the true self to become hidden [355].

-   False-self behavior can emerge when parents provide approval contingent on the child meeting their unrealistic standards [355].

The child engages in false-self behavior to gain the desired approval [355]. This results in the development of contingent self-esteem, where one's feeling of worth depends heavily on external approval and validation [355]. This type of self-esteem is unstable, fragile, and plummets in the face of setbacks [355]. This highlights that in addition to having self-worth, how a person derives self-worth is important.

As children grow, they begin to describe themselves in terms of their adequacy in specific domains such as social skills and cognitive abilities [355]. They also become more aware of how others perceive them [355].

By late childhood, children's self-descriptions become increasingly interpersonal, reflecting the growing importance placed on relationships [355]. Children also begin to engage in comparative self-evaluation [355]. Additionally, they are now able to verbally evaluate their overall self-worth based on their success and failure in domains they view as important [355]. This is accompanied by their growth in cognitive abilities that allow self-enhancements, such as putting others down to feel superior [355].

During adolescence, domains of self-evaluation encompassed cognitive competence, athleticism, physical appearance, job competence, romantic appeal, and the social success in getting others to accept and like them [356]. It was noted that global self-esteem is not just the sum of these domain-specific self-concepts, as each domain may have a different relationship with global self-worth [356].

A study showed that while global self-esteem was strongly associated with psychological well-being, specific self-esteem was a better predictor of school performance [357]. This suggests that specific self-esteem may play a more significant role in behavior [357].

- To elaborate, global self-esteem was negatively associated with depression, anxiety, irritability, and resentment, and positively associated with life satisfaction and happiness [357]. In contrast, academic self-esteem was only weakly and negatively associated with depression and resentment, and weakly and positively associated with life satisfaction and happiness [357].

- In addition, global self-esteem and academic self-esteem were found to have a reciprocal but small effect [357]. Among the group who highly valued academic performance, academic self-esteem had a greater effect on global self-esteem [357]. This was not the case for those who valued academic performance less [357]. These findings provided evidence that the degree to which academic self-esteem affected global self-esteem was influenced by how much academic performance was personally valued [357]. Furthermore, evidence suggested that changes in academic self-esteem can bring about improvement in school performance [357].

- In one study, a robust relationship was found between low global self-esteem and delinquency, including both aggression and non-aggression behaviors, such as drug and alcohol use [358]. The relationship between self-esteem and delinquency was not accounted for by factors such as academic achievement or whether supportive parenting was received [358].

- The same study found that self-esteem was negatively associated with externalizing behaviors [358]. Lower self-esteem at age 11 predicted increased externalizing problems at age 13 [358]. The relationship between self-esteem and externalizing problems was not explained by the individual's relationship with their parents and peers [358].

- At the same time, self-esteem was moderately and positively related to narcissism [358]. Narcissism, in turn, was positively related to aggression [358]. Further investigation revealed that both low self-esteem and narcissism contributed independently to aggression [358]. The impact of self-esteem, however, may not end there.

234

- One study found that self-worth was positively related to the quality of friendship [359]. Specifically, self-worth was positively associated with having companionship and help from a best friend [359]. Self-worth was also linked to 'security,' meaning friends are able to make up easily, and 'closeness,' meaning friends make each other feel special [359]. On the other hand, self-worth was negatively related to conflicts with one's best friend [359].

- Furthermore, reciprocated friendship was positively associated with self-worth, as well as the 'companionship' and 'help' components of friendship quality [359]. Unsurprisingly, reciprocated friendship was also negatively associated with relationship conflict [359].

- However, the study found that the number of reciprocated friendships did not predict self-worth when friendship quality was taken into consideration [359]. This suggests that the quality of relationships may be more significant in this context.

- A meta-analysis affirmed the link between relationships and self-worth, finding that relationships and self-esteem reciprocally predicted one another over time [360]. The meta-analysis also found that while high-quality relationships had a positive effect on self-esteem, low-quality relationships could have a negative effect instead [360]. These changes in self-esteem may then go on to influence social relationships [360]. Thus, the cycle continues.

With all that said, higher self-esteem does not automatically equate to healthy self-esteem. What makes up that esteem is also crucial.

One study asserted that pursuing contingent self-worth, such as through external validation or the satisfaction of certain standards, can be very costly [361]. The study found that self-esteem levels had little effect on how much time students spent on activities [361]. However, contingencies of self-worth did [361].

For example, students who based self-esteem on their appearance were more likely to join fraternities [361]. Similarly, basing self-esteem on academics predicted the hours spent studying each week [361]. However, basing self-esteem on academics and appearance also predicted academic problems, which included developmental challenges and academic alienation [361].

In addition, basing self-esteem on appearance and outdoing others predicted aggression-related problems and social problems, including friendship problems, social mistreatment, and hostility [361]. Furthermore, basing self-esteem on appearance predicted whether students had an experience with sexual victimization [361]. Meanwhile, students who based their self-esteem on appearance or family love and support showed higher levels of alcohol and drug use [361].

In contrast, internal contingencies of worth, such as virtue, were found to be associated with lower levels of these problems, with the exception of academic problems [361].

The study went on to control for personality characteristics such as narcissism and neuroticism, and the organizations that participants joined.

After accounting for these factors, the study found that basing self-esteem on appearance was no longer significantly related to social problems, academic problems, aggression, sexual victimization, and drug use [361]. Similarly, the relationship between drug and alcohol use and basing self-esteem on family support also lost significance [361]. These results suggest that personality development and the type of organization one joins may play a role in explaining the links between external contingencies of self-worth and negative outcomes.

The study also found that contingencies of self-worth led to self-esteem that was reactive towards successes and failures [361]. This instability of self-esteem, in turn, increased the level of depressive symptoms [361].

A separate study investigated from a different angle and found that personal self-esteem, relational self-esteem, and collective self-esteem were uncorrelated [362]. This means that individuals can derive their sense of self-worth not only from personal attributes but also from their relationships with significant others and membership in larger groups or identities [362].

Among the sample of college students from Macau, personal self-esteem was found to predict life satisfaction and meaning [362]. However, after controlling for relational self-esteem, personal self-esteem was no longer a significant predictor for life satisfaction [362]. On the other hand, relational self-esteem was found to be a predictor of positive emotions and life meaning [362].

Even after considering individualistic and collectivistic orientations, both personal and relational self-esteem remained significant predictors of life satisfaction [362].

In contrast, the study found that collective self-esteem was not a significant predictor for life satisfaction [362]. Additionally, the relationship between collective self-esteem and life meaning was only marginally significant [362]. However, these findings do not rule out the possibility that self-esteem may fluctuate based on relationship changes and threats to collective identity.

In addition to how self-esteem is derived, self-esteem level is also important. One study found that low adolescent self-esteem predicted negative adulthood consequences [363].

- Specifically, adolescents with low self-esteem experienced increased risks of depression, anxiety, tobacco dependence, poorer physical health, and criminal convictions [363]. These outcomes were not explained by gender, depression, or family socio-economic status [363].

- Furthermore, adolescents with low self-esteem experienced poorer economic prospects, such as being more likely to leave school early and less likely to attend university [363]. These outcomes were not explained by gender, family socio-economic status, depression, and IQ [363]. While adolescents with low self-esteem also experienced increased long-term unemployment, this effect was no longer significant after accounting for the above [363].

- In addition, low self-esteem predicted cumulative problems [363]. However, this link was partially mediated by the control factors [363]. Only 17% of low self-esteem adolescents did not experience these problems during adulthood [363].

- To elaborate, 56% of low self-esteem adolescents had multiple problems during adulthood, whereas only 17% of high self-esteem adolescents had multiple problems [363]. The risk for negative outcomes decreased with increased self-esteem [363]. So what, then, is conducive to higher self-esteem?

One study found that the parent-adolescent attachment was positively associated with adolescent self-esteem [364]. Parent-adolescent attachment included factors such as communication quality, trust in parental availability and sensitivity, and inversely, the extent of anger and alienation within the relationship [364]. An example of communication quality could be described as, 'if my parents know that something is bothering me, they ask me. [364]'

- The study also found that the quality of parent-adolescent attachment was negatively associated with adolescent aggression and delinquency [364]. However, self-esteem did not mediate this relationship [364].

- Instead, it was cognitive distortions that mediated the link between parent-adolescent attachment and aggression [364]. Specifically, the quality of parent-adolescent attachment was negatively associated with cognitive distortions, which, in turn, were positively associated with aggression [364].

- Cognitive distortions were measured in four categories. The first category was self-centeredness [364]. An example of the self-centered cognitive distortion could be thinking, such as 'if someone was careless enough to lose their wallet, they deserved to have it stolen' [364]. The second category was blaming others (e.g., "people 'forced' me") [364]. The third category was minimizing (e.g., 'it is not a big deal') [364]. The last category was assuming the worst (e.g., 'you should hurt others before they hurt you') [364].

- In contrast, the link between parent-adolescent attachment and delinquency was found to be mediated by affiliation with deviant peers, rather than aggression [364].

Given that low self-esteem was linked to various risks, what about high self-esteem?

More accurately, we ask, where is the line drawn between high self-esteem and narcissism?

The distinction between 'explicit' and 'implicit' self-esteem may shed light on this.

Explicit self-esteem refers to an individual's deliberate and controllable self-feelings [365]. Implicit self-esteem, on the other hand, refers to automatic and uncontrollable self-feelings [365].

A review reported that a few studies found that individuals with high explicit self-esteem but low implicit self-esteem reported the highest levels of narcissism [365]. This was higher than those who had high levels of both explicit and implicit self-esteem [365].

Furthermore, one of those studies found that explicit and implicit self-esteem interacted to predict narcissistic tendencies [365]. However, not all studies replicated these results [365]. A meta-analysis conducted as part of the review found no consistent support for this relationship [365].

One reason for the inconsistent findings may be the unreliability of implicit measurements [365]. This includes issues with retest unreliability and the uncorrelatedness of different measurement methods [365].

Another reason could be the lack of differentiation between 'agentic' and 'communal' forms of implicit self-evaluations [365]. In its simplest form, being agentic means being assertive and dominant, rather than reserved and inhibited [365]. On the other hand, being communal means being kind, cooperative, and nurturing, rather than mean [365].

One study found that narcissism was positively related to the implicit agency, but not implicit communion [365]. This suggests that narcissism may be related to implicit agentic self-evaluations rather than the previously mentioned interaction between high explicit and low implicit self-esteem [365].

To put it simply, a narcissist may have positive self-evaluations based on their domineering achievements rather than their kindness or nurturing of others. The same review found consistent evidence that narcissists valued agency and devalued communion [365]. In particular, narcissists may exhibit higher levels of competitiveness and lower levels of cooperation when there is something to be gained at the expense of others [365].

A third reason for the inconsistent findings could be the lack of differentiation between grandiose narcissism and vulnerable narcissism

[365]. Grandiose narcissism is characterized by arrogance and self-absorption, while vulnerable narcissism is characterized by feelings of inferiority and high reactivity during 'evaluative' events [365]. Vulnerable narcissists may also covertly crave for others' approval [365].

A fourth reason could be the lack of differentiation between fragile and secure self-esteem [365]. Fragile self-esteem requires constant validation, while secure self-esteem reflects honest self-acceptance [365].

High self-esteem that is dependent on one's accomplishments is considered fragile because it can be easily shattered by failure or poor performance in the valued domains [365]. Some researchers have suggested that the high self-esteem of narcissists may be contingent on their ability to garner admiration [365].

A past meta-analysis found that narcissism was positively associated with contingent self-esteem in competitive domains and negatively in affiliative ones [365]. However, there was no significant relationship between narcissism and overall contingent self-esteem [365].

In sum, these findings highlight the importance of differentiating agentic and communal implicit self-esteem, grandiose and vulnerable narcissism, and contingent and non-contingent self-esteem in order to gain a better understanding of narcissism.

With that said, the relationship of narcissism with explicit and implicit self-esteem is likely a complex one. After all, explicit and implicit self-esteem come with their own set of repercussions.

In one study, individuals with low implicit self-esteem but high explicit self-esteem exhibited more unrealistic optimism about their future and perceived flattering profiles as more self-descriptive compared to those who had high levels of both explicit and implicit self-esteem [366]. This supports the notion that individuals with high explicit self-esteem may engage in self-enhancement to conceal their low implicit self-esteem.

A review reported that people may engage in self-enhancements even when public image is not a concern [367]. Peoples naturally desire to see themselves as worthy, competent, and good, regardless of how others perceive them [367].

Additionally, a study found that individuals can distort information to align with their self-concept when presented with ambiguous task feedback that is relevant to their self-concept [367].

In one experiment, individuals with high self-esteem rated their evaluator as more competent and valid when the received evaluation was positive as opposed to negative [367]. In contrast, the ratings from those with low self-esteem were not influenced by their received evaluations [367]. In other words, people with high self-esteem interpreted information or searched for an explanation that was consistent with their self-esteem.

This raises the question, if self-esteem can be linked to self-enhancements and distortions, what about narcissism?

A study investigated this and found that narcissism was indeed linked to self-enhancement [368]. Within the four groups of participants, 'grandiosity' self-enhancement was positively and moderately associated with narcissism [368].

Here, grandiosity self-enhancement was defined as one seeing themselves in idealized terms [368]. This can include narratives like, 'I am a special agent of God' [368].

In contrast, 'social desirability' self-enhancement was negatively linked to narcissism in one of the four groups and unrelated in the remaining three [368]. This seemed to affirm the previous analyses that social desirability, defined as the need for others' acceptance, recognition, and approval, was unrelated to narcissism [368].

But to further clarify, social desirability self-enhancement referred to one's impression management of how others view them so as to validate their self-image [368]. For example, one may aim to win admiration, which, in turn, enhances their sense of self-importance [368].

Both grandiosity and social desirability self-enhancement were found to make up defensive self-enhancement [368]. Defensive self-enhancement can be said to be a self-deception, an unconscious evaluative bias that is used to defend the self against a psychological threat [368]. For example, when a grandiose person is threatened with failure, that person may unconsciously adopt a stance that is consistent with their aggrandized self [368].

With this understanding, it was found that narcissism was linked to the use of defensive self-enhancement [368].

Given that self-esteem and narcissism were both linked to positive illusions, the question remains, 'are positive illusions necessary for self-esteem?'

A study found that 10.5% of its participants had high self-esteem but low illusion [369]. In addition, their infrequent use of positive illusions was not associated with depression [369]. Nevertheless, positive illusions may be where the similarities end for self-esteem and narcissism.

One study embarked on making comparisons between explicit self-esteem and grandiose narcissism in terms of developmental experiences, personality traits, interpersonal functioning, and psychopathology, as well as adaptive and maladaptive outcomes [370]. The study clearly distinguished between grandiose narcissism and vulnerable narcissism, where the latter is characterized by emotional reactivity, entitlement, distrust, hypersensitivity to criticism, and low self-esteem [370].

To begin, the study found that there was little to no relationship between narcissism and adverse developmental experiences [370]. On the other hand, self-esteem was positively associated with parental warmth and monitoring, and negatively with abuse, parental intrusiveness, and the anxious and avoidant attachment styles [370].

There was, however, a small negative correlation between the Entitlement/ Exploitativeness sub-scale of Narcissism and parental warmth and monitoring, and a small positive correlation with parental intrusiveness [370].

In terms of personality traits, the study found that narcissism was negatively related to agreeableness, whereas self-esteem was strongly and negatively related to neuroticism [370]. Both narcissism and self-esteem were negatively related to behavioral inhibition [370].

When it comes to interpersonal functioning, the study found that narcissism was associated with responses such as yelling, rudeness, threat, and physical aggression when faced with hostile, ambiguous, or unintentional transgression [370]. On the other hand, self-esteem was weakly and negatively associated with these responses [370].

On top of aggressive social responses, narcissism was found to be positively related to bids for disproportionate resources within a resource-sharing situation, whereas self-esteem was unrelated [370]. However, the interpersonal issues of narcissism go beyond this.

The study found that narcissism was positively related to a whole range of indicators for interpersonal problems, including being domineering, revengeful, cold, intrusive, and arrogant-calculating [370]. However, self-esteem was also positively related to these characteristics, but to a much smaller extent [370].

Regarding relationship dynamics, narcissism was positively related to more frequent arguing and self-comparisons with others, whereas self-esteem was negatively related to such dynamics and positively related to feelings of closeness with one's social network [370].

In terms of psychopathology, narcissism was weakly and negatively related to anxiety and depression [370]. This highlights the protective effects of narcissism, potentially due to defensive self-enhancements. However, narcissism was also weakly but positively related to the constructs of anxiety, paranoia, and schizophrenia [370]. In contrast, self-esteem had negative relations with anxiety, depression, and the constructs of paranoia and schizophrenia [370].

In terms of externalizing behavior, narcissism was weakly but positively related to alcohol use, substance use, and anti-social behavior, whereas self-esteem was weakly but negatively related [370]. Additionally, self-esteem was moderately and negatively related to the construct of suicide [370].

Self-esteem was, in general, negatively related to various pathological traits, including anxiousness, separation insecurity, hostility, and detachment [370].

Self-esteem was also, in general, negatively related to pathological traits that narcissism was positively associated with. These traits included antagonism, which encompasses manipulativeness, deceitfulness, grandiosity, and callousness, and the disinhibition trait, which encompasses irresponsibility and impulsivity [370]. In terms of the entitlement trait, self-esteem was weakly but positively related, while narcissism was moderately and positively related [370].

Ultimately, the study affirmed that self-esteem and narcissism diverged strongly in terms of interpersonal style. Specifically, narcissism was characterized by an antagonistic and non-communal interpersonal style [370].

- One potential explanation for the differences between narcissism and self-esteem is that narcissists may perceive their social network as self-centered and unkind. As a result, they may consider those traits as necessary for maintaining a sense of superiority and a higher social status [370]. Moreover, narcissists may view the world from a zero-sum perspective and have a desire for admiration, meaning to be evaluated highly, and a desire for rivalry, meaning a desire for others to be evaluated poorly [370]. This could explain why narcissism is linked to an inclination to claim an unfair share of resources.

- In contrast to the 'superiority' held by narcissists, individuals with high self-esteem have a sense of adequacy [370]. This means that they can have positive evaluations of themselves and others, and without denigrating others [370].

Lastly, in terms of personality disorders, narcissism was positively associated with Psychopathy and Machiavellianism, whereas self-esteem was weakly and negatively associated [370]. Narcissism, along with Psychopathy and Machiavellianism, makes up what is known as the dark triad of personality.

Machiavellianism, as a concept, seemed to be characterized by a tumultuous history of inconsistency. Specifically, low internal reliability plagued its traditional measurements and definitions [371]. One study embarked on finding a more consistent definition and found that four factors satisfactorily defined Machiavellianism [371]. The four factors were: distrust for others, amoral manipulativeness, desire for status, and desire for control over others [371].

To elaborate, 'distrust' was defined as beliefs that people are motivated solely by personal gain and that they would backstab one another for their own benefit [371].

'Amoral manipulativeness' referred to the willingness to manipulate impressions to advance one's personal goals, even if it means acting unethically or cheating if the risk of being caught is low [371]. In other words, the appropriateness or morality of their behavior is irrelevant.

In contrast, the 'desire for status' referred to a desire to accumulate external indicators of success such as wealth, power, and of course, status [371].

Finally, the 'desire for control' referred to a desire to dominate others, including the enjoyment of control over others [371].

In general, Machiavellianism were positively associated with a need to achieve by outperforming others, rather than through personal excellence [371]. It was also positively linked to the frequency of performing counterproductive work behaviors toward an organization and toward others, such as verbally abusing a co-worker [371].

A study combined the concepts of the dark triad (Narcissism, Psychopathy, and Machiavellianism) and found that the dark triad was positively associated with self-enhancing values, such as power, achievement, and hedonism [372]. Conversely, the dark triad was negatively associated with self-transcendent values, such as benevolence and universalism [372].

These findings suggest that the dark triad could lead individuals to ruthlessly and guiltlessly pursue power, status, enjoyment, and success through the unremorseful exploitation of others. The development of such behavior could pose dangers to society.

Possible Initiatives

✓ School programs can offer opportunities to explore healthy aspects of self-esteem, where individuals may gain an awareness of how they form their self-esteem. These programs may aim to dispel the need for comparisons, positive illusions, and the tying of achievements to one's self-worth.

- At the same time, individuals can learn to differentiate self-esteem and narcissism, and discuss the narratives of the dark triad and their societal repercussions.

- Additionally, teachers and parents can be taught to differentiate between sensitive and insensitive communication, where the former seeks to encourage children to express their thoughts and feelings rather than force them to put on a false self. Parents should communicate unconditional love, one that is not dependent on a child's achievement, to their children.

- By doing so, we can prevent unhealthy forms of self-esteem and minimize the risk of individuals developing the dark triad of personality.

<u>What must Human Beings know about being human?</u>

<u>#20</u>

How does one's identity formation lead to risky outcomes?

An individual's identity formation is influenced by the satisfaction of their basic psychological needs, which include autonomy, competence, and relatedness [373]. The need for relatedness refers to a desire for a sense of mutual respect and connection with significant others [373]. It has been found that there is a reciprocal relationship between the satisfaction of these needs and the formation of one's identity [373].

Additionally, identity achievement, which involves finding identity commitment after exploring different values and goals, was related to the satisfaction of all three psychological needs [373].

On the other hand, those with low identity commitment and a ruminative approach to identity exploration experienced the greatest deficits in satisfying their psychological needs [373]. This suggests personal distress.

Moreover, to understand the identity that will be formed, it is important to consider what identity will fulfill a person's needs. This is significant because an individual's early identity can shape their later life outcomes.

A study found that social identities in high school were predictive of adult substance use, education attainment outcomes, and psychological adjustment [374]. Additionally, both identity and activity choices during adolescence were linked to various outcomes in adulthood [374].

However, the results should be interpreted with caution. This is because the 1983 Michigan study reflected cultural effects that may not be generalizable to other cultures and cultures may have also changed over time. Furthermore, the study categorized social identity in a stereotypical manner rather than measuring it reliably.

The study found that among adolescents who participated in prosocial activities, their frequency of drinking and marijuana use was lower between the ages of 16 and 24 [374]. On the other hand, adolescents who participated in sports teams reported a higher frequency of drinking compared to non-athletes [374]. Additionally, those involved in performing arts showed a higher rate of increased drinking compared to those not involved [374]. For marijuana use, those in performing arts also showed an increase over time, with a gender difference observed [374].

Although these activities were linked to increased substance use, participation in all activity types was positively associated with a higher number of completed years of education [374]. The exception was prosocial activity which was no longer a significant predictor after controlling for maternal education level and the adolescents' prior verbal and numerical ability [374].

Additionally, adolescents in performing arts reported lower levels of psychological adjustment during young adulthood [374]. 11% of them had attempted suicide, compared to the 6% of non-participants [374]. 22% had visited a psychologist, compared to the 11% of non-participants [374]. However, this correlation cannot be considered causal, as the underlying reasons remain unclear.

The study found that among high school social identities, 'jocks,' who were highly represented in team sports, reported the most frequent alcohol use going into adulthood [374]. This was also the case for 'criminals,' who were not involved in any extracurricular activities and had the largest proportion of friends who used alcohol and drugs [374].

On the other hand, 'brains', who were academic-oriented and had the most academic-oriented peers, reported the lowest frequency of drinking [374]. Additionally, in contrast to the high marijuana use of 'criminals', 'brains' reported the lowest usage [374].

Moreover, 'princesses,' who were highly represented in 'school spirit' activities, showed a sharp increase in marijuana use between the ages of 18 and 21, which then dropped dramatically by age 24 [374].

The study also found that social identity was a significant predictor of whether a person would be in drug or alcohol rehabilitation by age 24 [374]. The highest rates of rehabilitation was observed among 'criminals' and 'jocks' [374].

In contrast, 'brains' were the most likely to have graduated college by age 24, whereas 'criminals' were the least likely [374]. However, the study found that social identity did not have a significant effect on whether a person was in a job with a perceived career path [374].

In terms of psychological adjustment, 'criminals' and 'princesses' reported a higher frequency of depressed moods as they entered adulthood [374]. 'Criminals' also reported the lowest self-esteem, as well as the highest levels of worry and discouraged feelings about their future [374].

Given that high school social identities can have long-term effects on substance use, education attainment, and psychological adjustment, it is worth considering, 'could gang identity also have effects?'

In one study, gang identification, which was predicted by in-group cohesion, was positively related to criminal and violent activity [375].

In contrast, the study found that for non-gang individuals, in-group cohesion was positively related to group identification, but this identification was not linked to criminal or violent activity [375].

252

Deterrence concerns, such as the perceived likelihood of being caught, were weakly but negatively related to gang identification, criminal behavior, and violence [375].

These findings suggest that gangs, which are said to offer emotional stability, friendship, and street survival, may also normalize expectations for group behavior, including criminal and violent behavior [375].

In one review, gangs were further said to offer youths a chance to attain identity, status, companionship, and respect from others [376]. It was noted that those who joined gangs could be individuals who were the most alienated from their families, education systems, and communities [376]. As a result, they would embrace gang norms in order to gain acceptance, even if they initially felt uneasy [376]. Over time, criminal activity becomes a valued activity that enhances one's personal reputation and status within the group [376].

To cope with their initial discomfort, individuals may engage in moral disengagement [376]. Other gang members may also provide approval [376]. This endorsement reinforces the individual's moral disengagement strategies, which is in addition to their gang-cultivated hostile attributions and ruminations [376], that further support detrimental actions.

A similar phenomenon was observed in prison, where individuals who held non-conformist attitudes toward the inmate subculture and were not integrated into the inmate system, such as those who did not participate in a prison gang, were noted to be at increased risk of being bullied [377].

Conversely, for the bullies, the same study found that bullying was positively related to the perceived importance of social status [377]. In particular, prisoners who engaged in bullying valued social status more than those who did not bully [377].

In addition, moral disengagement was positively linked to the perceived importance of social status [377]. Further analysis revealed that moral disengagement partially mediated the relationship between bullying and the perceived importance of social status [377]. To put it simply, prisoners who have a strong need for social status may engage in moral disengagement to fulfill that need through bullying.

So what could have led to such a need for status or gang identity?

It is possible that gang identity is an extension of a person's marginalization, where they struggle to achieve an identity. Unfortunately, gang membership can exacerbate this marginalization and amplify their developmental deficits. Of course, that is not to say we can condone one's detrimental behavior.

With that said, the correlates of gang involvement may offer insight into the underlying marginalization.

A study found that gang involvement was linked to poorer self-esteem and impaired emotional regulation [378]. Specifically, those in gangs exhibited increased emotional reactivity, such as yelling at others, and poorer emotional coping mechanisms, such as rumination [378]. Furthermore, gang involvement was linked to higher exposure to traumatic events [378].

The study also revealed that there were lower levels of parental monitoring and communication with parents among those involved in gangs [378]. This was in addition to higher housing instability, such as running away from home or being forced to leave [378]. These factors suggest poor relationships and a lack of nurturing.

A city-level study also discovered that economic disadvantage had an independent effect on gang membership [379]. Specifically, a higher level of economic disadvantage was associated with higher levels of gang membership [379]. Furthermore, when there was a high degree of racial and ethnic heterogeneity, increased economic disadvantage was found to correspond with a larger increase in gang membership [379]. In sum, both economic disadvantage and heterogeneity had independent, additive, and multiplicative effects [379]. This suggests at two things.

Firstly, gang identity may not exist in isolation and may confound with one's ethnic and racial identities. Secondly, economic disadvantage may be concentrated amongst certain racial and ethnic groups or are perceived as such.

One study delved deeper into the precursors of gang involvement and found that gang members tended to be individuals who struggled with identity issues [380].

Compared to non-gang members, gang members felt poorer about themselves, perceived their academic abilities as weaker, felt less purpose in life, and were less integrated into their societal institutions [380]. Similarly, gang 'wannabes' experienced poorer integration with their societal institutions [380].

Poor integration was defined as weak bonding with parents, education, and the police [380]. For instance, family bonding was assessed by evaluating the attachment between the individual and their parents, including whether the parents ever understood the individual [380].

Education bonding was defined as one's attitude on how much education they would like to complete, as well as their view on the importance of good grades and career prospects [380]. Meanwhile, police bonding referred to an individual's beliefs on whether the police would prefer to help them or catch them doing something wrong [380].

In other words, gang 'wannabes' and members experienced greater detachment from their families, greater alienation from the police, and lower academic aspirations [380]. Additionally, confidence in academic abilities predicted education bonding, which was, in turn, negatively related to gang involvement [380].

Furthermore, people who wanted to join gangs had the lowest levels of general self-esteem, in addition to poor academic self-concept [380]. Non-gang members, on the other hand, had the highest self-esteem [380]. However, joining a gang seemed to improve the self-esteem of 'wannabes' [380]. Additionally, both 'wannabes' and gang members reported having less ability to resist peer pressures [380]. These findings support the notion that gangs provide their members with self-esteem and status.

In sum, gang members may be individuals who are struggling to understand themselves and their devaluation within societal institutions [380]. To prevent gang involvement, it may be beneficial to enhance each individual's bonding with their family, education, and the police, as well as improve their academic self-concept and global self-esteem. These efforts may help individuals find a positive sense of identity.

One study found that difficulties in finding identity could have additional consequences. Specifically, the study found that ruminative exploration was positively related to depressive symptoms across different age groups, including adolescence, young adulthood, and the late twenties [381].

On the other hand, identity resolution during young adulthood was found to predict a consistently high level of intimacy, generativity, and integrity later in life [382]. In contrast, those with lower identity resolution initially had lower levels of intimacy, generativity, and integrity, but eventually caught up during their sixties [382].

- Intimacy refers to the capacity to be open, empathetic, vulnerable, and welcoming toward authentic and close relationships [382]. Generativity means making efforts to nurture future generations and leave behind positive impacts [382]. Lastly, integrity refers to a person's ability to look back and see that they have achieved their main goals and lived according to their principles and without regret [382]. Those with strong integrity are said to overcome their fear of aging and death [382].

As can be seen, an individual's identity formation can be linked to their psychosocial development. Furthermore, a reason why people may engage in rumination and struggle to achieve a positive identity could be because their environments do not satisfy their need for autonomy, competence, and relatedness. However, one study offered a different perspective.

This study found that identity maturity at age 17, 19, and 23 was associated with more sophisticated meaning-making at age 23 [383]. Although the direction of effect is unclear, it does not rule out the possibility that identity maturity could be the result of increasing sophistication in meaning-making from age 17 to 23.

Additionally, the study suggested that events relating to mortality, relationship, and autonomy were the most relevant for meaning-making, whereas achievement was the least relevant [383].

To clarify, meaning-making refers to a person's ability to connect a turning point in life with some form of self-understanding [383]. Specifically, stories that involve redemptive turning points were positively related to meaning-making [383]. This, in turn, was positively linked to generativity and life optimism [383].

On the other hand, social rejection was found to reduce the perceived meaningfulness of life [384]. Individuals who experienced ostracism rated their lives as more meaningless [384]. However, social rejection did not impact their search for meaning [384].

In another study, participants felt that they had more control, more meaningful existence, and higher self-esteem when they ostracized a stranger [385]. In other words, people may ostracize others in order to enhance their own sense of meaning.

Additionally, when ostracism was punitive and in response to something about the target person, participants felt more control, self-esteem, and meaningful existence, but also more anger and less apologeticness [385]. The study also found that the less ambiguous the reasons for ostracism, the better the participants felt in terms of self-esteem and meaningful existence [385]. This ambiguity was reduced when a group performed the ostracism [385]. These findings suggest that self-enhancement may be unconsciously performed, resulting in the marginalization of others.

To prevent the marginalization of identities, it is crucial to investigate the mechanisms by which identities become marginalized.

A study found that child participants from different cultures had different levels of acceptance towards gender norm violations [386]. Additionally, individuals who violate gender norms may experience misclassification of their identities [387]. For example, heterosexual men who engage in stereotypically female behavior can be labeled as 'gay' [387]. These lead them to be assigned with a stigmatized status and become targets of regular social punishments, such as ostracism, ridicule, dislike, and aggression [387]. In some cases, the individuals may even be treated as less than fully human [387].

- A review found evidence that child gender behavior and development are influenced by genes and prenatal testosterone exposure [388]. The review found that child testosterone levels were largely genetic, and that puberty testosterone levels also had an effect on gender identity [388]. This was in addition to environmental influences, such as parental socialization [388]. Small associations were also found between the parents' gender schemas and their children's [388]. These findings suggest that one's gender identity and behavior may not be as changeable as previously thought.

At the same time, identities may become marginalized through myth construction.

A review noted that one woman was estimated to be raped every six minutes and that one in four women may become rape victims during their lifetime [389]. One contributing factor to this phenomenon could be Rape Myth Acceptance (RMA).

The review noted that considerable research has shown that there is a significant association between RMA and sexually aggressive behavior [389]. Moreover, higher RMA was linked to a lower likelihood of a community convicting a person accused of rape [389]. However, these findings were not replicated within another sample [389].

To clarify, rape myths are persistent and inaccurate beliefs that people use to justify and deny their sexual aggression [389]. People may even look for 'evidence' to suggest that a victim instigated or deserved the assault [389]. For example, one might say, 'With the way she was dressed, she was asking for it' [389]. It was noted that higher levels of RMA were found in individuals who reported a higher likelihood of committing rape [389].

The review also noted that a study conducted factor analysis and found that RMA can include the disbelief toward rape claims, and views that rape reports are manipulative [389]. Additionally, another study stated that RMA can include a denial of the seriousness of rape [389].

In another review, rape myths were reported to include, 'men cannot stop once they become aroused,' 'rapists are different,' and 'only certain women are raped, such as those who drink, sleep around, or hang out in the wrong places' [390]. However, it is important to note that while many studies focused on the rape of women, it is not to say that men cannot be raped. RMA likely supports rape behavior regardless of the gender of the target.

Further examples of rape myths include, 'husbands cannot rape their wives,' 'women enjoy rape,' 'women ask to be raped,' 'women lie about being raped,' and 'women put up token resistance' [391]. The term 'Token resistance' refers to the belief that a person's 'No' actually means a 'Yes' [391].

In a study on token resistance, participants who were informed that a woman had previously objected to a man touching her genitals and then stopped resisting took significantly longer to decide if the same man should stop further sexual behavior when the woman resisted again during a subsequent encounter [392].

Given that rape can occur after consensual sexual activity [392], this finding highlights that people may misinterpret an individual's resistance as sexual willingness, even if that person is unable to resist or changes their mind.

Given the damaging repercussions of RMA and rape, it is important to ask, what are the risk factors of RMA?

One study found that higher levels of gender role stereotyping, acceptance of relationship violence, and adversarial sexual beliefs were associated with higher levels of RMA [393].

To clarify, people with adversarial sexual beliefs hold the view that sexual relationships have an inherently exploitative nature, and therefore, neither party can be trusted [393].

A meta-analysis found that higher RMA was associated with lower levels of education and higher levels of prejudicial beliefs [394]. These prejudicial beliefs included sexism, classism, ageism, racism, religious intolerance, hatred towards white people, and hostility towards a specific gender [394]. These findings indicate that other problematic beliefs may co-exist with RMA.

In addition, the meta-analysis found that higher RMA was linked to sexual conservatism [394]. Furthermore, the prostitution myth was found to be positively related to RMA [394]. The prostitution myth refers to beliefs that justify the existence and exploitation of prostitutes [394].

In addition to prejudicial beliefs and other subscribed myths, the pursuit of status was found to be positively related to RMA [394]. Conversely, social competence and positive identification with one's race were negatively related to RMA [394]. This highlights that personal development and identity can affect RMA.

One study went further to investigate if identifying with a 'masculinity ideology' would be linked to date rape myth acceptance (DRMA). The study found that identifying with a combination of masculinity variables indeed predicted DRMA [395].

Masculinity ideology here included subscribing to the importance of respect and status from others, avoiding 'feminine' behaviors, having the need to display toughness and independence, and believing that physical violence is sometimes necessary [395].

In addition to the link between masculinity ideology and DRMA, DRMA was found to be positively correlated with the self-reported likelihood of committing rape if one would not get caught or punished [395]. (Basically, preconventional morality.)

It is important to recognize that RMA is not limited to prejudicial and adversarial attitudes towards a particular gender or identity, nor is it solely associated with the subscription to a masculinity identity. Alcohol-specific narratives, for example, can also contribute to instances of rape.

One review noted that alcohol use during dates can lead to misinterpretation of friendly cues as sexual invitations [396]. Men may also perceive women who are drinking alcohol to be more sexually available [396]. Additionally, a date may choose a drinking activity to increase the likelihood of sexual intercourse [396].

To put this into perspective, it was reported that 80% to 90% of rapes were committed by acquaintances [396]. Furthermore, a study found that over half of the reported sexual assaults on college-age victims occurred after alcohol consumption [396].

Given that narratives can endorse rape and result in harmful consequences, it is crucial to investigate how harmful myths and sexual beliefs are constructed. Sexual media may shed light on this matter.

One study found that increased exposure to sexual media, such as those depicting fondling or sex, was related to a multi-fold increase in the odds of adolescents experiencing 'coerced sex victimization,' meaning they gave in to sex when they did not want to [397].

In the study, the odds of coercive sex victimization was higher when there was increased exposure to sexual material in movies and television, but not games, music, or the internet [397]. Conversely, higher exposure to sexual material in music was associated with an increased number of sexual partners [397].

Furthermore, the odds of encountering attempted or completed rape were elevated among youths who reported that a high proportion of their consumed media depicted sexual situations [397]. However, this does not mean that these youths invited the rape. Instead, it is possible that sexual material was a popular viewing among their peers or acquaintances. The same study noted that 19 previous studies found a significant relationship between sexual media and adolescent sexual behavior, with some studies finding that media influenced youth sex attitudes [397].

262

In the worst-case scenario, sexual media may construct behaviors and attitudes that support sexual victimization against groups, including women and children. Alternatively, sexual media may construct a sexual desire that is so strong that people rely on its promiscuous narrative and various justifications and distortions to satisfy that desire. Or perhaps, a person's identity needs, such as those that underlie a masculinity identity, had led them to engage in harmful behavior. Further research is needed to determine the underlying causes.

In conclusion, people can become marginalized through myth construction, unconscious self-enhancement, and intolerance towards norm violation. This can result in a complex web of myths, prejudice, and justifications that lead to traumatic experiences.

As such, overcoming the risks that are associated with identities may not only entail the identity that is formed or how that identity is formed, but also how individuals and groups treat a perceived identity. This includes avoiding the misidentifications of individuals with identities that they may not actually identify with.

Possible Initiatives

✓ Schools can help students gain an understanding of how identities are formed. Moreover, by providing opportunities to critically evaluate positive and anti-social stories and discern the underlying needs of an identity, schools can enhance the identity process of students. This is aimed at promoting positive identity resolution and reducing exploratory rumination.

✓ School programs can actively promote the students' ability to handle interpersonal differences and foster the recognition and understanding of stereotyping, identity misclassification, prejudice, and ethnocentric judgments. By exploring how these narratives can contribute to issues like racism, classism, ageism, and the acceptance of rape myths, students can better understand their consequences.

<u>PART IV</u>

The Final Problem

<u>What must Human Beings know about being human?</u>

#The Final Problem

Can detrimental development arise from experiencing power?

The saying goes, 'power corrupts absolutely.' But is that really true? This is a crucial question because power disparities exist within lifespan institutions.

A study found that the perception of power over others positively predicted verbal aggression [398]. Conversely, the perception of control over one's own life was a negative predictor [398]. Similarly, power over others positively predicted exploitativeness, whereas personal control negatively predicted it [398].

However, it was noted that power over others and personal control were positively related [398].

But despite that, personal control was found to suppress the effect of power over others [398]. This implies that previous research may have underestimated the corruptive effect of power as this suppression effect was not taken into consideration [398].

Moving forward, it has been reported that individuals in higher organizational positions were responsible for the majority of workplace bullying [398]. As such, it is natural to ask, 'could power corruption be at play?'

To begin answering that question, one study found that a higher organizational position predicted both a higher perception of power over others and a greater sense of personal control [398].

However, the study did not find a statistically significant difference in the self-reported levels of aggression and exploitativeness between individuals at different organizational levels [398].

This could be because a higher organizational position was simultaneously associated with both power and personal control [398]. We have already seen that power and personal control have opposite effects on aggression and exploitativeness [398]. As a result, power alone may be insufficient for workplace bullying. However, this does not mean that power does not contribute to malefic development that may lead to bullying behavior.

A study found that individuals with high power exhibited a reduced inclination to adopt someone else's visual perspective [399]. They also tended to assume that others had the same privileged knowledge that they do [399]. Furthermore, individuals with high power demonstrated less accuracy in recognizing the emotional expressions of others [399].

In essence, having more power appears to result in a reduced tendency to comprehend how others see, think, and feel [399]. People with power are said to have impeded empathy and may also be insensitive to the repercussions of their actions [399]. The above findings seem to support this notion.

A study investigated further and found that individuals with a greater sense of power experienced less distress and compassion in response to the suffering of others [400]. This could be because people with higher-power have a weaker desire to get to know others, form friendships, and become emotionally invested in them [400]. Findings suggest that individuals with high power may not necessarily be insensitive to the emotions of others [400]. Instead, they may be reacting selectively to further their own goals [400].

In addition to ignoring others and having a limited perspective-taking ability, having more power may reduce an individual's willingness to accept advice. A study found that power was negatively associated with advice-taking [401]. This relationship was explained by self-confidence [401]. To elaborate, power increased one's confidence in their initial judgment, which then decreased the amount of advice taken [401]. Despite this, individuals with higher power had lower accuracy in their judgment but overestimated the number of correct answers they gave [401].

- In contrast, individuals who were perceived as good leaders had higher self-confidence but were also seen by their co-workers to be taking more advice [401].

On the other hand, reduced advice-taking implies impaired self-improvement. People may become unable to acknowledge or correct their mistakes. Furthermore, there may be a significant distortion in how they evaluate themselves and others.

One meta-analysis examined the relationship between power and performance evaluation [402]. The results showed that as power increased, evaluations of lower-ranked others became more derogatory [402]. At the same time, self-evaluations became more positive [402].

This meta-analysis included a famous 1972 experiment by David Kipnis which found that 'supervisors', who were given power over the reward and punishment of their 'subordinates', were more likely to devalue their subordinates' ability and worth to the company [403]. Moreover, more supervisors viewed their subordinates as objects of manipulation, displayed less concern, and attributed their subordinates' efforts to their own power and control, rather than their subordinates' motivation [403].

In addition, very few supervisors who were given power relied on persuasion [403]. Instead, many relied on threats and reward promises [403]. These findings demonstrated that power control can alter a power-holder's self-perception and their perception of others [403].

However, this change in perception may not be limited to favorable self-perceptions and unfavorable perceptions of others.

In one study, it was found that high-power conditions led to cynical attributions of favors received from others [404]. Participants in high-power conditions believed that a favor was motivated by self-interest rather than selfless concern [404]. These attributions reduced gratitude, trust, and the desire to reciprocate within work relationships [404].

Similarly, people in high-power conditions were less committed to their marriage partners due to cynical attributions of the favors they received from their spouses [404]. As can be seen, power can lead to cynical views of others' intentions, which can hinder the healthy responses that are necessary for nurturing healthy relationships [404].

Given that power can affect perception, can power also affect behavior?

Yes, it can. One study demonstrated that power increased moral hypocrisy [405]. The study revealed that powerful individuals were more critical toward the cheating of others, but also cheated more themselves [405]. They were also more strict in their judgments of others' moral transgressions compared to their own [405]. Interestingly, those who did not feel entitled to their high-power position did not exhibit moral hypocrisy [405].

In addition to moral hypocrisy, power can influence behavior through objectification.

Objectification is defined as the act of approaching social targets when they are viewed as useful for a goal [406]. This behavior can lead to a disregard for the value of other human qualities [406]. In other words, individuals in high-power positions may view people as mere objects, viewing them solely in terms of their usefulness.

Moreover, objectification can serve as a tool to subordinate the needs and interests of those with less power to those who have more [406]. This facilitates the use of others to further one's goals [406].

In the same study, it was found that individuals in high-power conditions were more likely to approach others based on their usefulness [406]. They also tended to objectify their subordinates and peers more [406]. The study controlled for the participants' Social Dominance Orientation and found that the effect of power on objectification remained unchanged [406].

Furthermore, when performance goals and sexual goals were both present, male individuals with high power were more inclined to prefer working with a female partner who was useful for sexual goals, but not necessarily for their ability to perform the task [406].

It is important to note that simply having power or sexual thoughts did not result in male participants choosing an attractive female for task performance [406]. Participants only acted on their sexual goal when they also held power [406].

Additionally, power increased one's willingness to interact with an unkind individual when the individual was useful for an active performance goal [406]. However, individuals in a high-power condition reduced their approach when the unkind individual was no longer useful and the performance goal was no longer active [406]. It was noted that other participants were more sensitive to the individual's kindness rather than their usefulness [406].

In essence, power combined with an active performance goal can result in a greater desire to interact with an unkind but competent individual [406]. This finding suggests that individuals in positions of power may have a higher tolerance for unkind behavior. However, once the unkind individual has served their purpose, the appreciation for them may diminish.

A review indicated that dehumanizing attitudes and behaviors are common in organizations and are often seen as acceptable or necessary for achieving personal or organizational goals [407]. However, these behaviors have significant consequences.

Even subtle forms of dehumanization, such as condescension, disrespect, ostracism, and neglect, are not innocent [407]. They have consequences. The same holds true for status-reducing treatments, such as treating someone as incompetent, embarrassing, or unintelligent [407].

Dehumanizing a person can result in increased anti-social and aggressive behaviors towards that individual [407]. Everyday maltreatments can leave victims feeling degraded and demoralized [407]. Ultimately, dehumanization impairs the victim's ability to meet their basic psychological needs, such as autonomy, competence, and relatedness, which can potentially lead to mental illness [407].

But the question remains, does suppressing one's empathy truly lead to better problem-solving and goal achievement?

Evidence shows that empathy is crucial for problem-solving within the social domains [407]. However, there is also evidence that problem-solving in both social and mechanistic domains can interfere with one another during complex tasks due to their competition for limited cognitive resources [407]. In other words, if people have enough cognitive capacity, they would not need to compromise one for the other.

Additionally, mechanistic problems often have a social aspect. For instance, work is done by people. Therefore, empathy suppression and dehumanization that ignore the social dimension of problems are unlikely to yield effective problem-solving.

A study ventured further and looked into the cognitive and emotional effects of dehumanization.

The study began by separating dehumanization into two constructs: the denial of human nature and the denial of human uniqueness [408].

Denial of human nature encompassed experiences such as, 'the other person treated me as a means to an end as if I was an object without feelings.' [408]

In contrast, Denial of human uniqueness encompassed experiences such as, 'the other person saw me as immature, unintelligent, and incompetent, and treated me like a child.' [408]

Participants who experienced the denial of human nature reported higher levels of identity denial, characterized by narratives such as, 'I felt like my life was meaningless' [408]. Furthermore, these participants reported higher levels of cognitive deconstructive states, which were characterized by numbing and difficulties in thinking clearly [408]. These persons also reported higher levels of anger and sadness [408].

In contrast, participants who experienced the denial of human uniqueness reported higher levels of status loss, characterized by narratives such as, 'they viewed me as having lower status' [408]. Furthermore, these participants reported higher levels of aversive self-consciousness, as well as guilt and shame [408].

Think that patronizing interactions or treating someone as hopeless or stupid does not constitute interpersonal maltreatment? Think again. All of these behaviors constitute interpersonal maltreatment [408]. These day-to-day maltreating interactions are often referred to as 'micro-aggressions' [408].

Micro-aggressions can be more insidious than overt aggression because they are often small and subtle, and may appear harmless at first glance. Consequently, they can be unconsciously perpetrated and downplayed.

In conclusion, the evidence suggests that power can lead to malevolent outcomes such as aggression, exploitation, and dehumanizing behavior. Such behavior can have serious consequences, including impairments to an individual's mental health and personhood.

<u>Possible Initiatives</u>

✓ Moral education programs can offer ongoing opportunities for students to acknowledge power disparities and the responsibilities that come with their power, thereby developing their ability to make moral considerations even when there is a power imbalance.

✓ At the same time, students can gain a greater awareness of the corrupting effects of power on development and behavior. They can then critically examine moral rationales and behaviors that challenge the self-centered narratives that drive exploitation and dehumanization, and replace them with more ethical alternatives.

✓ Ultimately, the goal is for individuals to gain control over their power, avoid its corruption, and develop the moral fortitude to resist the immoral use of power.

All of these goals align with the spirit of human development.

We strive to give people the freedom of choice and prevent them from being limited by debilitating life trajectories.

Moreover, we also want people to understand how they can develop various aspects of their lives rather than resigning themselves to them.

Most importantly, we want people to know how they can rein in the dark side of human nature and bring out its positive side instead. With this knowledge in hand, people can make informed choices in their human development, and the world will surely become a better place.

The Finishing Line

Congratulations.

You have completed what is essentially a crash course on human development. You now know what human beings must know about being human.

Most importantly, armed with this knowledge, you now have the necessary tools to achieve positive human development and address the root issues underlying many societal problems.

All of this did not come easy.

I would like to take this opportunity to thank the scientists around the world who have given numerous years of their lives to provide this knowledge.

I also want to thank you, the reader, for persevering and achieving the feat of reaching the end of this book. You have just absorbed the findings of approximately four hundred scientific papers curated from more than a thousand.

With that said, many developmental problems continue to plague our generation and the next. Now, it is up to us to make the necessary improvements to create environments that unleash positive human potential. This is a highest accomplishment each and every one of us can attain, a mark we can leave behind, and one that is passed down through the generations.

End Note

Prologue

[1] Zhang, T. Y., & Meaney, M. J. (2010). Epigenetics and the environmental regulation of the genome and its function. Annual Review of Psychology, 61 (1), 439–466.

[2] Stephanie A. Tammen, Simonetta Friso, Sang-Woon Choi. (2013). Epigenetics: The link between nature and nurture. Molecular Aspects of Medicine, 34 (4), 753-764.

[3] Champagne, F. A., Mashoodh, R. (2009). Genes in context: Gene – environment interplay and the origins of individual differences in behavior. Current Directions in Psychological Science, 18 (3), 127–131.

[4] Vidrascu, E.M., Bashore, A.C., Howard, T.D. et al. (2019). Effects of early- and mid-life stress on DNA methylation of genes associated with subclinical cardiovascular disease and cognitive impairment: a systematic review. BMC Med Genet, 20, 39.

[5] Byom, L. J., & Mutlu, B. (2013). Theory of mind: mechanisms, methods, and new directions. Frontiers in human neuroscience, 7, 413.

[6] Charlotte Ruhl. (2020). Theory of mind. Published on 07 August 2020. Retrieved on 01 April 2022 from: https://www.simplypsychology.org/theory-of-mind.html#

[7] Meins, E., Fernyhough, C., Wainwright, R., Das Gupta, M., Fradley, E., & Tuckey, M. (2002). Maternal Mind-Mindedness and Attachment Security as Predictors of Theory of Mind Understanding. Child Development, 73 (6), 1715–1726.

[8] Cerniglia, L., Bartolomeo, L., Capobianco, M., Lo Russo, S., Festucci, F., Tambelli, R., Adriani, W., & Cimino, S. (2019). Intersections and Divergences Between Empathizing and Mentalizing: Development, Recent Advancements by Neuroimaging and the Future of Animal Modeling. Frontiers in behavioral neuroscience, 13, 212.

[9] Meng, K., Yuan, Y., Wang, Y., Liang, J., Wang, L., Shen, J., & Wang, Y. (2020). Effects of parental empathy and emotion regulation on social competence and emotional/behavioral problems of school-age children. Pediatric investigation, 4 (2), 91–98.

[10] Bartsch, K., & Estes, D. (1996). Individual differences in children's developing theory of mind and implications for metacognition. Learning and Individual Differences, 8 (4), 281–304.

[11] Earley, P. Christopher. (2002). Redefining interactions across cultures and organizations: moving forward with cultural intelligence. Research in Organizational Behavior, 24, 271–99.

[12] Guay, F., Marsh, H. W., & Boivin, M. (2003). Academic self-concept and academic achievement: Developmental perspectives on their causal ordering. Journal of Educational Psychology, 95 (1), 124–136.

[13] Michelle S. Fortier, Robert J. Vallerand, Frédéric Guay. (1995). Academic Motivation and School Performance: Toward a Structural Model. Contemporary Educational Psychology, 20 (3), 257-274.

[14] The Japan Reporter. (2021). Japan is Dying by its Student Loan Crisis. Retrieved on 9 December 2022 from:
https://www.youtube.com/watch?v=BUFsm3bWiE0&ab_channel=NobitafromJapan

#1

[15] Totsika, V., & Sylva, K. (2004). The Home Observation for Measurement of the Environment Revisited. Child and Adolescent Mental Health, 9 (1), 25–35.

[16] Molfese, V. J., DiLalla, L. F., & Bunce, D. (1997). Prediction of the Intelligence Test Scores of 3- to 8-Year-Old Children by Home Environment, Socioeconomic Status, and Biomedical Risks. Merrill-Palmer Quarterly, 43 (2), 219–234.

[17] Espy, K. A., Molfese, V. J., & DiLalla, L. F. (2001). Effects of environmental measures on intelligence in young children: Growth curve modeling of longitudinal data. Merrill-Palmer Quarterly, 47, 42-73.

[18] Bartels M, Rietveld MJ, Van Baal GC, Boomsma DI. (2002). Genetic and environmental influences on the development of intelligence. Behav Genet, 32 (4), 237-249.

[19] Greenough, W. T., Black, J. E., & Wallace, C. S. (1987). Experience and brain development. Child Development, 58 (3), 539–559.

#2

[20] Patton, J. R. (2000). Educating students with mild mental retardation. Focus on Autism and Other Developmental Disabilities, 15 (2), 80–89.

[21] Weisz, J. R. (1990). Cultural-familial mental retardation: A developmental perspective on cognitive performance and "helpless" behavior. In R. M. Hodapp, J. A. Burack, & E. Zigler (Eds.), Issues in the developmental approach to mental retardation (pp. 137–168). Cambridge University Press.

[22] Grossman, H. (1983). Classification in Mental Retardation. Washington DC: AAMD, EUA.

[23] Breslau N, DelDotto J E, Brown G G, Kumar S, Ezhuthachan S, Hufnagle K G, Peterson E L. (1994). A gradient relationship between low birth weight and IQ at age 6 years. Arch Pediatr Adolesc Med, 148 (4), 377-383.

[24] Streissguth, A. P., Herman, C. S., & Smith, D. W. (1978). Intelligence, behavior, and dysmorphogenesis in the fetal alcohol syndrome: a report on 20 patients. The Journal of pediatrics, 92 (3), 363–367.

[25] Streissguth, A. P., Randels, S. P., & Smith, D. F. (1991). A Test-Retest Study of Intelligence in Patients with Fetal Alcohol Syndrome: Implications for Care. Journal of the American Academy of Child & Adolescent Psychiatry, 30 (4), 584–587.

[26] Wehman, P., Kregel, J., & Seyfarth, J. (1985). Transition from School to Work for Individuals with Severe Handicaps: A Follow-Up Study. Journal of the Association for Persons with Severe Handicaps, 10 (3), 132–136.

[27] Kumar, I., Singh, A. R., & Akhtar, S. (2009). Social development of children with mental retardation. Industrial psychiatry journal, 18 (1), 56–59.

[28] Hall, I., Strydom, A., Richards, M., Hardy, R., Bernal, J., & Wadsworth, M. (2005). Social outcomes in adulthood of children with intellectual impairment: evidence from a birth cohort. Journal of Intellectual Disability Research, 49 (3), 171–182.

[29] Reschly DJ, Myers TG, Hartel CR. (2002). Mental Retardation: Determining Eligibility for Social Security Benefits. Chapter 4, The Role of Adaptive Behavior Assessment. National Research Council (US). Committee on Disability Determination for Mental Retardation. Washington (DC): National Academies Press (US). Retrieved on 30 May 2022 from: https://www.ncbi.nlm.nih.gov/books/NBK207541/

[30] Zheng S, LeWinn K, Ceja T, Hanna-Attisha M, O'Connell L & Bishop S. (2021). Adaptive Behavior as an Alternative Outcome to Intelligence Quotient in Studies of Children at Risk: A Study of Preschool-Aged Children in Flint, MI, USA. Front. Psychol, 12, 692330.

<u>#3</u>

[31] Abrantes, Jose Luis & Seabra, Claudia & Lages, Luis Filipe. (2007). Pedagogical affect, student interest, and learning performance. Journal of Business Research, 60 (9), 960-964.

[32] Langat, A. C. (2015). Students' Attitudes and Their Effects on Learning and Achievement in Mathematics: A Case Study of Public Secondary Schools in Kiambu County, Kenya. Unpublished Master's Thesis, Nairobi: Kenyatta University.

[33] Newman, R. S. (1990). Children's help-seeking in the classroom: The role of motivational factors and attitudes. Journal of Educational Psychology, 82 (1), 71–80.

[34] Ray Hembree (1988). Correlates, Causes, Effects, and Treatment of Test Anxiety. Review of Educational Research, 58 (1), 47–77.

[35] Akey, Theresa. (2006). School Context, Student Attitudes and Behavior, and Academic Achievement: An Exploratory Analysis. MDRC. Retrieved on 01 June 2022 from: https://files.eric.ed.gov/fulltext/ED489760.pdf

[36] Skinner, Ellen & Wellborn, J.G. & Connell, J.P.. (1990). What It Takes to Do Well in School and Whether I've Got It: A Process Model of Perceived Control and Children's Engagement and Achievement in School. Journal of Educational Psychology, 82 (1), 22-32.

[37] Wang, H., & Hall, N. C. (2018). A systematic review of teachers' causal attributions: Prevalence, correlates, and consequences. Frontiers in Psychology, 9, Article 2305.

[38] National Research Council. (2003). Engaging Schools: Fostering High School Students' Motivation to Learn. Committee on Increasing High School Students' Engagement and Motivation to Learn. Chapter 1: Student Engagement and Disengagement in Urban High Schools, Pg 18. National Research Council. Washington, DC: National Academy Press.

[39] Covington, M. V. (2000). Goal theory, motivation, and school achievement: An integrative review. Annual Review of Psychology, 51 (1), 171–200.

[40] Diener, C. I., & Dweck, C. S. (1978). An analysis of learned helplessness: Continuous changes in performance, strategy, and achievement cognitions following failure. Journal of Personality and Social Psychology, 36 (5), 451–462.

[41] Elliott, E. S., & Dweck, C. S. (1988). Goals: An approach to motivation and achievement. Journal of Personality and Social Psychology, 54 (1), 5–12.

[42] Elliot, A., and Church, M. (1997). A hierarchical model of approach and avoidance achievement motivation. J. Person. Soc. Psychol, 72 (1), 218–232.

[43] Nolen, S. B. (1988). Reasons for Studying: Motivational Orientations and Study Strategies. Cognition and Instruction, 5 (4), 269–287.

[44] McGrath, E. P., & Repetti, R. L. (2000). Mothers' and fathers' attitudes toward their children's academic performance and children's perceptions of their academic competence. Journal of Youth and Adolescence, 29 (6), 713–723.

[45] Akey, Theresa. (2006). School Context, Student Attitudes and Behavior, and Academic Achievement: An Exploratory Analysis. Mdrc.

[46] Stipek, D., Recchia, S., McClintic, S., & Lewis, M. (1992). Self-Evaluation in Young Children. Monographs of the Society for Research in Child Development, 57 (1), 39 – 59.

[47] Siegel, A., & Burton, R.V. (1999). Effects of baby walkers on motor and mental development in human infants. Journal of developmental and behavioral pediatrics : JDBP, 20 (5), 355-61.

[48] Gutman, L. M. (2006). How student and parent goal orientations and classroom goal structures influence the math achievement of African Americans during the high school transition. Contemporary Educational Psychology, 31 (1), 44-63.

[49] Blackwell, L. S., Trzesniewski, K. H., & Dweck, C. S. (2007). Implicit Theories of Intelligence Predict Achievement Across an Adolescent Transition: A Longitudinal Study and an Intervention. Child Development, 78 (1), 246–263.

[50] Aronson, J., Lustina, M. J., Good, C., Keough, K., Steele, C. M., & Brown, J. (1999). When white men can't do math: Necessary and sufficient factors in stereotype threat. Journal of Experimental Social Psychology, 35 (1), 29–46.

[51] Schneider, W., Bjorklund, D. F., & Maier-Bruckner, W. (1996). The effects of expertise and IQ on children's memory: When knowledge is, and when it is not enough. International Journal of Behavioral Development, 19 (4), 773–796.

[52] Schneider, W.. (1993). Domain-specific knowledge and memory performance in children. Educ Psychol Rev, 5, 257–273.

[53] Convention on the Rights of the Child Adopted and opened for signature, ratification and accession by General Assembly resolution 44/25 of 20 November 1989 entry into force 2 September 1990, in accordance with article 49. Retrieved: https://www.ohchr.org/en/professionalinterest/pages/crc.aspx

[54] Barnett, L. A. (1990). Developmental Benefits of Play for Children. Journal of Leisure Research, 22 (2), 138–153.

[55] Rubin, Kenneth & Bukowski, William & Parker, Jeffrey & Bowker, Julie. (2008). Peer Interactions, Relationships, and Groups. In book: Child and Adolescent Development: An Advanced Course (pp.141-180). Wiley.

[56] Brown, F. and Webb, S. (2005). Children without play. Journal of Education, 35 (1), 139-158.

[57] Walden, T., Lemerise, E., & Smith, M. C.. (1999). Friendship and Popularity in Preschool Classrooms. Early Education & Development, 10 (3), 351–371.

[58] Terman, L. M. (1954). The discovery and encouragement of exceptional talent. American Psychologist, 9(6), 221–230.

[59] Véronneau, M-H., Vitaro, F., Pedersen, S., & Tremblay, R. E. (2008). Do peers contribute to the likelihood of secondary school graduation among disadvantaged boys?. Journal of Educational Psychology, 100 (2), 429–442.

[60] Ladd, Gary & Troop-Gordon, Wendy. (2003). The Role of Chronic Peer Difficulties in the Development of Children's Psychological Adjustment Problems. Child development, 74 (5), 1344-1367.

[61] Wentzel, Kathryn. (2003). Sociometric Status and Adjustment in Middle School: A Longitudinal Study. Journal of Early Adolescence, 23 (1), 5-28.

[62] Brendgen, M., Vitaro, F., & Bukowski, W. M. (1998). Affiliation with Delinquent Friends. The Journal of Early Adolescence, 18 (3), 244–265.

[63] Fordham, S., & Ogbu, J. U. (1986). Black students' school success: Coping with the "burden of 'acting white'". Urban Review, 18 (3), 176–206.

[64] Kinney, D. A. (1993). From Nerds to Normals: The Recovery of Identity among Adolescents from Middle School to High School. Sociology of Education, 66(1), 21-40.

[65] Vialle, Wilma & Heaven, Patrick & Ciarrochi, Joseph. (2007). On Being Gifted, but Sad and Misunderstood: Social, emotional, and academic outcomes of gifted students in the Wollongong Youth Study. Educational Research and Evaluation, 13 (6), 569-586.

[66] Maeda, R. (1999). "Ijime": An Exploratory Study of a Collective Form of Bullying among Japanese Students. Paper presented at the Biennial Meeting of the Society for Research in Child Development.

[67] Barker, E. D., Arseneault, L., Brendgen, M., Fontaine, N., & Maughan, B. (2008). Joint development of bullying and victimization in adolescence: Relations to delinquency and selfharm. Journal of the American Academy of Child and Adolescent Psychiatry, 47 (9), 1030–1038.

[68] Black, J. K. (1981). Are Young Children Really Egocentric? Young Children, 36 (6), 51–55.

[69] Yarrow, M. R., and Zahn-Waxler, C. (1977). The Emergence and Functions of Prosocial Behaviors in Young Children. In Readings in Child Development and Relationships, ed. R. Smart and M. Smart. New York: Macmillan.

[70] Riva F, Triscoli C, Lamm C, Carnaghi A and Silani G (2016) Emotional Egocentricity Bias Across the Life-Span. Front. Aging Neurosci, 8, 74.

[71] Royzman, E. B., Cassidy, K. W., & Baron, J. (2003). "I know, you know": Epistemic egocentrism in children and adults. Review of General Psychology, 7 (1), 38–65.

[72] Menesini, E., Sanchez, V., Fonzi, A., Ortega, R., Costabile, A., & Lo Feudo, G. (2003). Moral emotions and bullying: A cross-national comparison of differences between bullies, victims and outsiders. Aggressive Behavior, 29 (6), 515–530.

[73] Guy A, Lee K and Wolke D. (2019). Comparisons Between Adolescent Bullies, Victims, and Bully-Victims on Perceived Popularity, Social Impact, and Social Preference. Front. Psychiatry, 10:868.

[74] Olweus, Dan. (1994). Bullying at School: Basic Facts and Effects of a School Based Intervention Program. Journal of child psychology and psychiatry, and allied disciplines, 35 (7), 1171 –1190.

[75] Dijkstra, Jan & Lindenberg, Siegwart & Veenstra, René. (2008). Beyond the Class Norm: Bullying Behavior of Popular Adolescents and its Relation to Peer Acceptance and Rejection. Journal of abnormal child psychology, 36 (8), 1289 –1299.

[76] Saxe, R., & Kanwisher, N. (2003). People thinking about thinking people: The role of the temporoparietal junction in "theory of mind". NeuroImage, 19 (4), 1835–1842.

[77] Kochanska, G., & Aksan, N. (2006). Children's conscience and self-regulation. Journal of Personality, 74 (6), 1587–1617.

[78] Morris, A. S., Silk, J. S., Steinberg, L., Myers, S. S., & Robinson, L. R. (2007). The Role of the Family Context in the Development of Emotion Regulation. Social Development, 16 (2), 361–388.

[79] Buckholdt, K. E., Kitzmann, K. M., & Cohen, R. (2014). Parent emotion coaching buffers the psychological effects of poor peer relations in the classroom. Journal of Social and Personal Relationships, 33 (1), 23–41.

#5

[80] Deary, I. J., Strand, S., Smith, P., & Fernandes, C. (2007). Intelligence and educational achievement. Intelligence, 35 (1), 13–21.

[81] K. Warner Schaie. (1997). Intellectual Development in Adulthood: The Seattle Longitudinal Study. Ageing & Society, Vol. 17(2), 227 – 246.

[82] Gottfredson, L., & Saklofske, D. H. (2009). Intelligence: Foundations and issues in assessment. Canadian Psychology/Psychologie canadienne, 50(3), 183–195.

[83] Ericsson, K. A., & Kintsch, W. (1995). Long-term working memory. Psychological Review, 102 (2), 211–245.

[84] Carson, John. (2020). Quantification – Affordances and Limits. Scholarly Assessment Reports. 2 (1), 8.

[85] Ferrero, M., Vadillo, M. A., & León, S. P. (2021). A valid evaluation of the theory of multiple intelligences is not yet possible: Problems of methodological quality for intervention studies. Intelligence, 88, 101566.

[86] Davis, Katie & Christodoulou, Joanna & Seider, Scott & Gardner, Howard. (2011). The Theory of Multiple Intelligences. In book: Cambridge Handbook of Intelligence (pp. 485-503). Chapter: 24. Cambridge University Press. Editors: R.J. Sternberg, S.B. Kaufman.

[87] Halpern, D. F., & Dunn, D. S. (2021). Critical Thinking: A Model of Intelligence for Solving Real-World Problems. Journal of Intelligence, 9(2), 22.

[88] Harding, Colleen. (2006). Using the Multiple Intelligences as a learning intervention: a model for coaching and mentoring. International Journal of Evidence Based Coaching and Mentoring, 4 (2), 19 – 42.

[89] Geake, John. (2008). Neuromythologies in Education. Educational Research. 50 (2), 123-133.

[90] Naomi Breslau, Howard D. Chilcoat, Ezra S. Susser, Thomas Matte, Kung-Yee Liang, Edward L. Peterson. (2001). Stability and Change in Children's Intelligence Quotient Scores: A Comparison of Two Socioeconomically Disparate Communities. American Journal of Epidemiology, 154 (8), 711–717.

[91] M. P. Honzik, J. W. Macfarlane & L. Allen. (1948). The Stability of Mental Test Performance Between two and Eighteen Years. The Journal of Experimental Education, 17(2), 309-324.

[92] Mansukoski, L., Hogervorst, E., Fúrlan, L., Galvez-Sobral, J. A., Brooke-Wavell, K., & Bogin, B. (2019). Instability in longitudinal childhood IQ scores of Guatemalan high SES individuals born between 1941-1953. PloS one. 14(4).

[93] Sternberg, R. J. (2006). The nature of creativity. Creativity Research Journal, 18 (1), 87–98.

#6
[94] Dodge, K. A., Greenberg, M. T., Malone, P. S., & Conduct Problems Prevention Research Group. (2008). Testing an idealized dynamic cascade model of the development of serious violence in adolescence. Child Development, 79, 1907–1927.

[95] Finn, J. D. (1989). Withdrawing From School. Review of Educational Research, 59 (2), 117–142.

[96] Lippman, L., Burns, S., and McArthur, E. (1996). Urban schools: The challenge of location and poverty. (Rep. No. NCES 96-184). Washington, DC: U.S. Department of Education. 18- 82.

[97] Sameroff AJ, Seifer R, Baldwin A, Baldwin C. (1993). Stability of intelligence from preschool to adolescence: the influence of social and family risk factors. Child Dev, 64(1), 80-97.

[98] Bogenschneider, K. (1997). Parental involvement in adolescent schooling: A proximal process with transcontextual validity. Journal of Marriage and the Family, 59 (3), 718–733.

[99] Klineberg, O. (1963). Negro–white differences in intelligence test performance: A new look at an old problem. American Psychologist, 18 (4), 198–203.

[100] Berkman, DS, Lescano, AG, Gilman, RH, Lopez, S & Black, MM. (2002) Effects of stunting, diarrhoeal disease and parasitic infection during infancy on cognition in late childhood: A follow-up study. Lancet 359, 364 -371.

[101] Warsito Oktarina,Khomsan Ali,Hernawati Neti,Anwar Faisal. (2012). Relationship between nutritional status, psychosocial stimulation, and cognitive development in preschool children in Indonesia. Nutr Res Pract. 6(5), 451-457.

[102] Ensminger, M. E., & Slusarcick, A. L. (1992). Paths to high school graduation or dropout: A longitudinal study of a first-grade cohort. Sociology of Education, 65 (2), 95–113.

[103] Rumberger, R. W. (1995). Dropping out of middle school: A multilevel analysis of students and schools. American Educational Research Journal, 32 (3), 583–625.

[104] DeRidder, L. M. (1991). How Suspension and Expulsion Contribute to Dropping Out. Education Digest, 56 (6), 44-50.

[105] Franklin, C., & Streeter, C. L. (1995). Assessment of middle class youth at-risk to dropout: School, psychological and family correlates. Children and Youth Services Review, 17 (3), 433–448.

[106] Steinberg, L., & Dornbusch, S. M. (1991). Negative correlates of part-time employment during adolescence: Replication and elaboration. Developmental Psychology, 27 (2), 304–313.

[107] Sum, Andrew & Khatiwada, Ishwar & McLaughlin, Joseph. (2009). The consequences of dropping out of high school: Joblessness and Jailing for High School Dropouts and the High Cost for Taxpayers. Center for Labor Market Studies Publications.

[108] Ceci, S. J., & Williams, W. M. (1997). Schooling, intelligence, and income. American Psychologist, 52 (10), 1051–1058.

[109] Kaplan, D. S., Damphousse, K. R., & Kaplan, H. B. (1994). Mental health implications of not graduating from high school. Journal of Experimental Education, 62 (2), 105–123.

[110] Ladd, G. W., Buhs, E. S., & Seid, M. (2000). Children's initial sentiments about kindergarten: Is school liking an antecedent of early classroom participation and achievement?. Merrill-Palmer Quarterly, 46 (2), 255–279.

[111] Gottlieb, G., & Blair, C. (2004). How early experience matters in intellectual development in the case of poverty. Prevention Science, 5 (4), 245–252.

[112] Drotar, D., Robinson, J., Jeavons, L., & Kirchner, H. L. (2008). A randomized, controlled evaluation of early intervention: the Born to Learn curriculum. Child: Care, Health, and Development, 35 (5), 643–649.

[113] Hirsh-Pasek, K. (1991). Pressure or challenge in preschool? How academic environments affect children. In L. Rescorla, M. C. Hyson, & K. Hirsh-Pasek (Eds.), Academic instruction in early childhood: Challenge or pressure? (pp. 39–46). Jossey-Bass.

[114] Nelson, G., Westhues, A., & MacLeod, J. (2003). A Meta-Analysis of Longitudinal Research on Preschool Prevention Programs for Children. Prevention & Treatment, 6 (1), 31.

<u>#7</u>

[115] Kiesner, J., Dishion, T. J., & Poulin, F. (2001). A reinforcement model of conduct problems in children and adolescents: Advances in theory and intervention. In J. Hill & B. Maughan (Eds.), Conduct disorders in childhood and adolescence (Pg. 264–291). Cambridge University Press.

[116] Snyder, J., Edwards, P., McGraw, K., Kilgore, K., & Holton, A. (1994). Escalation and reinforcement in mother-child conflict: Social processes associated with the development of physical aggression. Development and Psychopathology, 6 (2), 305–321.

[117] Snyder, J., Horsch, E., & Childs, J. (1997). Peer relationships of young children: Affiliative choices and the shaping of aggressive behavior. Journal of Clinical Child Psychology, 26 (2), 145–156.

[118] Boxer, P., Huesmann, L. R., Bushman, B. J., Moceri, D., & O'Brien, M. (2009). The role of violent media preference in cumulative developmental risk for violence and general aggression. Journal of Youth and Adolescence, 38 (3), 417–428.

<u>#8</u>

[119] Tsang, Jo-Ann. (2002). Moral rationalization and the integration of situational factors and psychological processes in immoral behavior. *Review of General Psychology, 6* (1), 25-50.

[120] Garrigan, B., Adlam, A. L.R., & Langdon, P. E. (2018). Moral decision-making and moral development: Toward an integrative framework. Developmental Review, 49, 80–100.

[121] Ma H. K. (2013). The moral development of the child: an integrated model. Frontiers in public health, 1, 57.

[122] Ellemers, N., van der Toorn, J., Paunov, Y., & van Leeuwen, T. (2019). The psychology of morality: A review and analysis of empirical studies published from 1940 through 2017. Personality and Social Psychology Review, 23 (4), 332–366.

[123] Cohen, T.R. & Morse, L. (2014). Moral character: What it is and what it does. In A.P. Brief & B.M. Staw (eds.). Research in Organizational Behavior. Elsevier.

[124] Haidt, Jonathan. (2001). The Emotional Dog and Its Rational Tail: A Social Intuitionist Approach to Moral Judgment. Psychological review, 108, 814-34.

[125] Colby, A., Kohlberg, L., Gibbs, J., & Lieberman, M. (1983). A longitudinal study of moral judgment. Monographs of the Society for Research in Child Development, 48 (1–2, Serial No. 200).

[126] Koenig, A. L., Cicchetti, D., & Rogosch, F. A. (2004). Moral development: The association between maltreatment and young children's prosocial behaviors and moral transgressions. Social Development, 13(1), 87–106.

[127] Klimes-Dougan, Bonnie & Kistner, Janet. (1990). Physically Abused Preschoolers' Responses to Peers' Distress. Developmental Psychology, 26 (4), 599-602.

[128] Kaufman, Joan & Cicchetti, Dante. (1989). Effects of Maltreatment on School-Age Children's Socioemotional Development: Assessments in a Day-Camp Setting. Developmental Psychology, 25 (4), 516-524.

[129] Straker, G., & Jacobson, R. S. (1981). Aggression, emotional maladjustment, and empathy in the abused child. Developmental Psychology, 17(6), 762–765.

[130] McColgan, E. B., Rest, J. R., & Pruitt, D. B. (1983). Moral judgment and antisocial behavior in early adolescence. Journal of Applied Developmental Psychology, 4(2), 189–199.

[131] Steinberg, L. (2007). Risk Taking in Adolescence. Current Directions in Psychological Science, 16(2), 55–59.

[132] Giedd, J. N. (2004). Structural magnetic resonance imaging of the adolescent brain. Annals of the New York Academic of Sciences, 1021, 77–85.

[133] Bjork, J. M., Knutson, B., Fong, G. W., Caggiano, D. M., Bennett, S. M., & Hommer, D. W. (2004). Incentive-elicited brain activation in adolescents: Similarities and differences from young adults. The Journal of Neuroscience, 24 (8), 1793–1802.

[134] Hansen, E. B., & Breivik, G. (2001). Sensation seeking as a predictor of positive and negative risk behaviour among adolescents. Personality and Individual Differences, 30 (4), 627–640.

[135] Merline, A. C., O'Malley, P. M., Schulenberg, J. E., Bachman, J. G., & Johnston, L. D. (2004). Substance use among adults 35 years of age: prevalence, adulthood predictors, and impact of adolescent substance use. American journal of public health, 94 (1), 96–102.

[136] Walker, L. J., Hennig, K. H., & Krettenauer, T. (2000). Parent and Peer Contexts for Children's Moral Reasoning Development. Child Development, 71(4), 1033–1048.

[137] Prehn, K., Korczykowski, M., Rao, H., Fang, Z., Detre, J. A., & Robertson, D. C. (2015). Neural correlates of post-conventional moral reasoning: a voxel-based morphometry study. PloS one, 10(6), e0122914.

#9

[138] Tillman CJ, Gonzalez K, Whitman MV, Crawford WS and Hood AC. (2018). A Multi-Functional View of Moral Disengagement: Exploring the Effects of Learning the Consequences. Front. Psychol, 8, 2286.

[139] Bandura, A. (2002). Selective moral disengagement in the exercise of moral agency. J. Moral Educ. 31 (2), 101–119.

[140] Bandura, A., Barbaranelli, C., Caprara, G. V., and Pastorelli, C. (1996). Mechanisms of moral disengagement in the exercise of moral agency. J. Pers. Soc. Psychol. 71 (2), 364–374.

[141] Sznitman SR, Kolobov T, Bogt TT, Kuntsche E, Walsh SD, Boniel-Nissim M, Harel-Fisch Y. (2013). Exploring substance use normalization among adolescents: a multilevel study in 35 countries. Soc Sci Med, 97, 143-51.

[142] Beres, Nicole & Frommel, Julian & Reid, Elizabeth & Mandryk, Regan & Klarkowski, Madison. (2021). Don't You Know That You're Toxic: Normalization of Toxicity in Online Gaming. CHI '21: CHI Conference on Human Factors in Computing Systems, 1-15.

[143] Diener, E., Lusk, R., DeFour, D., & Flax, R. (1980). Deindividuation: Effects of group size, density, number of observers, and group member similarity on self-consciousness and disinhibited behavior. Journal of Personality and Social Psychology, 39(3), 449–459.

[144] Zimmerman, A. G., & Ybarra, G. J. (2016). Online aggression: The influences of anonymity and social modeling. Psychology of Popular Media Culture, 5(2), 181-193.

#10

[145] Minnes, S., Singer, L. T., Kirchner, H. L., Short, E., Lewis, B., Satayathum, S., & Queh, D. (2010). The effects of prenatal cocaine exposure on problem behavior in children 4-10 years. Neurotoxicology and teratology, 32(4), 443–451.

[146] Twomey, J., LaGasse, L., Derauf, C., Newman, E., Shah, R., Smith, L., Arria, A., Huestis, M., DellaGrotta, S., Roberts, M., Dansereau, L., Neal, C., & Lester, B. (2013). Prenatal methamphetamine exposure, home environment, and primary caregiver risk factors predict child behavioral problems at 5 years. The American journal of orthopsychiatry, 83(1), 64–72.

[147] Sen, Bisakha & Swaminathan, Shailender. (2008). Maternal prenatal substance use and behavior problems among children in the U.S. The journal of mental health policy and economics, 10 (4), 189-206.

[148] Mattson, S. N., Crocker, N., & Nguyen, T. T. (2011). Fetal alcohol spectrum disorders: neuropsychological and behavioral features. Neuropsychology review, 21 (2), 81–101.

[149] Mattson, S. N., Riley, E. P., Gramling, L., Delis, D. C., & Jones, K. L. (1998). Neuropsychological comparison of alcohol-exposed children with or without physical features of fetal alcohol syndrome. Neuropsychology, 12 (1), 146–153.

[150] Goldschmidt, L., Richardson, G. A., Stoffer, D. S., Geva, D., & Day, N. L. (1996). Prenatal alcohol exposure and academic achievement at age six: A nonlinear fit. Alcoholism: Clinical and Experimental Research, 20 (4), 763–770.

[151] Schonfeld, Amy & Mattson, Sarah & Riley, Edward. (2005). Moral maturity and delinquency after prenatal alcohol exposure. Journal of studies on alcohol, 66 (4), 545-54.

[152] D. K., Conry, J., & Loock, C. A. (1999). Identifying fetal alcohol syndrome among youth in the criminal justice system. Journal of Developmental and Behavioral Pediatrics, 20 (5), 370–372.

[153] Baer, J. S., Sampson, P. D., Barr, H. M., Connor, P. D., & Streissguth, A. P. (2003). A 21-Year Longitudinal Analysis of the Effects of Prenatal Alcohol Exposure on Young Adult Drinking. Obstetrical & Gynecological Survey, 58 (10), 638–639.

[154] O'Connor, M. J., Portnoff, L. C., Lebsack-Coleman, M., & Dipple, K. M. (2019). Suicide risk in adolescents with fetal alcohol spectrum disorders. Birth defects research, 111 (12), 822–828.

[155] Cicero, T. J. (1994). Effects of paternal exposure to alcohol on offspring development. Alcohol Health & Research World, 18(1), 37–41.

[156] Parker, S. E., Collett, B. R., Speltz, M. L., & Werler, M. M. (2016). Prenatal smoking and childhood behavior problems: is the association mediated by birth weight?. Journal of developmental origins of health and disease, 7(3), 273–281.

[157] Habek, Dubravko & Čerkez Habek, Jasna & Ivanisevic, Marina & Djelmis, Josip. (2002). Fetal Tobacco Syndrome and Perinatal Outcome. Fetal diagnosis and therapy, 17 (6), 367-71.

[158] Reeves, Shane & Bernstein, Ira. (2008). Effects of maternal tobacco-smoke exposure on fetal growth and neonatal size. Expert review of obstetrics & gynecology, 3 (6), 719-730.

[159] Hartkopf, Julia & Schleger, Franziska & Keune - Née Muenssinger, Jana & Wiechers, Cornelia & Pauluschke-Fröhlich, Jan & Weiss, Magdalene & Conzelmann, Annette & Sara Yvonne, Brucker & Preissl, Hubert & Kiefer-Schmidt, Isabelle. (2018). Impact of Intrauterine Growth Restriction on Cognitive and Motor Development at 2 Years of Age. Frontiers in Physiology, 9, 1278.

[160] Roigé-Castellví, J., Murphy, M. M., Voltas, N., Solé-Navais, P., Cavallé-Busquets, P., Fernández-Ballart, J., Canals-Sans, J. (2021). A Prospective Study of Maternal Exposure to Smoking during Pregnancy and Behavioral Development in the Child. Journal of Child and Family Studies, 30 (9), 2204–2214.

[161] Gatzke-Kopp, L., Willoughby, M. T., Warkentien, S., Petrie, D., Mills-Koonce, R., & Blair, C. (2020). Association between environmental tobacco smoke exposure across the first four years of life and manifestation of externalizing behavior problems in school-aged children. Journal of child psychology and psychiatry, and allied disciplines, 61 (11), 1243–1252.

[162] Anderko, L., Braun, J., & Auinger, P. (2010). Contribution of tobacco smoke exposure to learning disabilities. Journal of obstetric, gynecologic, and neonatal nursing: JOGNN, 39 (1), 111–117.

[163] Quinn, P. D., Rickert, M. E., Weibull, C. E., Johansson, A., Lichtenstein, P., Almqvist, C., Larsson, H., Iliadou, A. N., & D'Onofrio, B. M. (2017). Association Between Maternal Smoking During Pregnancy and Severe Mental Illness in Offspring. JAMA psychiatry, 74 (6), 589–596.

[164] Van den Bergh, B. R., & Marcoen, A. (2004). High antenatal maternal anxiety is related to ADHD symptoms, externalizing problems, and anxiety in 8- and 9-year-olds. Child development, 75(4), 1085–1097.

[165] Bland VJ, Lambie I, Best C. (2018). Does childhood neglect contribute to violent behavior in adulthood? A review of possible links. Clinical Psychology Review, 60, 126-135.

[166] Lamborn, S. D., Mounts, N. S., Steinberg, L., & Dornbusch, S. M. (1991). Patterns of competence and adjustment among adolescents from authoritative, authoritarian, indulgent, and neglectful families. Child Development, 62 (5), 1049–1065.

[167] Burt, C. H., Simons, R. L., & Simons, L. G. (2006). A longitudinal test of the effects of parenting and the stability of selfcontrol: Negative evidence for the general theory of crime. Criminology, 44 (2), 353-396.

[168] Burt, Callie & Simons, Ronald. (2013). Self-Control, Thrill Seeking, and Crime Motivation Matters. Criminal Justice and Behavior, 40 (11), 1326-1348.

[169] Young, R., Lennie, S., & Minnis, H. (2011). Children's perceptions of parental emotional neglect and control and psychopathology. Journal of child psychology and psychiatry, and allied disciplines, 52 (8), 889–897.

[170] Baumrind, D. (1991). The Influence of Parenting Style on Adolescent Competence and Substance Use. The Journal of Early Adolescence, 11 (1), 56–95.

[171] Hosokawa, R., & Katsura, T. (2018). Role of Parenting Style in Children's Behavioral Problems through the Transition from Preschool to Elementary School According to Gender in Japan. International journal of environmental research and public health, 16 (1), 21.

[172] Berzonsky, Michael. (2004). Identity Style, Parental Authority, and Identity Commitment. Journal of Youth and Adolescence, 33 (3), 213-220.

[173] Angela Ramsey, P. J. Watson, Michael D. Biderman & Amy L. Reeves. (1996). Self-Reported Narcissism and Perceived Parental Permissiveness and Authoritarianism. The Journal of Genetic Psychology, 157 (2), 227-238.

[174] Oindrilla Ghosh. (2021). Effect of Authoritarian Parenting Style on Psychopathology. International Journal of Humanities and Social Science Invention, 10 (9) (II), 37-45.

[175] Weiss, B., Dodge, K. A., Bates, J. E., & Pettit, G. S. (1992). Some consequences of early harsh discipline: child aggression and a maladaptive social information processing style. Child development, 63 (6), 1321–1335.

[176] Chang, L., Schwartz, D., Dodge, K. A., & McBride-Chang, C. (2003). Harsh Parenting in Relation to Child Emotion Regulation and Aggression. Journal of Family Psychology, 17 (4), 598–606.

[177] Conger, R. D., Neppl, T., Kim, K. J., & Scaramella, L. (2003). Angry and aggressive behavior across three generations: A prospective, longitudinal study of parents and children. Journal of Abnormal Child Psychology, 31 (2), 143–160.

[178] O'Connor, T. G., Deater-Deckard, K., Fulker, D., Rutter, M., & Plomin, R. (1998). Genotype–environment correlations in late childhood and early adolescence: Antisocial behavioral problems and coercive parenting. Developmental Psychology, 34(5), 970–981.

[179] Larsson, H., Viding, E., Rijsdijk, F. V., & Plomin, R. (2008). Relationships between parental negativity and childhood antisocial behavior over time: A bidirectional effects model in a longitudinal genetically informative design. Journal of Abnormal Child Psychology. 36 (5), 633–645.

[180] Smith, J. D., Dishion, T. J., Shaw, D. S., Wilson, M. N., Winter, C. C., & Patterson, G. R. (2014). Coercive family process and early-onset conduct problems from age 2 to school entry. Development and psychopathology, 26 (4 Pt 1), 917–932.

[181] P. Nieman, S. Shea. (2004). Effective discipline for children. Paediatrics & child health, 9(1), 37–50.

[182] Lawrence J. Walker & Karl H. Hennig. (1999). Parenting Style and the Development of Moral Reasoning. Journal of Moral Education, 28(3), 359-374.

[183] Lansford, J. E., Miller-Johnson, S., Berlin, L. J., Dodge, K. A., Bates, J. E., & Pettit, G. S. (2007). Early physical abuse and later violent delinquency: A prospective longitudinal study. Child Maltreatment, 12 (3), 233–245.

[184] Lansford, J. E., Dodge, K. A., Pettit, G. S., Bates, J. E., Crozier, J., & Kaplow, J. (2002). A 12-Year Prospective Study of the Long-term Effects of Early Child Physical Maltreatment on Psychological, Behavioral, and Academic Problems in Adolescence. Archives of Pediatrics & Adolescent Medicine, 156(8), 824 -830.

[185] Weiler, B. L., & Widom, C. S. (1996). Psychopathy and violent behaviour in abused and neglected young adults. Criminal Behaviour and Mental Health, 6(3), 253–271.

[186] Krupić, D., Ručević, S., & Vučković, S. (2020). From parental personality over parental styles to children psychopathic tendencies. Current Psychology.

[187] Moffitt, T. E. (1993). Adolescence-limited and life-course-persistent antisocial behavior: A developmental taxonomy. Psychological Review, 100(4), 674–701.

#11

[188] Flouri, E., & Midouhas, E. (2017). Environmental adversity and children's early trajectories of problem behavior: The role of harsh parental discipline. Journal of family psychology. Journal of the Division of Family Psychology of the American Psychological Association (Division 43), 31(2), 234–243.

[189] Conger, R. D., Conger, K. J., Elder, G. H., Lorenz, F. O., Simons, R. L., & Whitbeck, L. B. (1992). A family process model of economic hardship and adjustment of early adolescent boys. Child Development, 63(3), 526–541.

[190] Owen, Margaret & Cox, Martha. (1997). Marital conflict and the development of infant–parent attachment relationship. Journal of Family Psychology, 11 (2), 152-164.

[191] Wallerstein, J. S. (1991). The Long-Term Effects of Divorce on Children: A Review. Journal of the American Academy of Child & Adolescent Psychiatry, 30(3), 349–360.

[192] Poortman, Anne-Rigt. (2005). How Work Affects Divorce : The Mediating Role of Financial and Time Pressures. Journal of Family Issues, 26 (2), 168 - 195.

[193] Ilies, R., Schwind, K. M., Wagner, D. T., Johnson, M. D., DeRue, D. S., & Ilgen, D. R. (2007). When can employees have a family life? The effects of daily workload and affect on work-family conflict and social behaviors at home. The Journal of applied psychology, 92 (5), 1368–1379.

[194] Whiteside-Mansell, L., Bradley, R. H., Casey, P. H., Fussell, J. J., & Conners-Burrow, N. A. (2009). Triple risk: do difficult temperament and family conflict increase the likelihood of behavioral maladjustment in children born low birth weight and preterm?. Journal of pediatric psychology, 34 (4), 396–405.

[195] Campbell, S. B., Shaw, D. S., & Gilliom, M. (2000). Early externalizing behavior problems: toddlers and preschoolers at risk for later maladjustment Development and psychopathology, 12 (3), 467–488.

#12

[196] Kupersmidt JB, Griesler PC, DeRosier ME, Patterson CJ, Davis PW. (1995). Childhood aggression and peer relations in the context of family and neighborhood factors. Child Development, 66 (2), 360–375.

[197] Durant, R. H., Pendergrast, R. A., & Cadenhead, C. (1994). Exposure to violence and victimization and fighting behavior by urban black adolescents. The Journal of adolescent health: official publication of the Society for Adolescent Medicine, 15 (4), 311–318.

[198] Colder, C. R., Mott, J., Levy, S., & Flay, B. (2000). The relation of perceived neighborhood danger to childhood aggression: a test of mediating mechanisms. American journal of community psychology, 28(1), 83–103.

[199] Guerra, N. G., Huesmann, L. R., Tolan, P. H., Van Acker, R., & Eron, L. D. (1995). Stressful events and individual beliefs as correlates of economic disadvantage and aggression among urban children. Journal of Consulting and Clinical Psychology, 63 (4), 518–528.

[200] Li, Y., Wright, M.F. (2014). Adolescents' Social Status Goals: Relationships to Social Status Insecurity, Aggression, and Prosocial Behavior. J Youth Adolescence, 43 (1), 146–160.

[201] Wright MF, Wachs S and Huang Z (2021) Adolescents' Popularity-Motivated Aggression and Prosocial Behaviors: The Roles of Callous-Unemotional Traits and Social Status Insecurity. Front. Psychol, 12:606865.

[202] Sijtsema, J.J., Lindenberg, S.M., Ojanen, T.J. et al. (2020). Direct Aggression and the Balance between Status and Affection Goals in Adolescence. J Youth Adolescence, 49 (7), 1481–1491.

[203] Zahn-Waxler, C., Friedman, R. J., Cole, P. M., Mizuta, I., & Himura, N. (1996). Japanese and United States preschool children's responses to conflict and distress. Child Development, 67 (5), 2462–2477.

[204] Rowell Huesmann, L. (1988). An information processing model for the development of aggression. Aggr. Behav, 14 (1), 13-24.

[205] Margolin G, Gordis E.B. (2000). The effects of family and community violence on children. Annual Review of Psychology, 51(1), 445–479.

[206] Kellam, S. G., Ling, X., Merisca, R., Brown, C. H., & Ialongo, N. (1998). The effect of the level of aggression in the first grade classroom on the course and malleability of aggressive behavior into middle school. Development and psychopathology, 10 (2), 165–185.

[207] Espelage, D. L., Holt, M. K., & Henkel, R. R. (2003). Examination of peer-group contextual effects on aggression during early adolescence. Child development, 74(1), 205–220.

[208] Thomas, D. E., Bierman, K. L., Powers, C. J., & Conduct Problems Prevention Research Group (2011). The influence of classroom aggression and classroom climate on aggressive-disruptive behavior. Child development, 82 (3), 751–757.

[209] Malik, S., Fatima, S. (2015). Causes of Students' Aggressive Behavior at Secondary School Level. Journal of Literature, Languages and Linguistics, 11, 49-65.

[210] Estévez E, Inglés CJ, Martínez-Monteagudo MC. (2013). School Aggression: Effects of Classroom Environment, Attitude to Authority and Social Reputation Among Peers. European Journal of Investigation in Health, Psychology and Education, 3(1), 15-28.

[211] Emler, N., & Reicher, S. (2005). Delinquency: Cause or Consequence of Social Exclusion?. In D. Abrams, M. A. Hogg, & J. M. Marques (Eds.). The social psychology of inclusion and exclusion (Pg 211–241). Psychology Press.

[212] Hamre, B. K., & Pianta, R. C. (2001). Early teacher–child relationships and the trajectory of children's school outcomes through eighth grade. Child Development, 72 (2), 625–638.

[213] DeRosier, M. E., Kupersmidt, J. B., & Patterson, C. J. (1994). Children's academic and behavioral adjustment as a function of the chronicity and proximity of peer rejection. Child development, 65 (6), 1799–1813.

[214] Steenbergen-Hu, S., Makel, M. C., & Olszewski-Kubilius, P. (2016). What One Hundred Years of Research Says About the Effects of Ability Grouping and Acceleration on K–12 Students' Academic Achievement: Findings of Two Second-Order Meta-Analyses. Review of Educational Research, 86 (4), 849–899.

[215] Belfi, Barbara & Goos, Mieke & Fraine, Bieke & Damme, Jan. (2011). The effect of class composition by gender and ability on secondary school students' school well-being and academic self-concept: A literature review. Educational Research Review, 7 (1), 62-74.

[216] Papachristou, E., Flouri, E., Joshi, H., Midouhas, E., & Lewis, G. (2022). Ability-grouping and problem behavior trajectories in childhood and adolescence: Results from a U.K. population-based sample. Child Development, 93 (2), 341– 358.

[217] Kozina, A. (2015). Aggression in primary schools: The predictive power of the school and home environment. Educational Studies, 41(1-2), 109–121.

[218] Thomas W. Miller. (2008). School-Related Violence and Primary Prevention. SpringerLink.

[219] Thunfors, Peter & Cornell, Dewey. (2008). The Popularity of Middle School Bullies. Journal of School Violence, 7(1), 65-82.

<u>#13</u>

[220] Hofstra, M. B., Van der Ende, J., & Verhulst, F. C. (2000). Continuity and change of psychopathology from childhood into adulthood: a 14-year follow-up study. Journal of the American Academy of Child and Adolescent Psychiatry, 39 (7), 850–858.

[221] Windle M. (1991). The difficult temperament in adolescence: associations with substance use, family support, and problem behaviors. Journal of clinical psychology, 47 (2), 310–315.

[222] Caspi, A. (2000). The child is father of the man: personality continuities from childhood to adulthood. Journal of personality and social psychology, 78 (1), 158-172.

[223] Morizot, J., & Le Blanc, M. (2003). Continuity and change in personality traits from adolescence to midlife: a 25-year longitudinal study comparing representative and adjudicated men. Journal of personality, 71 (5), 705–755.

[224] Borkenau, P., Riemann, R., Angleitner, A., & Spinath, F. M. (2001). Genetic and environmental influences on observed personality: evidence from the German Observational Study of Adult Twins. Journal of personality and social psychology, 80 (4), 655–668.

[225] Robins, Richard & Caspi, Avshalom & Moffitt, Terrie. (2000). Two personalities, one relationship: Both partners' personality traits shape the quality of their relationship. Journal of personality and social psychology, 79 (2), 251-259.

[226] Johnson, V., & Pandina, R. J. (1991). Effects of the Family Environment on Adolescent Substance Use, Delinquency, and Coping Styles. The American Journal of Drug and Alcohol Abuse, 17 (1), 71–88.

[227] Thomas, R., & Zimmer-Gembeck, M. J. (2007). Behavioral Outcomes of Parent-Child Interaction Therapy and Triple P—Positive Parenting Program: A Review and Meta-Analysis. Journal of Abnormal Child Psychology, 35 (3), 475–495.

[228] Forgatch, M. S., & DeGarmo, D. S. (1999). Parenting through change: An effective prevention program for single mothers. Journal of Consulting and Clinical Psychology, 67 (5), 711–724.

[229] Hosseini-Nasab SD, Fathiazar E, Vahedi S, Moghaddam M, Kiani A. (2007). The Effect of Social Skills Training on Decreasing the Aggression of Pre-school Children. Iran J Psychiatry, 1;2(3), 108-114.

[230] Beelmann, A., Lösel, F. (2021). A Comprehensive Meta-Analysis of Randomized Evaluations of the Effect of Child Social Skills Training on Antisocial Development. J Dev Life Course Criminology, 7, 41–65.

[231] Wilson, H. K., Pianta, R. C., & Stuhlman, M. (2007). Typical classroom experiences in first grade: The role of classroom climate and functional risk in the development of social competencies. The Elementary School Journal, 108 (2), 81–96.

[232] Guerra, N. G., & Slaby, R. G. (1990). Cognitive mediators of aggression in adolescent offenders: II. Intervention. Developmental Psychology, 26 (2), 269–277.

[233] Bank, L., Marlowe, J., Reid, J., Patterson, G., & Weinrott, M. (1991). A comparative evaluation of parent-training interventions for families of chronic delinquents. Journal of Abnormal Child Psychology, 19 (1), 15–33.

[234] Demir M, Jaafar J, Bilyk N, Ariff MR. (2012). Social skills, friendship and happiness: a cross-cultural investigation. J Soc Psychol, 152 (3), 379-85.

#14

[235] Kessler, R. C., Adler, L., Barkley, R., Biederman, J., Conners, C. K., Demler, O., Faraone, S. V., Greenhill, L. L., Howes, M. J., Secnik, K., Spencer, T., Ustun, T. B., Walters, E. E., & Zaslavsky, A. M. (2006). The prevalence and correlates of adult ADHD in the United States: Results from the National Comorbidity Survey Replication. American Journal of Psychiatry, 163 (4), 716–723.

[236] Faraone SV, Biederman J, Mick E. (2006). The age-dependent decline of attention deficit hyperactivity disorder: a meta-analysis of follow-up studies. Psychol Med, 36 (2), 159-165.

[237] Barkley, R. A. (1997). Behavioral inhibition, sustained attention, and executive functions: Constructing a unifying theory of ADHD. Psychological Bulletin, 121 (1), 65–94.

[238] Shaw, M., Hodgkins, P., Caci, H., Young, S., Kahle, J., Woods, A. G., & Arnold, L. E. (2012). A systematic review and analysis of long-term outcomes in attention deficit hyperactivity disorder: effects of treatment and non-treatment. BMC medicine, 10, 99.

[239] Mayo Clinic. Intermittent explosive disorder. Retrieved on 7 September 2022 from: https://www.mayoclinic.org/diseases-conditions/intermittent-explosive-disorder/symptoms-causes/syc-20373921#

[240] Pollak, Y., Dekkers, T. J., Shoham, R., & Huizenga, H. M. (2019). Risk-Taking Behavior in Attention Deficit/Hyperactivity Disorder (ADHD): a Review of Potential Underlying Mechanisms and of Interventions. Current psychiatry reports, 21(5), 33.

[241] Horvath, P., & Zuckerman, M. (1993). Sensation seeking, risk appraisal, and risky behavior. Personality and Individual Differences, 14(1), 41–52.

[242] Retz, W., & Rosler, M. (2010). Association of ADHD with reactive and proactive violent behavior in a forensic population. ADHD Attention Deficit Hyperactivity Disorder, 2 (4), 195-202.

[243] Schmidt, S., & Petermann, F. (2009). Developmental psychopathology: Attention deficit hyperactivity disorder (ADHD). BMC Psychiatry, 9, Article 58.

[244] Kyle Redford. (2018). Daydreaming or Distracted? What Teachers Misunderstand About ADHD. Education Week. Retrieved on 8 September 2022 from:
https://www.edweek.org/teaching-learning/opinion-daydreaming-or-distracted-what-teachers-misunderstand-about-adhd/2018/05

[245] Fried, R., Petty, C., Faraone, S. V., Hyder, L. L., Day, H., & Biederman, J. (2016). Is ADHD a Risk Factor for High School Dropout? A Controlled Study. Journal of Attention Disorders, 20 (5), 383–389.

[246] Barkley, R. A., Fischer, M., Smallish, L., & Fletcher, K. (2006). Young adult outcome of hyperactive children: Adaptive functioning in major life activities. Journal of the American Academy of Child and Adolescent Psychiatry, 45 (2), 192–202.

[247] Kendall, J. (1999). Sibling Accounts of Attention Deficit Hyperactivity Disorder (ADHD). Family Process, 38 (1), 117–136.

[248] Banerjee, T. D., Middleton, F., & Faraone, S. V. (2007). Environmental risk factors for attention deficit hyperactivity disorder. Acta Paediatrica, 96 (9), 1269–1274.

[249] Lehn, H., Derks, E. M., Hudziak, J. J., Heutink, P., van Beijsterveldt, T. C. E. M., & Boomsma, D. I. (2007). Attention problems and attention-deficit/ hyperactivity disorder in discordant and concordant monozygotic twins: Evidence of environmental mediators. Journal of the American Academy of Child and Adolescent Psychiatry, 46(1), 83–91.

[250] Rioux, C., Murray, J., Castellanos-Ryan, N., Séguin, J., Tremblay, R., & Parent, S. (2020). Moderation of parenting by inhibitory control in the prediction of the common and unique variance of hyperactivity-impulsivity and inattention. Development and Psychopathology, 32(3), 909-921.

#15

[251] U.S. Department of Health & Human Services, Administration for Children and Families, Administration on Children, Youth and Families, Children's Bureau. (2019). Child Maltreatment 2017. Retrieved on 13 September 2022 from
https://www.acf.hhs.gov/cb/research-data-technology/ statistics-research/child-maltreatment.

[252] Cicchetti D, Lynch M. (1993). Toward an ecological/transactional model of community violence and child maltreatment: Consequences for children's development. Psychiatry-Interpersonal and Biological Processes, 56 (1), 96–118.

[253] Locke, T. F., & Newcomb, M. D. (2003). Childhood maltreatment, parental alcohol/drug-related problems, and global parental dysfunction. Professional Psychology: Research and Practice, 34 (1), 73–79.

[254] Widom, C. S., Czaja, S. J., & DuMont, K. A. (2015). Intergenerational transmission of child abuse and neglect: real or detection bias?. Science, 347(6229), 1480–1485.

[255] Wiehe, Vernon R. (2003). Empathy and narcissism in a sample of child abuse perpetrators and a comparison sample of foster parents. Child Abuse & Neglect, 27 (5), 541–555.

[256] Main, M., & George, C. (1985). Responses of abused and disadvantaged toddlers to distress in agemates: A study in the day care setting. Developmental Psychology, 21(3), 407–412.

[257] Straker, G., & Jacobson, R. S. (1981). Aggression, emotional maladjustment, and empathy in the abused child. Developmental Psychology, 17 (6), 762–765.

[258] Egeland, B. (1979). Preliminary results of a prospective study of the antecedents of child abuse. International Journal of Child Abuse and Neglect, 3 (1), 269–278.

[259] Johnson, M. P., & Ferraro, K. J. (2000). Research on domestic violence in the 1990s: Making distinctions. Journal of Marriage and the Family, 62 (4), 948–963.

[260] Hurlbert, D. F., & Apt, C. (1991). Sexual narcissism and the abusive male. Journal of Sex & Marital Therapy, 17 (4), 279–292.

[261] Cicchetti, D., & Valentino, K. (2006). An ecological-transactional perspective on child maltreatment: Failure of the average expectable environment and its influence on child development. In D. Cicchetti & D. J. Cohen (Eds.), Developmental psychopathology: Risk, disorder, and adaptation (Pg 129–201). John Wiley & Sons, Inc..

[262] Angelakis, I., Gillespie, E. L., & Panagioti, M. (2019). Childhood maltreatment and adult suicidality: a comprehensive systematic review with meta-analysis. Psychological medicine, 49 (7), 1057–1078.

[263] Min, M., Farkas, K., Minnes, S. and Singer, L.T. (2007). Impact of childhood abuse and neglect on substance abuse and psychological distress in adulthood. J. Traum. Stress, 20 (5), 833-844.

[264] Jonson-Reid, M., Kohl, P. L., & Drake, B. (2012). Child and adult outcomes of chronic child maltreatment. Pediatrics, 129 (5), 839–845.

[265] Horwitz, A. V., Widom, C. S., McLaughlin, J., & White, H. R. (2001). The Impact of Childhood Abuse and Neglect on Adult Mental Health: A Prospective Study. Journal of Health and Social Behavior, 42 (2), 184–201.

[266] Maxfield, M. G., & Widom, C. S. (1996). The cycle of violence. Revisited 6 years later. Archives of pediatrics & adolescent medicine, 150 (4), 390–395.

[267] Lynch, M., & Cicchetti, D. (1998). An ecological-transactional analysis of children and contexts: the longitudinal interplay among child maltreatment, community violence, and children's symptomatology. Development and psychopathology, 10 (2), 235–257.

[268] Perez CM, Widom CS. (1994). Childhood victimization and long-term intellectual and academic outcomes. Child Abuse & Neglect, 18 (8), 617–633.

[269] Diette, Timothy & Goldsmith, Arthur & Hamilton, Darrick & Darity, William. (2017). Child Abuse, Sexual Assault, Community Violence and High School Graduation. Review of Behavioral Economics, 4 (3), 215-240.

[270] Bulik, C. M., Prescott, C. A., & Kendler, K. S. (2001). Features of childhood sexual abuse and the development of psychiatric and substance use disorders. The British journal of psychiatry: the journal of mental science, 179, 444–449.

[271] Gunnar, M. R., Hostinar, C. E., Sanchez, M. M., Tottenham, N., & Sullivan, R. M. (2015). Parental buffering of fear and stress neurobiology: Reviewing parallels across rodent, monkey, and human models. Social Neuroscience, 10 (5), 474–478.

[272] Gonzalez A. (2013). The impact of childhood maltreatment on biological systems: Implications for clinical interventions. Paediatrics & child health, 18 (8), 415–418.

[273] Shields A, Cicchetti D. (2001). Parental maltreatment and emotion dysregulation as risk factors for bullying and victimization in middle childhood. Journal of Clinical Child Psychology, 30 (3), 349–363.

[274] Robinson, R., Roberts, W.L., Strayer, J. and Koopman, R. (2007), Empathy and Emotional Responsiveness in Delinquent and Non-delinquent Adolescents. Social Development, 16 (3), 555-579.

[275] Stuewig, J., & McCloskey, L. A. (2005). The relation of child maltreatment to shame and guilt among adolescents: psychological routes to depression and delinquency. Child maltreatment, 10 (4), 324–336.

[276] Hosser, D., Windzio, M., & Greve, W. (2008). Guilt and Shame as Predictors of Recidivism: A Longitudinal Study With Young Prisoners. Criminal Justice and Behavior, 35 (1), 138–152.

[277] Delsol, C., & Margolin, G. (2004). The role of family-of-origin violence in men's marital violence perpetration. Clinical psychology review, 24 (1), 99–122.

[278] Kwong, M. J., Bartholomew, K., Henderson, A. J., & Trinke, S. J. (2003). The intergenerational transmission of relationship violence. Journal of Family Psychology, 17 (3), 288–301.

[279] Dong, X., Li, G., & Simon, M. A. (2017). The Association Between Childhood Abuse and Elder Abuse Among Chinese Adult Children in the United States. The journals of gerontology. Series A, Biological sciences and medical sciences, 72 (suppl_1), S69–S75.

[280] World Health Organization. (2022). Abuse of older people. Published on 13 June 2022. Retrieved on 26 September 2022 from: http://www.who.int/news-room/fact-sheets/detail/elder-abuse

[281] Storey, Jennifer. (2019). Risk factors for elder abuse and neglect: A review of the literature. Aggression and Violent Behavior, 50 (2), 101339.

[282] Today. "Elderly prostitutes reveal dark side of South Korea's rise". Published on 25 September 2015. Retrieved on 10 January 2022 from: https://www.todayonline.com/world/asia/elderly-prostitutes-reveal-dark-side-south-koreas-rise

[283] Jaffee S.R., Gallop R. (2007). Social, emotional, and academic competence among children who have had contact with child protective services: Prevalence and stability estimates. Journal of the American Academy of Child and Adolescent Psychiatry, 46 (6), 757–765.

[284] Afifi, T. O., & Macmillan, H. L. (2011). Resilience following child maltreatment: a review of protective factors. Canadian journal of psychiatry. Revue canadienne de psychiatrie, 56 (5), 266–272.

[285] Collishaw, S., Pickles, A., Messer, J., Rutter, M., Shearer, C., & Maughan, B. (2007). Resilience to adult psychopathology following childhood maltreatment: evidence from a community sample. Child abuse & neglect, 31(3), 211–229.

[286] Egeland, B., Jacobvitz, D., & Sroufe, L. A. (1988). Breaking the cycle of abuse. Child Development, 59 (4), 1080–1088.

#16

[287] De Ruiter C, Burghart M, De Silva R, Griesbeck Garcia S, Mian U, et al. (2022) A meta-analysis of childhood maltreatment in relation to psychopathic traits. PLOS ONE 17(8), e0272704.

[288] Kiehl, K. A., & Hoffman, M. B. (2011). The Criminal Psychopath: History, Neuroscience, Treatment, And Economics. Jurimetrics, 51(4), 355–397.

[289] Coid, J., Yang, M., Ullrich, S., Roberts, A., & Hare, R. D. (2009). Prevalence and correlates of psychopathic traits in the household population of Great Britain. International journal of law and psychiatry, 32 (2), 65–73.

[290] Diagnostic and statistical manual of mental disorders : DSM-IV. (1994). Washington, DC :American Psychiatric Association.

[291] Sánchez de Ribera, O., Kavish, N., Katz, I. M., & Boutwell, B. B. (2019). Untangling intelligence, psychopathy, antisocial personality disorder, and conduct problems: A meta-analytic review. European Journal of Personality, 33 (5), 529–564.

[292] Gregory, S., Blair, R. J., Ffytche, D., Simmons, A., Kumari, V., Hodgins, S., & Blackwood, N. (2015). Punishment and psychopathy: a case-control functional MRI investigation of reinforcement learning in violent antisocial personality disordered men. The lancet. Psychiatry, 2(2), 153–160.

[293] Newman, J. P., Patterson, C. M., & Kosson, D. S. (1987). Response perseveration in psychopaths. Journal of abnormal psychology, 96 (2), 145–148.

[294] Shirtcliff, E.A., Vitacco, M.J., Graf, A.R., Gostisha, A.J., Merz, J.L. and Zahn-Waxler, C. (2009). Neurobiology of empathy and callousness: Implications for the development of antisocial behavior. Behav. Sci. Law, 27 (2), 137-171.

[295] Lasko, E. N., Chester, D. S., Martelli, A. M., West, S. J., & DeWall, C. N. (2019). An investigation of the relationship between psychopathy and greater gray matter density in lateral prefrontal cortex. Personality neuroscience, 2, e7.

#17

[296] Bowlby, J. (1973). Attachment and loss: Vol. 2. Separation. New York: Basic Books.

[297] Gallo, L. C., Smith, T. W., & Ruiz, J. M. (2003). An Interpersonal Analysis of Adult Attachment Style: Circumplex Descriptions, Recalled Developmental Experiences, Self-Representations, and Interpersonal Functioning in Adulthood. Journal of Personality, 71 (2), 141-181.

[298] Gunnar, M. R. (1998). Quality of early care and buffering of neuroendocrine stress reactions: Potential effects on the developing human brain. Preventive Medicine, 27 (2), 208–211.

[299] Movahed Abtahi, M., & Kerns, K. A. (2017). Attachment and emotion regulation in middle childhood: changes in affect and vagal tone during a social stress task. Attachment & human development, 19 (3), 221–242.

[300] Simpson, J. A., Collins, W. A., Tran, S., & Haydon, K. C. (2007). Attachment and the experience and expression of emotions in romantic relationships: A developmental perspective. Journal of Personality and Social Psychology, 92 (2), 355–367.

[301] Van IJzendoorn, M. H. (1995). Adult attachment representations, parental responsiveness, and infant attachment: A meta-analysis on the predictive validity of the Adult Attachment Interview. Psychological Bulletin, 117 (3), 387–403.

[302] Baer, J. C., & Martinez, C. D. (2006). Child maltreatment and insecure attachment: a meta-analysis. Journal of Reproductive and Infant Psychology, 24 (3), 187–197.

[303] van Ijzendoorn, M. H., Schuengel, C., & Bakermans-Kranenburg, M. J. (1999). Disorganized attachment in early childhood: meta-analysis of precursors, concomitants, and sequelae. Development and psychopathology, 11(2), 225–249.

[304] Risi, A., Pickard, J. A., & Bird, A. L. (2021). The implications of parent mental health and wellbeing for parent-child attachment: A systematic review. PloS one, 16 (12), e0260891.

[305] Weinfield, N. S., Sroufe, L. A., & Egeland, B. (2000). Attachment from infancy to early adulthood in a high-risk sample: Continuity, discontinuity, and their correlates. Child Development, 71 (3), 695–702.

[306] O'Connor, B. P. (1995). Family and friend relationships among older and younger adults: Interaction motivation, mood, and quality. International Journal of Aging and Human Development, 40 (1), 9–29.

[307] Krause, N., & Rook, K. S. (2003). Negative interaction in late life: issues in the stability and generalizability of conflict across relationships. The journals of gerontology. Series B, Psychological sciences and social sciences, 58 (2), 88–99.

[308] Newsom, J. T., Nishishiba, M., Morgan, D. L., & Rook, K. S. (2003). The relative importance of three domains of positive and negative social exchanges: A longitudinal model with comparable measures. Psychology and Aging, 18 (4), 746–754.

[309] Oliva, A., Jimenez, J. M., & Parra, A. (2009). Protective effect of supportive family relationships and the influence of stressful life events on adolescent adjustment. Anxiety, stress, and coping, 22 (2), 137–152.

[310] Maria Camara, Gonzalo Bacigalupe, & Patricia Padilla. (2017). The role of social support in adolescents: are you helping me or stressing me out?. International Journal of Adolescence and Youth, 22 (2), 123-136.

[311] Griffiths, K. M., Crisp, D. A., Barney, L., & Reid, R. (2011). Seeking help for depression from family and friends: a qualitative analysis of perceived advantages and disadvantages. BMC psychiatry, 11, 196.

[312] Cacioppo, J. T., & Hawkley, L. C. (2009). Perceived social isolation and cognition. Trends in cognitive sciences, 13 (10), 447–454.

#18

[313] GBD 2017 Disease and Injury Incidence and Prevalence Collaborators (2018). Global, regional, and national incidence, prevalence, and years lived with disability for 354 diseases and injuries for 195 countries and territories, 1990-2017: a systematic analysis for the Global Burden of Disease Study 2017. Lancet (London, England), 392(10159), 1789–1858.

[314] Kessler, R. C., Berglund, P., Demler, O., Jin, R., Merikangas, K. R., & Walters, E. E. (2005). Lifetime prevalence and age-of-onset distributions of DSM-IV disorders in the National Comorbidity Survey Replication. Archives of general psychiatry, 62(6), 593–602.

[315] Al-Asadi, A. M., Klein, B., & Meyer, D. (2015). Multiple comorbidities of 21 psychological disorders and relationships with psychosocial variables: a study of the online assessment and diagnostic system within a web-based population. Journal of medical Internet research, 17(2), e55.

[316] Kessler, Ronald & Angermeyer, Matthias & Anthony, James & Graaf, Ron & Demyttenaere, Koen & Gasquet, Isabelle & de Girolamo, Giovanni & Gluzman, Semyon & Gureje, Oye & Haro, Josep Maria & Kawakami, Norito & Karam, Aimee & Levinson, Daphna & Medina-Mora, Maria & Oakley Browne, Mark & Posada-Villa, Jose & Stein, Dan & Tsang, Cheuk & Aguilar-Gaxiola, Sergio & Ustun, Tevfik. (2007). Lifetime prevalence and age-of-onset distributions of mental disorders in the WHO World Mental Health (WMH) Surveys. World psychiatry: official journal of the World Psychiatric Association (WPA), 6(3), 168-76.

[317] Turner, R. J., & Lloyd, D. A. (2004). Stress burden and the lifetime incidence of psychiatric disorder in young adults: racial and ethnic contrasts. Archives of general psychiatry, 61(5), 481–488.

[318] Grant, K. E., Compas, B. E., Thurm, A. E., McMahon, S. D., Gipson, P. Y., Campbell, A. J., Krochock, K., & Westerholm, R. I. (2006). Stressors and child and adolescent psychopathology: evidence of moderating and mediating effects. Clinical psychology review, 26 (3), 257–283.

[319] Brent, D. A., Perper, J. A., Moritz, G., Liotus, L., Schweers, J., Balach, L., & Roth, C. (1994). Familial risk factors for adolescent suicide: a case-control study. Acta psychiatrica Scandinavica, 89 (1), 52–58.

[320] Goodyer, I. M., & Altham, P. M. E. (1991). Lifetime exit events and recent social and family adversities in anxious and depressed school-age children and adolescents — I. Journal of Affective Disorders, 21 (4), 219–228.

[321] Goodyer, I. M., & Altham, P. M. (1991). Lifetime exit events and recent social and family adversities in anxious and depressed school-age children and adolescents: II. Journal of Affective Disorders, 21(4), 229–238.

[322] Marttunen, M. J., Aro, H. M., & Lönnqvist, J. K. (1993). Precipitant stressors in adolescent suicide. Journal of the American Academy of Child and Adolescent Psychiatry, 32(6), 1178–1183.

[323] Liu, R. T., & Alloy, L. B. (2010). Stress generation in depression: A systematic review of the empirical literature and recommendations for future study. Clinical Psychology Review, 30 (5), 582–593.

[324] Reilly, L. C., Ciesla, J. A., Felton, J. W., Weitlauf, A. S., & Anderson, N. L. (2012). Cognitive vulnerability to depression: a comparison of the weakest link, keystone and additive models. Cognition & emotion. 26 (3), 521–533.

[325] Thwaites, R., & Dagnan, D. (2004). Moderating variables in the relationship between social comparison and depression: an evolutionary perspective. Psychology and psychotherapy, 77(Pt 3), 309–323.

[326] Reis, S., & Grenyer, B. F. S. (2002). Pathways to anaclitic and introjective depression. Psychology and Psychotherapy: Theory, Research and Practice, 75 (4), 445–459.

[327] Séguin, L., Potvin, L., St-Denis, M., & Loiselle, J. (1995). Chronic stressors, social support, and depression during pregnancy. Obstetrics and gynecology, 85(4), 583–589.

[328] Boyce, P. M. (2003). Risk factors for postnatal depression: A review and risk factors in Australian populations. Archives of Women's Mental Health, 6 Supplement 2, S43–S50.

[329] Chen, Y., Cheung, S., & Huang, C.-C. (2022). Intimate Partner Violence During Pregnancy: Effects of Maternal Depression Symptoms and Parenting on Teen Depression Symptoms. Journal of Interpersonal Violence, 37(9–10), NP7034–NP7056.

[330] Tiruye, T. Y., Harris, M. L., Chojenta, C., Holliday, E., & Loxton, D. (2020). Determinants of intimate partner violence against women in Ethiopia: A multi-level analysis. PloS one, 15 (4), e0232217.

[331] Sommer, J., Iyican, S., & Babcock, J. (2019). The Relation Between Contempt, Anger, and Intimate Partner Violence: A Dyadic Approach. Journal of Interpersonal Violence, 34 (15), 3059–3079.

[332] Wilson, A. E., Smith, M. D., Ross, H. S., & Ross, M. (2004). Young children's personal accounts of their sibling disputes. Merrill-Palmer Quarterly, 50 (1), 39–60.

[333] Baumeister, R. F., Stillwell, A., & Wotman, S. R. (1990). Victim and perpetrator accounts of interpersonal conflict: Autobiographical narratives about anger. Journal of Personality and Social Psychology, 59 (5), 994–1005.

[334] Hanington, L., Heron, J., Stein, A., & Ramchandani, P. (2012). Parental depression and child outcomes--is marital conflict the missing link?. Child: care, health and development, 38 (4), 520–529.

[335] Chang, J. J., Halpern, C. T., & Kaufman, J. S. (2007). Maternal depressive symptoms, father's involvement, and the trajectories of child problem behaviors in a US national sample. Archives of pediatrics & adolescent medicine, 161 (7), 697–703.

[336] Nkansah-Amankra, Stephen & Luchok, Kathryn & Hussey, James & Watkins, Ken & Liu, Xiaofeng. (2009). Effects of Maternal Stress on Low Birth Weight and Preterm Birth Outcomes Across Neighborhoods of South Carolina, 2000–2003. Maternal and child health journal, 14 (2), 215-226.

[337] Giscombé, C. L., & Lobel, M. (2005). Explaining disproportionately high rates of adverse birth outcomes among African Americans: the impact of stress, racism, and related factors in pregnancy. Psychological bulletin, 131(5), 662–683.

[338] Peralta-Carcelen, M., Bailey, K., Rector, R. et al. (2013). Behavioral and socioemotional competence problems of extremely low birth weight children. J Perinatol, 33 (11), 887–892.

[339] Grote, Nancy & Bridge, Jeffrey & Gavin, Amelia & Melville, Jennifer & Iyengar, Satish & Katon, Wayne. (2010). A Meta-analysis of Depression During Pregnancy and the Risk of Preterm Birth, Low Birth Weight, and Intrauterine Growth Restriction. Archives of general psychiatry, 67 (10), 1012- 1024.

[340] Chan, Chui Yi & Lee, Antoinette & Lam, Siu & Lee, Chin Peng & Leung, Kwok & Koh, Yee & Tang, So Kum. (2013). Antenatal anxiety in the first trimester: Risk factors and effects on anxiety and depression in the third trimester and 6-week postpartum. Open Journal of Psychiatry, 3 (3), 301-310.

[341] Davis, E. P., & Sandman, C. A. (2012). Prenatal psychobiological predictors of anxiety risk in preadolescent children. Psychoneuroendocrinology, 37 (8), 1224–1233.

[342] Ibanez, G., Bernard, J. Y., Rondet, C., Peyre, H., Forhan, A., Kaminski, M., Saurel-Cubizolles, M. J., & EDEN Mother-Child Cohort Study Group. (2015). Effects of Antenatal Maternal Depression and Anxiety on Children's Early Cognitive Development: A Prospective Cohort Study. PloS one, 10 (8), e0135849.

[343] Sheline, Y., Wany, P., Gado, Csernansky, J. & Vannier, M. (1996). Hippocampal atrophy in recurrent major depression. Proceedings of the National Academy of Sciences USA, 93 (9), 3908-3913.

[344] Renee J. Thompson, Jutta Mata, Susanne M. Jaeggi, Martin Buschkuehl, John Jonides, Ian H. Gotlib. (2010). Maladaptive coping, adaptive coping, and depressive symptoms: Variations across age and depressive state. Behaviour research and therapy, 48 (6), 459 – 66.

[345] Holdaway, A. S., Luebbe, A. M., & Becker, S. P. (2018). Rumination in relation to suicide risk, ideation, and attempts: Exacerbation by poor sleep quality?. Journal of affective disorders, 236, 6–13.

[346] Kamijo, N. & Yukawa, S. (2018). The Role of Rumination and Negative Affect in Meaning Making Following Stressful Experiences in a Japanese Sample. Front Psychol. 9, 2404.

[347] Park, Crystal. (2010). Making Sense of the Meaning Literature: An Integrative Review of Meaning Making and Its Effects on Adjustment to Stressful Life Events. Psychological bulletin, 136 (2), 257-301.

[348] Caprara, G. V., Paciello, M., Gerbino, M., & Cugini, C. (2007). Individual differences conducive to aggression and violence: trajectories and correlates of irritability and hostile rumination through adolescence. Aggressive behavior, 33(4), 359–374.

[349] Miller, T. R., & Taylor, D. M. (2005). Adolescent suicidality: Who will ideate, who will act?. Suicide and Life-Threatening Behavior, 35(4), 425–435.

[350] Shajari, Farzaneh & Sohrabi, Faramarz & Jomehri, Farhad. (2016). Relationship between Early Maladaptive Schema and Internet Addiction: A Cross-Sectional Study. Asian Journal of Pharmaceutical Research and Health Care, 8 (3), 84-91.

[351] Schmidt, N. B., Joiner, T. E., Young, J. E., & Telch, M. J. (1995). The schema questionnaire: Investigation of psychometric properties and the hierarchical structure of a measure of maladaptive schemas. Cognitive Therapy and Research, 19(3), 295–321.

[352] Aydm, B., & San, S.V. (2011). Internet addiction among adolescents: The role of self-esteem. Procedia - Social and Behavioral Sciences, 15 (3), 3500-3505.

308

[353] Berte, D.Z., Mahamid, F.A. & Affouneh, S. (2021). Internet Addiction and Perceived Self-Efficacy Among University Students. Int J Ment Health Addiction, 19, 162–176.

[354] Keeton, C. P., Perry-Jenkins, M., & Sayer, A. G. (2008). Sense of control predicts depressive and anxious symptoms across the transition to parenthood. Journal of family psychology : JFP : journal of the Division of Family Psychology of the American Psychological Association (Division 43), 22(2), 212–221.

#19

[355] Harter, S. (2012). Developmental Differences in Self-representations during Childhood. In The Construction of the Self: Developmental and Sociocultural Foundations, Second Edition (Pg 27 – 71). Guilford Publications.

[356] Harter, S. (2012). Self-perception profile for adolescents: Manual and Questionnaires. 2012 Revision. University of Denver, Department of Psychology. Retrieved on 19 January 2022 from: https://portfolio.du.edu/downloadItem/221931

[357] Rosenberg, Morris & Schooler, Carmi & Schoenbach, Carrie & Rosenberg, Florence. (1995). Global Self-Esteem and Specific Self-Esteem: Different Concepts, Different Outcomes. American Sociological Review, 60 (1), 141-156.

[358] Donnellan, M & Trzesniewski, Kali & Robins, Richard & Moffitt, Terrie & Caspi, Avshalom. (2005). Low Self-Esteem Is Related to Aggression, Antisocial Behavior, and Delinquency. Psychological science, 16 (4), 328-335.

[359] Maunder, R., & Monks, C. P. (2019). Friendships in middle childhood: Links to peer and school identification, and general self-worth. The British journal of developmental psychology, 37 (2), 211–229.

[360] Harris, M. A., & Orth, U. (2020). The link between self-esteem and social relationships: A meta-analysis of longitudinal studies. Journal of Personality and Social Psychology, 119 (6), 1459-1477.

[361] Crocker, J. (2002). The Costs of Seeking Self–Esteem. Journal of Social Issues, 58 (3), 597-615.

[362] Du H, King RB, Chi P. (2017). Self-esteem and subjective well-being revisited: The roles of personal, relational, and collective self-esteem. PLoS ONE, 12(8), e0183958.

[363] Trzesniewski, Kali & Donnellan, M & Moffitt, Terrie & Robins, Richard & Poulton, Richie & Caspi, Avshalom. (2006). Low Self-Esteem During Adolescence Predicts Poor Health, Criminal Behavior, and Limited Economic Prospects during Adulthood. Developmental psychology, 42 (2), 381-390.

[364] de Vries, S. L., Hoeve, M., Stams, G. J., & Asscher, J. J. (2016). Adolescent-Parent Attachment and Externalizing Behavior: The Mediating Role of Individual and Social Factors. Journal of abnormal child psychology, 44(2), 283–294.

[365] Bosson, Jennifer & Lakey, Chad & Campbell, W. Keith & Zeigler-Hill, Virgil & Jordan, Christian & Kernis, Michael. (2008). Untangling the Links between Narcissism and Self-esteem: A Theoretical and Empirical Review. Social and Personality Psychology Compass, 2 (3), 1415 –1439.

[366] Bosson, J. K., Brown, R. P., Zeigler-Hill, V., & Swann, W. B., Jr. (2003). Self-enhancement tendencies among people with high explicit self-esteem: The moderating role of implicit self-esteem. Self and Identity, 2(3), 169–187.

[367] Blaine, Bruce & Crocker, Jennifer. (1993). Self-Esteem and Self-Serving Biases in Reactions to Positive and Negative Events: An Integrative Review. In 'Self Esteem' (Plenum Press), Chapter 4, 55-85.

[368] Raskin, R., Novacek, J. and Hogan, R. (1991). Narcissism, Self-Esteem, and Defensive Self-Enhancement. Journal of Personality, 59 (1), 19-38.

[369] Compton, William. (1992). Are positive illusions necessary for self-esteem: a research note. Personality and Individual Differences, 13 (12), 1343-1344.

[370] Hyatt, C. S., Sleep, C. E., Lamkin, J., Maples-Keller, J. L., Sedikides, C., Campbell, W. K., & Miller, J. D. (2018). Narcissism and self-esteem: A nomological network analysis. PloS one, 13(8), e0201088.

[371] Dahling, J. J., Whitaker, B. G., & Levy, P. E. (2008). The Development and Validation of a New Machiavellianism Scale. Journal of Management, 35(2), 219–257.

[372] Kajonius, Petri & Persson, Björn & Jonason, Peter. (2015). Hedonism, Achievement, and Power: Universal values that characterize the Dark Triad. Personality and Individual Differences, 77, 173-178.

#20

[373] Luyckx, Koen & Vansteenkiste, Maarten & Goossens, Luc & Duriez, Bart. (2009). Basic Need Satisfaction and Identity Formation: Bridging Self-Determination Theory and Process-Oriented Identity Research. Journal of Counseling Psychology, 56 (2), 276-288.

[374] Barber, B. L., Eccles, J. S., & Stone, M. R. (2001). Whatever happened to the jock, the brain, and the princess? Young adult pathways linked to adolescent activity involvement and social identity. Journal of Adolescent Research, 16(5), 429–455.

[375] Hennigan, Karen & Kelber, Marija. (2012). Gang Dynamics Through the Lens of Social Identity Theory. In "Youth Gangs in International Perspective (pp.127-149)". Springer.

[376] Wood, Jane L. (2014). Understanding gang membership: The significance of group processes. Group Processes & Intergroup Relations, 17 (6), 710-729.

[377] South, Catherine & Wood, Jane. (2006). Bullying in prisons: The importance of perceived social status, prisonization, and moral disengagement. Aggressive Behavior, 32 (5), 490 – 501.

[378] Voisin, D. R., King, K. M., Diclemente, R. J., & Carry, M. (2014). Correlates of gang involvement and health-related factors among African American females with a detention history. Children and youth services review, 44, 120–126.

[379] Pyrooz, David & Fox, Andrew & Decker, Scott. (2010). Racial and Ethnic Heterogeneity, Economic Disadvantage, and Gangs: A Macro-Level Study of Gang Membership in Urban America. Justice Quarterly, 27 (6), 867-892.

[380] Dukes, Richard & Martinez, Ruben & Stein, Judith. (1997). Precursors and Consequences of Membership in Youth Gangs. Youth & Society, 29 (2), 139-165.

[381] Luyckx, Koen & Klimstra, Theo & Duriez, Bart & Van Petegem, Stijn & Beyers, Wim. (2013). Personal Identity Processes from Adolescence Through the Late 20s: Age Trends, Functionality, and Depressive Symptoms. Social Development, 22 (4), 701-721.

[382] Mitchell, L. L., Lodi-Smith, J., Baranski, E. N., & Whitbourne, S. K. (2021). Implications of identity resolution in emerging adulthood for intimacy, generativity, and integrity across the adult lifespan. Psychology and aging, 36(5), 545–556.

[383] McLean, Kate & Pratt, Michael. (2006). Life's Little (and Big) Lessons: Identity Statuses and Meaning-Making in the Turning Point Narratives of Emerging Adults. Developmental psychology, 42 (4), 714 – 722.

[384] Stillman, T. F., Baumeister, R. F., Lambert, N. M., Crescioni, A. W., Dewall, C. N., & Fincham, F. D. (2009). Alone and Without Purpose: Life Loses Meaning Following Social Exclusion. Journal of experimental social psychology, 45 (4), 686–694.

[385] Nezlek, John & Wesselmann, Eric & Wheeler, Ladd & Williams, Kipling. (2015). Ostracism in Everyday Life: The Effects of Ostracism on Those Who Ostracize. The Journal of social psychology, 155 (5), 432- 451.

[386] Clare Conry-Murray, Jung Min Kimb, Elliot Turiel. (2015). Judgments of gender norm violations in children from the United States and Korea. Cognitive Development, 35, 122-136.

[387] Bosson, Jennifer & Taylor, Jenel & Prewitt-Freilino, Jennifer. (2006). Gender Role Violations and Identity Misclassification: The Roles of Audience and Actor Variables. Sex Roles, 55 (1-2), 13-24.

[388] Endendijk, J. J., Groeneveld, M. G., & Mesman, J. (2018). The Gendered Family Process Model: An Integrative Framework of Gender in the Family. Archives of sexual behavior, 47 (4), 877–904.

[389] Kimberly A. Lonsway & Louise F. Fitzgerald. (1994). RAPE MYTHS. In Review. Psychology of Women Quarterly, 18 (2), 133 – 164.

[390] Ryan, Kathryn. (2011). The Relationship between Rape Myths and Sexual Scripts: The Social Construction of Rape. Sex Roles, 65, 774 –782.

[391] Edwards, Katie & Turchik, Jessica & Dardis, Christina & Reynolds, Nicole & Gidycz, Christine. (2011). Rape Myths: History, Individual and Institutional-Level Presence, and Implications for Change. Sex Roles, 65, 761-773.

[392] Van Wie, V. E., Gross, A. M., & Marx, B. P. (1995). Females' Perception of Date Rape: An Examination of Two Contextual Variables. Violence Against Women, 1 (4), 351–365.

[393] Burt, M. R. (1980). Cultural myths and supports for rape. Journal of Personality and Social Psychology, 38(2), 217–230.

[394] Suarez, Eliana & Gadalla, Tahany. (2010). Stop Blaming the Victim: A Meta-Analysis on Rape Myths. Journal of interpersonal violence, 25 (11), 2010 - 2035.

[395] Truman, D.M., Tokar, D.M. and Fischer, A.R. (1996). Dimensions of Masculinity: Relations to Date Rape Supportive Attitudes and Sexual Aggression in Dating Situations. Journal of Counseling & Development, 74 (6), 555-562.

[396] V.I. Rickert, C.M. Wiemann. (1998). Date Rape Among Adolescents and Young Adults. Journal of pediatric & Adolescent gynecology. 11 (4), 167-175.

[397] Ybarra, M. L., Strasburger, V. C., & Mitchell, K. J. (2014). Sexual media exposure, sexual behavior, and sexual violence victimization in adolescence. Clinical pediatrics, 53 (13), 1239–1247.

#The Final Problem

[398] Cislak, A., Cichocka, A., Wojcik, A. D., & Frankowska, N. (2018). Power Corrupts, but Control Does Not: What Stands Behind the Effects of Holding High Positions. Personality and Social Psychology Bulletin, 44(6), 944–957.

312

[399] Galinsky, A. D., Magee, J. C., Inesi, M. E., & Gruenfeld, D. H. (2006). Power and Perspectives Not Taken. Psychological Science, 17(12), 1068–1074.

[400] van Kleef, G. A., Oveis, C., van der Löwe, I., LuoKogan, A., Goetz, J., & Keltner, D. (2008). Power, distress, and compassion: turning a blind eye to the suffering of others. Psychological science, 19 (12), 1315–1322.

[401] See K. E., Morrison E. W., Rothman N. B., Soll J. B. (2011). The detrimental effects of power on confidence, advice taking, and accuracy. Organizational Behavior and Human Decision Processes, 116 (2), 272-285.

[402] Georgesen, J. C., & Harris, M. J. (1998). Why's My Boss Always Holding Me Down? A Meta-Analysis of Power Effects on Performance Evaluations. Personality and Social Psychology Review, 2(3), 184–195.

[403] David Kipnis. (1972). Does power corrupt?. Journal of Personality and Social Psychology, 24(1), 33 – 41.

[404] Inesi M. E., Gruenfeld D. H., Galinsky A. D. (2012). How power corrupts relationships: Cynical attributions for others' generous acts. Journal of Experimental Social Psychology, 48 (4), 795-803.

[405] Lammers, J., Stapel, D. A., & Galinsky, A. D. (2010). Power increases hypocrisy: moralizing in reasoning, immorality in behavior. Psychological science, 21 (5), 737–744.

[406] Gruenfeld, D. H., Inesi, M. E., Magee, J. C., & Galinsky, A. D. (2008). Power and the objectification of social targets. Journal of Personality and Social Psychology, 95(1), 111–127.
[407] Christoff, K. (2014). Dehumanization in organizational settings: some scientific and ethical considerations. Frontiers in Human Neuroscience, 8, 748.

[408] Bastian, B., & Haslam, N. (2011). Experiencing Dehumanization: Cognitive and Emotional Effects of Everyday Dehumanization. Basic and Applied Social Psychology, 33 (4), 295–303.

www.ingramcontent.com/pod-product-compliance
Lightning Source LLC
Chambersburg PA
CBHW051245250726
48656CB00004B/1139